Berlin 1900–1933

Architecture and Design
Architektur und Design

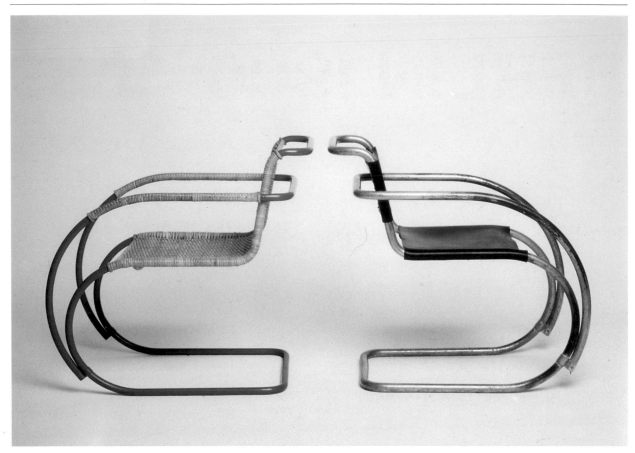

Fig. 1 *Ludwig Mies van der Rohe. Tubular-steel armchairs, 1927. Produced by Berliner Metallgewerbe Joseph Müller, Berlin. Private collection.*
The chair on the right is a bit smaller and narrower with thicker steel tubing than the model that was finally marketed on the left. Since it originally came from the Berlin house that Mies inhabited in 1926, it may well have been an early experimental prototype.

Abb. 1 *Ludwig Mies van der Rohe. Stahlrohrsessel mit Armlehnen, 1927. Hersteller: Berliner Metallgewerbe Joseph Müller, Berlin. Privatbesitz.*
Der rechte Sessel ist etwas kleiner und schmaler und besitzt ein dickeres Stahlrohr. Die Provenienz aus dem Berliner Haus, in dem Mies wohnte, spricht für ein frühes Versuchsstück.

BERLIN 1900–1933

ARCHITECTURE AND DESIGN

ARCHITEKTUR UND DESIGN

General Editor   Herausgeber
Tilmann Buddensieg

Contributions by   Mit Beiträgen von
Tilmann Buddensieg
Fritz Neumeyer
Angela Schönberger
Michael Esser

Cooper-Hewitt Museum
The Smithsonian Institution's
National Museum of Design
New York

Gebr. Mann Verlag
Berlin

Text Editor / Textredaktion: Nancy Aakre

Translations into English /
Übersetzungen ins Englische: John Gabriel

Cover:

Wertheim Department Store, 1896
Alfred Messel (1853–1909)

Horseshoe Development, 1927–29
Bruno Taut (1880–1938)

Umschlagfotos:

Kaufhaus Wertheim, 1896
Alfred Messel (1853–1909)

Großsiedlung Britz
Bruno Taut (1880–1938)

Library of Congress Cataloging-in-Publication Data

Berlin, 1900–1933: Architecture and Design.
Bibliography: p.
1. Modernism (Art) – Berlin (Germany) 2. Architecture – Berlin (Germany) 3. Architecture, Modern – 20th century – Berlin (Germany) 4. Design – Berlin (Germany) – History – 20th century. I. Buddensieg, Tilmann. II. Neumeyer, Fritz. III. Schönberger, Angela. IV. Esser, Michael. V. Cooper-Hewitt Museum.
N6885.B36 1987 709'.431'55

LC Number 87-6766
ISBN 0-910503-55-9

CIP – Kurztitelaufnahme der Deutschen Bibliothek

[Berlin nineteen hundred to nineteen hundred and thirty-three, architecture and design]
Berlin 1900–1933, architecture and design, Architektur und Design / Cooper-Hewitt Museum, the Smithsonian Institution's National Museum of Design, New York. General Ed. Tilmann Buddensieg. Contributions by Tilmann Buddensieg ... [Transl. into Engl.: John Gabriel]. – Berlin: Mann, 1987.
ISBN 3-7861-1507-9
NE: Buddensieg, Tilmann [Hrsg.]: Cooper-Hewitt Museum of Decorative Arts and Design ‹New York, NY›; Berlin neunzehnhundert bis neunzehnhundertdreiunddreißig, Architektur und Design; Berlin nineteen hundred to nineteen hundred and thirty-three, architecture and design, Architektur und Design.

Alle Rechte einschließlich Fotokopie und Mikrokopie vorbehalten
Lithos: O. R. T. Kirchner & Graser
Satz und Druck: Druckerei Hellmich KG
Verarbeitung: Lüderitz & Bauer, alle in Berlin
Printed in Germany.
ISBN 3-7861-1507-9

Contents   Inhalt

Foreword

This publication and the exhibition out of which it grew celebrate the 750th anniversary of the City of Berlin and the 10th anniversary of the Cooper-Hewitt's rebirth as the Smithsonian Institution's National Museum of Design. Of the more than 150 subjects explored by the Museum during the past decade, this is for me the most personal because my own parents were among the young artists and architects who flocked to Berlin in the twenties. Why Berlin? What made this city such a magnet?

One would think that the socio-political climate – a terrible war, humiliating defeat, massive unemployment, astronomical inflation, and frequent civil disturbances – would have made Berlin the place *not* to be. Yet, the city was bursting with creative energy and had great intellectual appeal. How that energy manifested itself in architecture and design is the concern of this publication. While American audiences are familiar with the development of the Modern movement, the rich array of material presented in *Berlin 1900–1933: Architecture and Design* includes work not widely known outside Germany, such as the poetic unbuilt projects of the Expressionist architects. Even for the Germans who may be more conversant with them, they hold new interest as Berlin reexamines her illustrious past.

Few cities, if any, have had as strong an impact on the twentieth century as Berlin. The ideas generated there spread quickly around the world. To the degree that we readily embraced them, we share a special bond with Berlin. Friends and colleagues on both sides of the ocean have enabled us to experience this extraordinary city at an exciting time in her history. We are deeply grateful to the German Foreign Office, the Berlin Senate for Cultural Affairs, and the Regents of the Smithsonian Institution, as well as to the authors and the other institutions and individuals listed elsewhere. A generous grant from the J. M. Kaplan Fund made the production of this publication possible. We

Vorwort

Die vorliegende, aus einer Ausstellung hervorgegangene Veröffentlichung gedenkt des 750. Geburtstages der Stadt Berlin sowie des 10. Jahrestages der Neugründung des Cooper-Hewitt Museums als Smithsonian Institution's National Museum of Design. Mehr als 150 Ausstellungen sind während der vergangenen zehn Jahre von unserem Museum organisiert worden, doch ist diese für mich mit der persönlichsten Anteilnahme verbunden, da meine Eltern ebenfalls zu den jungen Künstlern und Architekten gehörten, welche während der Zwanziger Jahre nach Berlin strömten. Warum Berlin? Was war es, das diese Stadt so anziehend machte?

Man sollte doch meinen, daß das sozio-politische Klima – ein schrecklicher Krieg, eine demütigende Niederlage, Massenarbeitslosigkeit, eine astronomische Inflation und bürgerkriegsartige Unruhen – Berlin zu einem Ort gemacht hatte, wo man sich besser nicht aufhalten sollte. Indes, die Stadt barst förmlich vor kreativer Energie und übte eine große intellektuelle Anziehungskraft aus. Obwohl Amerika mit der Entwicklung des Modernismus vertraut ist, beinhaltet das reichhaltige Material der Publikation ›Berlin 1900–1933: Architecture and Design‹ Arbeiten, welche außerhalb Deutschlands nicht allzu gut bekannt sind, beispielsweise die Projekt gebliebenen phantastischen Bauten der expressionistischen Architekten. Aber auch für die Deutschen, welche mehr mit diesen Werken vertraut sind, bietet die Veröffentlichung vor dem Hintergrund der glanzvollen Vergangenheit Berlins neuartige Aspekte.

Wenige Städte, wenn überhaupt, hatten einen so starken Einfluß auf das Zwanzigste Jahrhundert wie Berlin. Die dort entstandenen Ideen verbreiteten sich schnell über die ganze Welt, und in dem gleichen Maße, wie wir sie gerne aufgenommen haben, sind wir Berlin in besonderer Weise verbunden. Freunde und Kollegen auf beiden Seiten des Ozeans haben uns geholfen, diese ungewöhnliche Stadt in einer aufregenden Zeit ihrer Geschichte zu entdecken.

also wish to express our appreciation to Lufthansa German Airlines for their enormous assistance.

Lisa Taylor
Director, Cooper-Hewitt Museum
The Smithsonian Institution's National Museum of Design

Wir danken dem Deutschen Auswärtigen Amt, dem Berliner Senator für Kulturelle Angelegenheiten, den Verantwortlichen der Smithsonian Institution, sowie den Autoren, anderen Institutionen und Einzelpersonen, welche an anderer Stelle aufgeführt sind. Eine großzügige Spende des J. M. Kaplan Fund hat die vorliegende Veröffentlichung möglich gemacht. Ebenso gebührt unser Dank der Deutschen Lufthansa.

Lisa Taylor
Director, Cooper-Hewitt Museum
The Smithsonian Institution's National Museum of Design

Acknowledgments

Danksagung

We would like to thank the participants who have made this project a reality.

Wir danken allen, die zur Verwirklichung dieses Projektes beigetragen haben.

Akademie der Künste, Abteilung Baukunst, Berlin
AEG AG, Aus- und Weiterbildungszentrum, Berlin
AEG AG, Abteilung Öffentlichkeitsarbeit –
    Firmenarchiv, Frankfurt
Auswärtiges Amt, Politisches Archiv, Bonn
Avery Architectural and Fine Arts Library, Columbia
    University, New York
Badisches Landesmuseum, Karlsruhe
Bauhaus-Archiv, Museum für Gestaltung, Berlin
Kenneth Barlow Ltd., London
Bayerisches Nationalmuseum, München
Berlin Museum, Berlin
Berlin-Porzellansammlung Belvedere, Berlin
Berliner Kraft- und Licht-Aktiengesellschaft
    (BEWAG), Berlin
Berliner Verkehrs-Betriebe (BVG), Berlin
Berlinische Galerie, Berlin
Bezirksamt Reinickendorf, Bauaufsicht, Berlin
Bezirksamt Tiergarten, Bauaufsicht, Berlin
Bröhan-Museum, Berlin
Collection Centre Canadien d'Architecture/Canadian
    Centre for Architecture, Montreal
Columbia University, Department of Art History and
    Archeology, New York
Deutsches Archäologisches Institut, Berlin
Deutsches Patentamt, München
Deutsches Textilmuseum, Krefeld
Ex Libris, New York
Fischer Fine Arts, London
Barry Friedman Ltd., New York
Galerie Aedes, Berlin
Galerie Geitel, Berlin
Geheimes Staatsarchiv Preussischer Kulturbesitz,
    Berlin
Generallandesarchiv, Karlsruhe
Gruppe Nord Wohnungsunternehmen GmbH, Berlin
Wolfgang Gützlaf, Antiquitäten, Berlin
Harvard University Art Museums (Busch–Reisinger
    Museum), Cambridge, Massachusetts
Hessisches Landesmuseum, Darmstadt
Internationales Design Zentrum, Berlin
KPM–Archiv, Schloss Charlottenburg, Berlin

Kunstbibliothek, Staatliche Museen Preussischer
    Kulturbesitz, Berlin
Kunstgewerbemuseum, Staatliche Museen
    Preussischer Kulturbesitz, Berlin
Münchner Stadtmuseum, München
The Museum of Modern Art, New York
The New York Public Library, New York
Pfalzgalerie, Kaiserslautern
Der Regierende Bürgermeister von Berlin,
    Senatskanzlei – Protokoll
Rheineck-Apotheke, Berlin
Siemens Museum, München
Verwaltung der Staatlichen Schlösser und Gärten,
    Berlin
Stiftung Deutsche Kinemathek, Berlin
Stiftung Deutsche Klassenlotterie, Berlin
Universitätsbibliothek der Technischen Universität,
    Berlin
Versuchs- und Lehranstalt für Brauerei, Berlin
Westfälisches Landesmuseum für Kunst- und
    Kulturgeschichte, Münster
Wenzel-Hablik-Stiftung, Itzehoe
Werkbund-Archiv, Berlin
Wissenschaftskolleg zu Berlin
Nancy Aakre
Thomas Albrecht
Frederik Bernett
Dr. Sabine Bohle-Heintzenberg
Horst Brinkmann
Mark Butler
Annette Ciré
Bernd H. Dams
Robert Davis
Larry Deemer
Ann Dorfsman
Bernhard Dreyer
Chris Fremantle
Tom Freudenheim
Dorothy Twining Globus
Rose Gottschalk
Elizabeth Hall
Constance Herndon
George King

Renate Klotz
Steven Langehough
James Lee
Bernhard Leitner
Manfred Ludewig
David McFadden
George Nichols
Dr. Jürgen Ohlau
Robin Parkinson
Anne Patterson
Knud Peter Petersen
Harold F. Pfister
Rolf Punitzer
Cordelia Rose

Daniela Sannwald
Ute Scheibe
Hanna Schnackenberg
Dr. Carl Wolfgang Schümann
Barbara Schulz
Rudolf Stilcken
Dr. Paul Tauchner
Andrea Thym
UKZ: Simon Ungers
    Laszlo Kiss
    Todd Zwigard
Wolfgang Volz
Jörg-Ingo Weber
Christoph Wecker

and especially
und besonders

O. M. Ungers

Essays

Essays

Fig. 2 *Erich Mendelsohn. Administration building of the metalworkers' union, 1929–30. Main staircase and lamp. Berlin-Kreuzberg, Lindenstrasse.*

Abb. 2 *Erich Mendelsohn. Verwaltungsgebäude der Metall-arbeiter-Gewerkschaft, 1929–30. Haupttreppe und Lampe. Berlin-Kreuzberg, Lindenstraße.*

Tilmann Buddensieg

Introduction: Aesthetic Opposition and International Style

"Paris is the capital of art" – the young Swiss architect Jeanneret, who would later call himself Le Corbusier, seems to have been confirmed in this belief after six months in Berlin, where he had arrived in June of 1910. But his experience in Peter Behrens's office had also taught him that Germany was "the great production plant" of the day. To Le Corbusier, Germany meant above all its capital city, Berlin, and "production plant" signified a new industrial architecture and design created to suit the requirements of mass production by machine.[1]

Berlin's superior position had humble origins little more than half a century earlier. "Having passed the prosperous domiciles of France and Austria," reported a German manufacturer upon viewing his country's entries at London's Crystal Palace Exhibition of 1851, "one enters a region where all cows are gray and all flowers black"; the "noble savagery of German fairground booths" was totally eclipsed by the "surpassing elegance" of French industry and the "utility" of English mass-produced goods.[2] The World Exhibition of 1873 in Vienna was considered in the official report "a defeat of Germany in the field of decorative arts." The exhibition architecture was described as homespun, and the exhibition itself as "pure flea market." Only the chemical products and the cannons manufactured by Krupp evaded this verdict.

At Philadelphia's Centennial Exposition of 1876, German observers were again chagrined to find that even America had a tremendous lead. Franz Reuleaux, a prominent Berlin engineer, wrote home from Philadelphia in 1876 that German commodities were generally "cheap and bad."[3] Here, for the first time, that demand for "quality goods" was voiced which would persist for the next fifty years.

From the innovations of 1900 to the mature conceptions of 1930, modern German design was the work of just two generations. The pioneer generation, born in the 1860s – Peter Behrens, Bruno Paul, Hermann Muthesius, August Endell, Alfred Grenander, Hans Poelzig, Heinrich Tessenow – grew up during a period of historical revival and worked sporadically in the Jugendstil before fomenting a major change with

Tilmann Buddensieg

Einleitung: Ästhetische Opposition und Internationaler Stil

»Paris ist die Hauptstadt der Kunst«, – das scheint dem jungen Schweizer Architekten Jeanneret, der sich später Le Corbusier nannte, ganz außer Frage zu stehen nach einem halbjährigen Aufenthalt in Berlin seit Juni 1910. Im Atelier von Peter Behrens hatte er aber gelernt, daß Deutschland »die große Produktionsstätte« der Gegenwart sei.[1]

Deutschland, das war für Le Corbusier vor allem seine Hauptstadt Berlin, und »Produktion« meinte für ihn eine neue Industriearchitektur und Massenproduktion. Der Weg dorthin war lang und steinig.

»Geht man«, so schildert ein deutscher Fabrikant seine Eindrücke auf der Londoner Weltausstellung von 1851, »an dem reichen Haus Frankreichs und Österreichs vorbei«, so kommt man »in eine Gegend, wo alle Kühe grau und alle Blumen schwarz sind«. Er sieht »die edle Einfachheit deutscher Jahrmarktbuden« neben der »unerreichten Eleganz« der französischen Industrie und der »Zweckmäßigkeit« der englischen »Massenproduktion«.[2]

Auf der Weltausstellung 1873 in Wien konstatierte der »Amtliche Bericht« eine »kunstgewerbliche Niederlage Deutschlands«. Die Ausstellungsarchitektur sei eine »tollgewordene Holzkonstruktion«, in einem »Haspel- und Kunkelstil«, die Ausstellung selbst sei der »reinste Trödelmarkt«. Nur die chemischen Produkte und die Kruppschen Kanonen entgingen diesem Urteil.

Auf der Weltausstellung von Philadelphia 1876 kam die Erfahrung hinzu, daß Deutschland auch im Vergleich mit den USA den kürzeren zog. Franz Reuleaux, der bedeutende Berliner Ingenieur, schilderte in seinen »Briefen aus Philadelphia« das deutsche Gewerbe als »billig und schlecht«.[3] Hier wurde erstmals der Ruf nach industrieller »Wertarbeit« laut, der die nächsten 50 Jahre bestimmen sollte.

Dieser Umschwung seit 1900 und sein Höhepunkt um 1930 ist das Werk zweier Generationen. Die erste Generation derer, die in den 60er Jahren des 19. Jahrhunderts geboren wurden – Peter Behrens, Bruno Paul, Hermann Muthesius, August Endell, Alfred Grenander, Hans Poelzig, Heinrich Tessenow – wuchs noch ganz in der Hochblüte der Gründerzeit auf und schuf im episo-

Fig. 3 *Max Taut. Dorotheen School, 1928–29. Berlin-Köpenick.*
Abb. 3 *Max Taut. Dorotheenschule, 1928–29. Berlin-Köpenick.*

the founding of the Deutsche Werkbund. Their students, children of the 1880s – Bruno and Max Taut, Walter Gropius, Mies van der Rohe, Erich Mendelsohn, Hans Scharoun, the Luckhardt brothers, Hugo Häring, Otto Bartning, Ludwig Hilberseimer, Otto Rudolf Salvisberg, and Erwin Gutkind – began their careers in the atmosphere of the late Jugendstil and early Werkbund. The ideals of this group were incarnated in Peter Behrens ("Mr. Werkbund himself," as he was called by his contemporaries) and his designs for the Allgemeine Elektricitätsgesellschaft (AEG). This second generation, along with the first, was also that of Expressionism, Neues Bauen, and the International Style. Only a very few members of a younger third generation, born around the turn of the century, were able to make a substantial contribution before 1933 – Marcel Breuer, Herbert Bayer, Wilhelm Wagenfeld, and Marguerite Friedlaender-Wildenhain are the best known. Many of the above-mentioned architects were also designers of products for everyday use.

There arose as well a new breed of professional designers in typography, advertising, interior and

dischen Jugendstil und im Werkbund den Umschwung gegen Hofstil und Akademie. Ihre in den achtziger Jahren geborenen Schüler Bruno und Max Taut, Walter Gropius, Mies van der Rohe, Erich Mendelsohn, Hans Scharoun, die Brüder Luckhardt, Hugo Häring, Otto Bartning, Ludwig Hilberseimer, Otto Rudolf Salvisberg, Erwin Gutkind begannen ihre Arbeit in dieser Atmosphäre des späten Jugendstils und des Werkbundes. Dieser fand in Berlin durch die Tätigkeit des »Mister Werkbund«, durch Peter Behrens und sein Engagement für die AEG, die Inkarnation seiner Ziele und Ideale. Diese zweite Generation war zusammen mit der ersten auch die des Expressionismus, des Neuen Bauens und des Internationalen Stiles. Nur wenige Angehörige einer jüngeren, um die Jahrhundertwende geborenen dritten Generation vermochten, noch vor 1933, einen substanziellen künstlerischen Beitrag zu leisten, wie Marcel Breuer oder Herbert Bayer, Wilhelm Wagenfeld oder Marguerite Friedlaender-Wildenhain. Neben den genannten Architekten, die oftmals auch Entwerfer von Produkten gewesen sind, entsteht der neue Typus eines Gestalters für Geräte und Produkte, Typographie und Werbung, für

Fig. 4 *Toaster, 1926–27. Produced by Deutsche Auergesellschaft (DEGEA), Berlin. Private collection.*
Abb. 4 *Toaster, vor 1927. Hersteller: Deutsche Auergesellschaft (DEGEA), Berlin. Privatbesitz.*

Fig. 5   *Leonhard Friedrich Fries. "Wotan Halbwatt Lampe" poster, circa 1912. SMPK Kunstbibliothek, Berlin.*

Abb. 5   *Leonhard Friedrich Fries. »Wotan Halbwatt Lampe«, Plakat, um 1912. SMPK Kunstbibliothek, Berlin.*

Fig. 6 *Peter Behrens. Imperial German Embassy, St. Petersburg, 1912 (early photo).*

Abb. 6 *Peter Behrens. Kaiserlich Deutsche Botschaft, St. Petersburg, 1912 (Ursprünglicher Zustand).*

industrial design that included Wagenfeld and Friedlaender-Wildenhain, along with Trude Petri, Eva Stricker-Zeisel, Emmy Roth, Lilly Reich, Jan Tschichold, Herbert Bayer, and even Moholy-Nagy.

The influence of their ideals only began to wane in the late 1960s, when the continuity and future of the "project of the modern" began to be questioned. Today, such authorities on Berlin architecture as Wolf Jobst Siedler see the Weimar dream of creating a classless society, the dream of being able to provide all people with the best of everything, as an impulse toward proletarianization.[4] To Siedler, the continuation of the Weimar vision after the Nazi era is responsible for the monotonous uniformity of the welfare architecture of the Federal Republic of Germany and of Berlin.

Not all of the above-mentioned architects and designers were, strictly speaking, Berlin artists. Some studied or worked there for relatively brief or intermittent periods. But the city touched each of them, and their work, in important ways. Karl Scheffler, journalist and critic, described the unique importance of Berlin as a marketplace as early as 1910: "Berlin's activity essentially consists in attracting finished products from all over Germany – popularizing them and making them marketable – materializing them, if you will.... All

Raumgestaltung, vertreten von Wilhelm Wagenfeld, Marguerite Friedlaender-Wildenhain, Trude Petri, Eva Stricker-Zeisel, Emmy Roth, Lilly Reich, Jan Tschichold, Herbert Bayer oder auch Moholy-Nagy. Sie alle haben einen fortwirkenden Einfluß auf das Gesicht unserer Umwelt gehabt. Ihre Ideale jedoch verlieren seit den späten 60er Jahren ihre universale Gültigkeit. Damit war Zukunft und Kontinuität des »Projektes der Moderne« in Frage gestellt.

Der Traum der Weimarer Moderne von der Klassenlosigkeit des Besten, von der Machbarkeit des Guten für jedermann überall ist für Wolf Jobst Siedler die Diktatur der Proletarisierung gewesen.[4] Das späte Fortleben dieses Traumes nach der Nazizeit sei schuld an der monotonen Uniformität der Wohlfahrtsarchitektur in der Bundesrepublik und Berlin.

Die genannten Namen schließen auch einige wenige Architekten und Designer ein, die keine Berliner gewesen sind. Die Rechtfertigung liegt in der überragenden Bedeutung Berlins als nationalem und internationalem Markt. Karl Scheffler hat das schon 1910 genau beschrieben: »Die Tätigkeit Berlins besteht im wesentlichen darin, aus ganz Deutschland die fertigen Werte an sich zu ziehen, sie zu nutzen, sie weiterzugeben, sie zu popularisieren und sie markt-

of the assets produced throughout the Empire must . . . pass through the channels of Berlin modernism in order to compete on the international market."[5]

A concern for mass production and the salability of products certainly predominated. Yet the commercial emphasis was tempered by aims of an educational and cultural kind: the aim of creating an "art for all" in the Jugendstil of the Imperial era, and the much more politically inspired desire for an "art for all classes of the population" during the Weimar Republic.

Scheffler had anticipated the importance of these "values of international civilization" in 1910, at a time when the arts and crafts in Berlin were just beginning to shed their eclectic character, their imitation of Parisian or Viennese objets d'art, their aesthetic packaging in costly materials and applied ornament. In this process of self-reform, the tenets of progressive architecture became the reference points for the good design of objects for daily use. Industrially produced teacups, coffeepots, and kitchenware, for instance, through the abstract quality of their design, the pure presence of their materials (whether porcelain, glass, or metal), or

fähig, sie sozusagen materiell zu machen . . . . So müssen alle im Reich erzeugten Werte durch die Kanäle des Berliner Modernismus gehen, um international marktfähig zu werden.«[5]

Der schlechterdings beherrschende Aspekt der massenhaften Produktion und der Verkäuflichkeit hatte neben dem ökonomischen aber auch einen volksbildnerischen und kulturpädagogischen Impuls: »Die Kunst für alle« im Jugendstil des Kaiserreiches, »die Kunst für alle Schichten des Volkes« in der Weimarer Republik, die klassenlose Formgebung der für »jedermann« erschwinglichen Gebrauchsgeräte auch über die nationalen Grenzen hinaus, für den Markt einer modernen Weltzivilisation.

Diese »internationalen Zivilisationswerte« hatte Karl Scheffler schon 1910 kommen sehen, zu einer Zeit, als das Gewerbe in Berlin den Charakter der Nachahmung deutscher Stile der Vergangenheit aufgab und ganz andere Ziele verfolgte als eine ästhetische Umhüllung mit kostbaren Materialien oder eine dekorative Ausschmückung wie die Pariser oder Wiener Objèts d'Art.

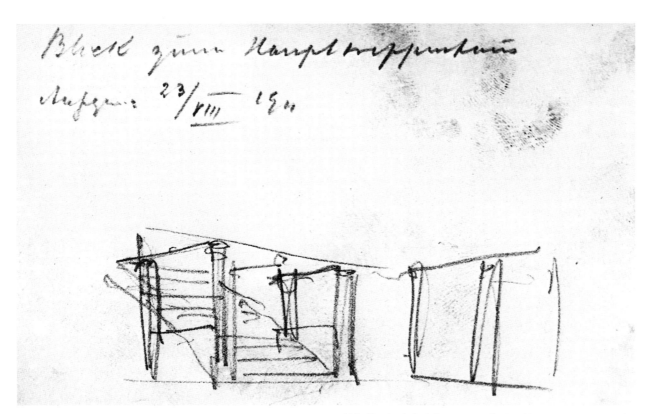

Fig. 7 *Ludwig Mies van der Rohe. Main staircase in the Imperial German Embassy, St. Petersburg, 1911. Pencil sketch on back of photograph. Foreign Office, Bonn, Political Archive.*

Abb. 7 *Ludwig Mies van der Rohe. Haupttreppenhaus der Kaiserlich Deutschen Botschaft, St. Petersburg, 1911. Bleistiftzeichnung auf der Rückseite einer Photographie. Auswärtiges Amt, Bonn, Politisches Archiv.*

their mechanically reproduced patterns derived from contemporary painting – all sought an analogy to architecture.

Eduard Berdel, influential director of the Bunzlau College of Ceramics, defined the task of designers of household pottery in 1926 by stating that "everything we create in the way of forms, shapes, colors, and decor" must be brought "into connection … with modern architecture." Artur Hennig, one of the great ceramists of his time, and teacher in Bunzlau, described his aim in 1928 as "creating things for use, which, in terms of integrity, can stand beside the technical products of our day. The path is the same as that followed by the New Architecture."[6] This ideal of creating a rationally designed and completely integrated environment to meet contemporary needs was the ultimate accomplishment of Weimar Berlin.

How different was the art of Vienna! The pervasiveness of luxurious materials, the extreme individualism of design, the attempts to express a profound emotional message, not only in individual works of art but in those manufactured in limited editions, and the sheer quality of the craftsmanship of Vienna's creations transport the beholder out of the banality of his everyday life. Exquisite silverwork of all sorts, jewelry, fine textiles, furniture – Vienna's treasures were marvelous and enchanting. Berlin's designs, however, evoke a far different world.

Instead of creating flowing transitions between ornament and expression, function and autonomy of form, pure and applied art as was done in Vienna, Berlin design from the end of the Jugendstil period was involved in a process of distinguishing between objects for daily use and art as creative individual expression. The conscious symbiosis of these functions in the mainstream of Viennese art led to ornamental excess and to an overloading of content. For example, one of Josef Hoffmann's textile patterns, titled *Outcry*, was expected, with a slight shift of decorative emphasis, to express "longing."[7] Coming across such subject matter in a sofa's upholstery, who would not prefer the superb symbolism of an Edvard Munch painting?

By contrast, the glassware designed by Peter Behrens as early as 1898, and distributed in Berlin by Keller & Reiner – unemotionally simple, with a calculated balance of form, purpose, and standard type – evinces a nonreferential beauty of form that enhances utility, transcends the material, and does so almost entirely without the obvious individuality of fine craftsmanship.

Again, the glassware designed by Wilhelm Wagenfeld during his short Berlin period for Schott/Jena *(figs. 78–80)*, and from 1935 for the Vereinigte Lausitzer

Die Architektur wurde in den zwanziger Jahren die übergreifende Orientierungsform für alle Geräte und Objekte ihrer Ausstattung. Industriell produziertes Tisch- und Küchengerät aus Steingut, Porzellan, Glas und Metall suchte in dem Abstraktionsgrad ihrer Formgebung, in einem maschinell erzeugten Dekor aus den Formerfindungen der gleichzeitigen Malerei die Analogie zur Architektur.

Eduard Berdel, der einflußreiche Direktor der keramischen Fachschule in Bunzlau, sah 1926 die Aufgabe der keramischen Gebrauchsgeräte darin, »alles, was wir an Formen, an Gestalten, an Farben und Dekoren schaffen, in Berührung mit der modernen Architektur« zu bringen. Artur Hennig, einer der großen Keramiker der Zeit und Lehrer in Bunzlau, nannte 1928 sein Ziel, »Dinge des Gebrauchs zu formen, die durch ihre Haltung neben den technischen Erzeugnissen unserer Zeit bestehen können. Der Weg ist der gleiche wie bei der neuen Architektur«.[6] In dieser einem leidenschaftlichen Gegenwartsbewußtsein verpflichteten Rationalität der Geräte und der Architektur und in allen Aspekten der Lebenswelt des modernen Menschen erfüllt sich das Weimarer Berlin.

Wie anders die Kunst der Donau-Metropole! Ihre Luxuskunst der Pracht im Material, eines extremen Individualismus der Formgebung und der Tiefe des Ausdrucks im Einzelstück oder in Kleinserien, entrückt jeden Betrachter der Banalität des Alltags, in der die silbernen Vitrinen, das kostbare Silbergerät und der Schmuck, die Stoffe und perlmuttverzierten Möbel keinen Platz finden.

Statt der fließenden Übergänge zwischen Ornament und Ausdruck, Gebrauchszweck und Autonomie der Form, freier und angewandter Kunst in den meisten Wiener Objekten, ist in Berlin seit dem Ende der Jugendstilepisode ein kontinuierlicher Prozeß der Scheidung zwischen Gebrauchsgerät und der großen Kunst der Expression im Gange. Die gewollte Symbiose dieser Bereiche in vorherrschenden Strömungen der Wiener Kunst führt zu ornamentalen Überformungen noch in den Meisterwerken von Klimt und zu inhaltlichen Überlastungen in Stoffmustern von Josef Hoffmann: »Aufschrei« heißt eines derselben. Geringfügige Ornamentverschiebungen verlangen von dem gleichen Stoff den Ausdruck der »Sehnsucht«.[7] Wer dächte bei solcher Thematik von Möbelstoffen nicht lieber an Bilderfindungen von Edvard Munch?

Schon der 1898 von Behrens in München entworfene Gläsersatz, den die Kunsthandlung Keller & Reiner in Berlin vertrieb, zeigt in seiner unpathetischen Schmucklosigkeit, in dem kalkulierten Zusammenklang von Form, Zweck und Typologie eine inhaltlose Schönheit der Form, die den Gebrauch verklärt, das Material

Glaswerke AG at Weisswasser, combines highly personal artistry with the unyielding requirements of mass production. Wagenfeld would later refine his designs to that ineffable point where his creative touch could be distinguished from the result of anonymous factory design only by a connoisseur's practiced eye. For Wagenfeld, an industrial product had a form that was "completely divested of its individual, personally determined character . . . an expression of collective labor and collective achievement."[8] With only slight variations that have been introduced since 1934 *(fig. 79)*, the extremely rare first version of his teapot of 1931 has been in continuous production to this day, in both East and West Germany.

The increasing anonymity of mass-produced commodities inspired the memorable Werkbund debate

transzendiert und fast schon auf das Pathos der handwerklichen Fertigung verzichten kann.

Die Glasgeschirre, die Wilhelm Wagenfeld während seiner kurzen Berliner Zeit für Schott/Jena *(Abb. 78–80)* und für die Glaswerke in Weißwasser ab 1935 entworfen hat, folgen dieser ureigenen Gewerbekunst auch noch in der industriellen Massenproduktion. Wagenfeld entwickelt das Entwurfskonzept bis zu einer gewollten Grenze, wo das Künstlerische des Entwurfs nur noch für das prüfende Auge des Kenners von namenlosen Werksprodukten zu unterscheiden ist. Das Industrieprodukt erschien ihm als eine Form, die »ihres individuellen, an den einzelnen gebundenen Charakters völlig entkleidet« sei, zum »Ausdruck kollektiver Arbeit und kollektiver Leistung« wird.[8] Der extrem seltene Prototyp der ersten Fassung seiner

Fig. 8   *Peter Behrens. Cloakroom, Wiegand Residence, 1911. Berlin-Dahlem, Peter-Lenné-Strasse (1986 photo).*

Abb. 8   *Peter Behrens. Garderobe, Wohnhaus Wiegand, 1911. Berlin-Dahlem, Peter-Lenné-Straße (Zustand 1986).*

between Henri van de Velde and Hermann Muthesius at Cologne in 1914. Their arguments naturally revolved around the consequences of industrial production. With the design of the AEG product line, the artist's signature was replaced by a company trademark; "Behrens style" became synonymous with "AEG style." Although in terms of function AEG products were only slightly better than those of the competition, by 1908 AEG had captured the market with its superior designs. Following an unprecedented press campaign, the AEG was hailed for its artistic designer and he for his work for that firm. No self-promotion was necessary. Twenty-five years later, Wilhelm Wagenfeld followed this strategy at Schott/Jena and then again at the Vereinigte Lausitzer Glaswerke at Weisswasser. It remains a valuable corporate tactic to our day.

The unprecedented collusion of artists in the erasure of their signatures, their unique styles, cannot be explained solely by the strictures of industrial manufacture, by the advertising and sales interests of the companies they worked for, nor surely out of a sympathy for Nietzsche's dictum that a subjective artist is a bad artist. Utopian hopes definitely played a part here.

Fig. 9 *Peter Behrens. AEG workers' housing, 1910–11. Berlin-Hennigsdorf (early photo).*
Abb. 9 *Peter Behrens. Arbeiterwohnhausanlage für die AEG, 1910–11. Berlin-Hennigsdorf (ursprünglicher Zustand).*

Teekanne von 1931 wurde von etwa 1934 an *(Abb. 79)* bis in unsere Tage in Ost- und Westdeutschland in immer neuen Varianten abgewandelt.

Dieser Prozeß der Anonymisierung der Warenproduktion war schon Thema der denkwürdigen Werkbund-Debatte in Köln 1914 zwischen van de Velde und Muthesius. Er kreist um das Jahrhundert-Problem der Konsequenzen industrieller Warenproduktion. In der Formgebung der AEG-Produkte findet der Ersatz einer Künstlersignatur durch eine Fabrikmarke statt. »Stil Behrens« wird identisch mit dem »Stil AEG«. Waren die AEG-Produkte in technischer Hinsicht kaum besser als die der wachsenden Konkurrenz, so gewinnt man Vorsprung und damit Umsatz durch das schon seit 1908 vergleichslos überlegene und umfassende AEG-Design. Infolge einer bis dahin unbekannten Presse-Werbung wird die Firma wegen ihres künstlerischen Beraters und dieser wegen seiner Arbeit für die Firma gelobt. Eigenwerbung war gar nicht mehr nötig. 25 Jahre später wiederholte Wilhelm Wagenfeld dieses AEG-Modell für Schott/Jena und die Vereinigten Lausitzer Glaswerke. Bis heute hat es seine Nützlichkeit erwiesen.

Diese erstaunliche Mitarbeit der Künstler an der Auslöschung ihrer Erkennbarkeit erklärt sich nicht allein aus den objektiven Zwängen der industriellen Produktion, den Werbe- und Verkaufsinteressen der Firmen, auch sicher nicht aus der Sympathie für Nietzsches Dictum, der subjektive Künstler sei der schlechte Künstler. Hier wirken durchaus utopische Hoffnungen mit. Die Anonymisierung der Formensprache war nicht als Verlust individuellen Ausdrucks zu beklagen. Nur die »großen modernen Künstler«, die Theo van Doesburg beschwört, vermochten in der Architektur und im Gewerbe den Prozeß der »Entformung«, die Dekomposition hinter die historische Stilkopie, hinter bürgerliche Geschmacksstereotypen und hinter die Selbstdarstellung des Künstlers zurückzuführen auf »Konstruktionsprinzipien nach Elementargesetzen«. Diese Art der »maschinellen Konstruktion von einfachen, klaren und in sich schönen Gegenständen« würde »der Herrschaft des Individualismus und dem Nationalismus in der menschlichen Produktion ein Ende bereiten«.[9] Diese Konstruktion nach Elementargesetzen sahen die holländischen Künstler des Stijl, die russischen Konstruktivisten, die ungarische, tschechische, Schweizer und italienische Avantgarde mit ihren Frankfurter, Hamburger, Celler und Berliner Genossen als den über Grenzen verbindenden Zeitstil an. Berlin war für wenig mehr als 10 Jahre die Metropole dieser Internationale der Avantgarde. Hier hatte sie ihre Vorgeschichte, hier gewann sie ihre polemische Kraft, hier verachtete und pries man sie, hier

Fig. 10   *Bruno Taut and Martin Wagner. Coffee terrace, Horseshoe Development, 1925–31. Berlin-Britz (early photo).*

Abb. 10   *Bruno Taut und Martin Wagner. Kaffeeterrasse, Hufeisensiedlung, 1925–31. Berlin-Britz (ursprünglicher Zustand).*

The complaint was frequently voiced that the anonymity of these new forms signaled a loss of individual expression. Indeed, only "great modern artists," Theo van Doesburg declared, were capable of applying the method of "de-design," peeling off the layers not only of historical revival plaster but of bourgeois stereotypes of taste and of the artists' glorification of ego to reveal beneath a substratum of "construction principles based on elementary laws." And conversely, a "mechanical construction of simple, clear, and intrinsically beautiful objects would "bring the regime of individualism and nationalism in human production to an end."[9] This interest in construction according to elementary laws cut across national borders and resulted in a *Zeitstil* that provided a unity to the works of artists internationally: the Dutch de Stijl artists, the Russian Constructivists, the Hungarian, Czech, Swiss, and Italian avant-garde can all be considered comrades of their Hamburg, Frankfurt, Celle, and Berlin fellow artists.

For little more than ten years Berlin was the seat of this internationale of the avant-garde. It was here that the avant-garde had its prehistory and here that it

lachte man über und lebte auch ohne sie. In Berlin gelang das Bündnis mit Presse, Publizistik, Literatur, Satire und Kabarett, mit Musik, Tanz und Theater, mit Film und Mode, ja sogar mit Bereichen der Wissenschaft und des Handels.

Es war nicht zuletzt der Fachhandel, der durch seine Werkbund-Ideale einer einfachen, sachlichen und soliden Formgebung einen Riesenschritt tat: von dem Massenkram des 19. Jahrhunderts über die kostbaren Kleinserien des Jugendstils zum Verkauf der Massenproduktion von guten und sehr guten Gebrauchsgütern, in Übereinstimmung mit dem Neuen Bauen und für einen internationalen Markt bestimmt.

Schon bei Messels Kaufhaus Wertheim meinte Walter Curt Behrendt, nun endlich seien auch die »Zwecke des Kaufmannes« zu einer »Sache der Kunst« geworden[10], und Max Osborn nennt das gleiche Warenhaus einen »bedeutsamen Faktor der demokratischen Kultur«[11].

Das gleiche galt für die gigantische Warenproduktion der AEG, die nach Karl Ernst Osthaus, »der Welt ihr Anrecht auf Kunst in der Produktion zurückgegeben« habe[12].

Fig. 11 *Olga Herber-Lieb-knecht. Drawing for fancy dress ball at the Reimann School, 1926. Pencil and watercolor. Private collection.* Abb. 11 *Olga Herber-Lieb-knecht. Zeichnung für Ballkostüm (»Pierrot«), Reimann-Schule, Berlin, 1926. Aquarell über Bleistift. Privatbesitz.*

acquired its polemic strength; it was in Berlin that the avant-garde was ridiculed and discredited, in Berlin that it was celebrated and ignored. It was also in this great metropolis that the avant-garde formed successful alliances with the press, publishers, literary circles, and cabaret, with the worlds of music, dance, and theater, film and fashion, and even with factions of the sciences and commerce.

Berlin's exclusive retail establishments championed the Werkbund ideal by leaving behind the mass-produced banalities of the nineteenth century, and the precious limited editions of the Jugendstil, to promote the simple, solid forms of the Werkbund and the superbly designed appliances and goods destined for the international market, in accordance with Neues Bauen ideals.

Walter Curt Behrendt, speaking of the Wertheim Department Store, commented, "Finally the concerns of the merchant are those of art."[10] Max Osborn considered the same department store "an important part of a democratic culture."[11] This was also thought to be true of AEG's appliances, which, according to Karl Ernst Osthaus "gave back to the world its right to have art incorporated in production."[12]

Nach Alfred Messels frühem Einzelwerk in der Sickingenstraße *(Abb. 105)*, dann durch Martin Wagner und Bruno Taut wird auch die Massenproduktion des Wohnungsbaus für das Volk der Minderbemittelten unternommen und zum eigentlichen Schrittmacher des Neuen Bauens. Es folgen die Gehäuse der Massenorganisationen, der Massenerholung, der Massenvergnügungen, der Massenerziehung und des Massenverkehrs: Gewerkschaftsbauten von Mendelsohn *(Abb. 2)* und Max Taut, das Kino von Mendelsohn, die Garage, das Krankenhaus von Bartning, das Strandbad von Martin Wagner, das Schwimmbad von Tessenow, Fabriken von Mendelsohn und Punitzer, Straßenbahndepots von Jean Krämer und U-Bahnhöfe von Grenander und Bruno Taut, Schulen von Bruno und Max Taut *(Abb. 3)* und Gutkind, Kaufhäuser von Mendelsohn und den Luckhardts, der Großstadtplatz von den Luckhardts, Mies, Behrens und Schaudt *(Abb. 17, 55–59)*, ein neues Regierungszentrum der Republik von Hugo Häring, Verwaltungs- und Geschäftshäuser von Behrens und Mies, eine Rundfunkanstalt von Poelzig, Messebauten von Wagner und Poelzig. Für all diese Bauaufgaben liefern die Berliner Architekten modellhafte Lösungen oder Projekte zu jedermanns Nutzen in einem einheitlichen »Stil« der Großstadt Berlin. Nur die Reichsregierung, Stadtverwaltungen, die Gerichtsgebäude, die weltberühmten Forschungsinstitute der Kaiser-Wilhelm-Gesellschaft (außer dem einzigen Einstein-Turm von Mendelsohn), die Hotels, die Häuser der Mittel- und Oberschicht bleiben in Berlin in ihrer Masse ohne moderne Lösungen. Das Landhaus für den großen Psychologen Kurt Lewin *(Abb. 19)* in Berlin-Schlachtensee von 1929–30, die Luckhardt- und Mendelsohn-Wohnhäuser *(Abb. 18, 53, 117)* sind Einzelstücke, aber blieben nie wieder erreichte Modelle.

In keiner anderen Metropole ist der Weg aus dem 19. Jahrhundert, von der preußischen Residenz zur Reichshauptstadt im 20. Jahrhundert von solchen Brüchen und Sprüngen, von solchen erbitterten und höhnischen Polemiken gekennzeichnet wie in Berlin. Der Streit um die Fakultätsbilder von Klimt in Wien ist ein Professorengezänk im Vergleich mit den feindseligen Auseinandersetzungen um Reichstag und Dom, Opernhaus und Zeilenbau, »kalte« Stahlrohrmöbel und »geisteskranke« Architektur-Utopien. Ein Kaiser, der den »Individualismus« der Künstler als den von vaterlandslosen Sozialdemokraten verfolgte, der sich in voller Montur mit Adlerhelm zwischen mythologischen Gestalten auf dem Dach des Reichs-Postmuseums darstellen ließ, war mit schuld, wenn der Großherzog von Hessen Ernst Ludwig im Tagebuch vermerkte: »Übrigens, wenn ich zu Kaisers Geburtstag

Fig. 12 / Abb. 12

Fig. 13 / Abb. 13

Fig. 14 / Abb. 14

Fig. 15 / Abb. 15

Figs. 12–15 *Mass-produced crockery, 1928–33. Various manufacturers. Private collection.*

Abb. 12–15 *Gebrauchskeramik, 1928–33. Verschiedene Hersteller. Privatbesitz.*

With Alfred Messel's early tenement house on Sickingenstrasse *(fig. 105)*, and the later work of Martin Wagner and Bruno Taut, mass production of housing for the working classes became the leading concern of the Neues Bauen. In this same spirit, Berlin's architects went on to design buildings for mass transportation, mass education, mass entertainment, mass recreation, and mass organizations such as unions and political parties. Functional structures of widely varying types rose up in the urban fabric of greater Berlin to meet public needs – union offices by Erich Mendelsohn *(fig. 2)* and Max Taut, movie theaters by Mendelsohn and Hans Poelzig, garages, public baths, and hospitals by Otto Bartning, Martin Wagner, and Heinrich Tessenow; factories by Mendelsohn and Martin Punitzer, train depots by Jean Krämer, subway stations by Alfred Grenander and Bruno Taut, schools by Bruno and Max Taut *(fig. 3)* and Erwin Gutkind, department stores by Mendelsohn and the Luckhardts, metropolitan squares by the Luckhardts, Mies, Peter Behrens, and Emil Schaudt, a new administration center for the Republic by Hugo Häring, administration and retail buildings by Behrens and Mies, a radio station by Poelzig, and exhibition buildings by Wagner and Poelzig.

Only government buildings, city administration buildings, law courts, the world-famous research institutes of the Kaiser Wilhelm Society (the one exception being Mendelsohn's unique Einstein Tower), hotels, and the mansions of the middle and upper classes remained, for the most part, without modern solutions. The 1929 country house in Berlin-Schlachtensee for the famous psychologist Kurt Lewin *(fig. 19)*, the houses by the Luckhardts *(figs. 18, 53, 117)* and Mendelsohn, were, like true works of art, single creations, models that have never been surpassed.

In no other great European city was the transition from the nineteenth century to the twentieth so beset by tensions and ruptures, so flawed by harsh and bitter polemics as it was in Berlin. The Viennese quarrel over Klimt's controversial pictures was a professorial tiff compared to the vitriolic battles that raged in Berlin over the Reichstag and Cathedral, the Opera, and row houses, "cold" tubular steel furniture and "insane" architectural utopias.

Kaiser Wilhelm II denounced artistic individualism as if it were Social Democratic sedition. His notion of art was to have himself portrayed in full regalia, complete with eagle-topped helmet, flanked by mythological figures, on the roof of the Imperial Post Museum. The Grand Duke of Hesse, Ernst Ludwig, noted in his diary: "When I stayed in Berlin during the birthday festivities of the Kaiser, I often felt that many of my

in Berlin weilte, fand ich oft, daß viele von meinen sogenannten Kollegen noch so rückständig in ihren Anschauungen waren, daß ich mich als reiner Sozialist fühlte«.[13]

Der Konflikt zwischen Hofstil und den von Handel und Industrie getragenen Kräften des Fortschritts brach offen aus in der Polemik um die Kaiserliche Deutsche Botschaft in St. Petersburg *(Abb. 5)*, entworfen von Behrens 1911/12. Die Projektleitung hatte Mies van der Rohe *(Abb. 6)*, der den Bau, wie Philipp Johnson überliefert, als sein »Gesellenstück« ansah, auf das er sein Leben lang stolz war. Für Max Osborn und Karl Scheffler war sie der erste offizielle Triumph der modernen, im Deutschen Werkbund und in der Berliner Sezession versammelten Kräfte der deutschen Kunst über altertümelnden Hofstil und dogmatische Akademie. Anläßlich des Antrages auf Ordensverleihung fragt der Kaiser im Zorn nach dem »Esel, der sich dieses Ungeheuer ausgedacht hat«, und er beschimpft die Botschaft als »Bauscheusal«, das »scheußlich im Jugendstyl« errichtet worden sei.[14]

Der Kaiser stand für Adolf Behne im Jahre 1912 »völlig außerhalb der Kunstentwicklung«[15]. Damit war die 300jährige Geschichte einer glorreichen Führungsrolle des Preußischen Königshauses in allen Belangen der Kunst zu Ende. Fast alle wesentlichen Impulse der Architektur und der gewerblichen Künste nach der Jahrhundertwende stammen von Künstlern, die sich solidarisch in einer einhelligen ästhetischen Opposition gegen die Kunstpolitik des Kaisers fühlten. Doch gilt es festzuhalten, daß die modernen Künstler wegen der Feindschaft des Kaisers und seiner akademischen Günstlinge kaum Förderung, aber auch kaum Behinderung erfuhren. »Zensur« gab es nur bei Aufträgen des Hofes. Einflußreiche Personen seines Vertrauens vermochten den Kaiser gelegentlich durchaus zum Richtigen in Sachen der Kunst zu beeinflussen und das Schlimmste zu verhindern. 1933 erliegt die gleiche Opposition, nicht selten der gleichen Personen, einer zu keiner Duldung bereiten, zur materiellen Zerstörung und zur Vertreibung entschlossenen Diktatur.

Die Lücken des Buches im Hinblick auf den geschichtlichen und wirtschaftlichen Hintergrund der Epoche, der unvermeidliche Verzicht auf eine Zusammenschau der Künste, sowie das Fehlen einiger ihrer einflußreichen Künstler wie Hermann Muthesius, August Endell, Bruno Paul, Heinrich Tessenow kann mit Hilfe anderer Bücher, ja Schulbüchern ausgeglichen werden. Unser vorherrschendes Interesse galt der Fülle der ästhetischen Gestaltungsversuche der materiellen Bedingungen des Lebens, der lange Weg von Jugendstilpreziosen zu alltäglichen Geräten, von den utopischen und prototypischen zu den praktischen

Fig. 16   *Fritz Brill. "Ein Pudding," 1932. Black-and-white photo with airbrushed color. Berlinische Galerie, Berlin.*

Abb. 16   *Fritz Brill. »Ein Pudding«, 1932. Schwarz-weiß Foto mit Spritztechnik. Berlinische Galerie, Berlin.*

so-called colleagues were so backward in their convictions that I considered myself a pure socialist."[13]

The conflict between the court style and that supported by the progressive forces of commerce and industry openly erupted in the polemics surrounding the Imperial German Embassy in St. Petersburg *(fig. 5)*, designed by Behrens between 1911 and 1912. Mies van der Rohe was in charge of the project *(fig. 6)*. According to Philip Johnson, Mies considered it his apprenticeship piece, and he remained proud of it all his life. For Max Osborn and Karl Scheffler, the Embassy building was the first "official" triumph of Germany's modern artistic forces against the retrogressive court style and the dogmatism of the academy. When the Kaiser was faced with the application to grant the expected awards for the building – normal procedure in such circumstances – he furiously asked for "the donkey who had conceived this monster." He called the Embassy an "architectural monstrosity, erected in a dreadful Jugendstil."[14]

und zugleich vollendet schönen Lösungen in Architektur und Design für jedermann. Wir wollten die einzelnen Prototypen und die einzigen Höchstleistungen erforschen, aber auch den allzu kurzen Kulturprozeß ihrer Vermittlung in die Gebrauchsgeräte für viele. Für die Autoren dieses Buches gliedert sich der große Stoff der Architektur und des Design in Berlin von 1900–1933 in sieben Etappen der Berliner Geschichte. Sie rekonstruieren eine künstlerische Topographie Berlins, wie sie sich in Ausstellungen, Aufträgen, Produktsystemen und Organisationsmethoden niedergeschlagen hat.

1. Mit den »Modernen Wohnräumen«, die das Kaufhaus Wertheim 1902 ausstellte, wurden einem großen Publikum zu vernünftigen Preisen Möbel, Porzellan, Gläser, Bestecke, Lampen, Tischdecken, Stoffe, Tapeten und Fliesen von mehreren Raumkünstlern angeboten: Peter Behrens *(Abb. 65–69)*, Curt Stoeving *(Abb. 63)* und August Endell *(Abb. 64)*. Sie stellten ihre Werke erstmals nicht in einem Museum, einer

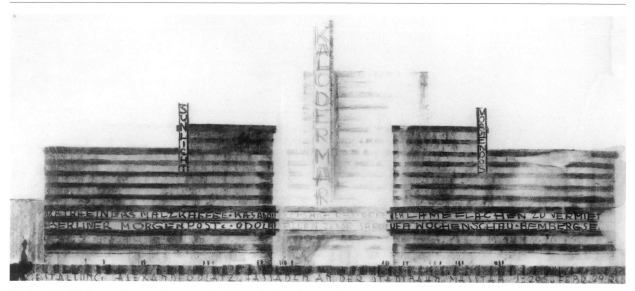

Fig. 17   *Emil Schaudt. Competition entry for the redesign of Alexanderplatz, Berlin, 1929. Drawn by R. Rettig. Charcoal and pencil. Private collection.*

Abb. 17   *Emil Schaudt. Entwurf für die Umgestaltung des Alexanderplatzes, Berlin, 1929. Gezeichnet von R. Rettig. Kohle und Bleistift. Privatbesitz.*

By 1912, as far as Adolf Behne was concerned, the Kaiser stood "totally outside developments in art."[15] Thus ended a three-hundred-year history of glorious support for the arts on the part of the Prussian royal house.

After the turn of the century, almost all of the important developments in architecture and the decorative arts came from artists who felt united in an aesthetic opposition against the artistic and cultural policy of the Kaiser. It should be emphasized, however, that although the artists of the modern movement never received any support from the Kaiser, because of his hostility and his academic favorites, they were never hindered by him, either. "Censorship" was applied only in cases of court commissions. More than likely, important persons who had the Kaiser's confidence were able to influence his opinions on art from time to time and to prevent the worst from happening. This was not the case in 1933, when artists and architects – many of them the same persons who had earlier opposed the Kaiser – were subdued by a dictatorship determined to destroy and expel them.

The present book's omissions in what concerns the historical and economic background of the period, as well as its neglect of a number of influential artists such as Hermann Muthesius, August Endell, Bruno Paul, and Heinrich Tessenow, to mention only those of the older generation, can easily be compensated for by referring to standard textbooks. Our prevailing interest is in the

Galerie oder zu Hause aus, sondern sahen ihre Produkte von dem führenden, als Meisterwerk der Architektur gepriesenen Warenhaus in der Hauptstadt »allen Schichten des Volkes« zum Verkauf angeboten.

Lichtwark schildert die Zimmereinrichtungen in einem Brief vom 17. Dezember 1902 an die Kommission für die Verwaltung der Hamburger Kunsthalle: Sie seien »in origineller Art auf die Brauchbarkeit zurückgeführt. Der Entwurf eines Speisezimmers von P. Behrens war fünfmal ausverkauft ... einzelne Möbel öfters. Wertheim läßt die ganze Ausstellung auf seine Rechnung herstellen«.

2. Daneben schufen Werkbundkünstler einen durchaus prunkvollen, an der preußischen Überlieferung, vor allem Schinkels, orientierten Wohnstil, der Zugang zur Wilhelminischen Oberschicht fand, wie 1912 im Wohnhaus Wiegand von Behrens *(Abb. 7)*, sowie im Ceres-Geschirr von Schmuz-Baudiss für die KPM *(Abb. 73)*. Fast ohne Kompromisse war dieser Werkbundstil für ein offizielles Geschenk wie das Tafelsilber für das Kronprinzenpaar geeignet. Kurz vor dem ersten Weltkrieg schien hier die Möglichkeit einer Versöhnung der Künstler mit dem Hof, kurz vor seiner Abdankung, nicht ausgeschlossen.

3. Erst die neuen Produkte der Elektroindustrie erschlossen einen großen und internationalen Markt für preisgünstige Gebrauchsgeräte wie Lampen, Uhren, Ventilatoren und Wasserkessel. An ihrer technischen Entwicklung beteiligten sich viele Firmen des In-

richness of the aesthetic models provided for shaping the material conditions of life – the long road from precious Jugendstil objects to everyday appliances – from the utopian and prototypical to the practical and at the same time the beautiful, in architecture and design destined for all. We have tried to present the prototypes and the masterpieces, and at the same time to explore the sadly short process of their transformation into commodities for the people. The authors of this book view the immense material on architecture and design in Berlin from 1900 to 1933 as having developed in seven stages. These seven stages are distinguished in terms of important exhibitions and architectural commissions, as well as by prevailing production methods and systems of organization.

1. Through the *Moderne Wohnräume* exhibition at the Wertheim Department Store in 1902, a broad public became acquainted with reasonably priced furniture, tableware, glass, lamps, tiles, textiles, and wallpapers by several designers: Peter Behrens *(figs. 65–69)*, Curt Stoeving *(fig. 63)*, and August Endell *(fig. 64)*. For the first time, these artists were not exhibiting their work in a museum or gallery or at home but offering objects for sale to "all levels of the population" at one of the capital's leading commercial establishments, one that was hailed as a masterpiece of architecture, as well. In a letter dated December 17, 1912, to the administration of his museum, Alfred Lichtwark, the famed director of the Hamburg Kunsthalle, described these rooms: "They are reduced to utility in an original manner. The dining room by P. Behrens has sold out five times, single pieces of furniture more often. Wertheim has produced the whole ensemble at his own expense."

2. In the next stage, Werkbund artists created a sumptuous style of furnishing derived from the Prussian tradition, particularly from Karl Friedrich Schinkel, and embodied in the 1912 Wiegand residence *(fig. 8)* by Behrens and in the "Ceres" tableware *(fig. 73)* by Schmuz-Baudiss for KPM. It seemed before the First World War that a reconciliation between Werkbund artists and the Hohenzollern throne (which was abdicated only a few years later) might be possible.

3. An extensive international market for German design did not develop until the electrical industry brought out new inexpensive appliances such as lamps, clocks, fans, and kettles. Many international firms contributed to their technical development. But nobody explored the new potential for shaping their shells and skins more thoroughly and with longer lasting influence than Peter Behrens for the AEG. The idea of conceiving a product line as a planned variation of und Auslandes. Die neuen Möglichkeiten der Formung der Hüllen und Gehäuse erforschte niemand so gründlich und folgenreich wie Behrens für die AEG. Die Idee einer Produktserie als geplante Variation der Form, des Materials und eines schlichten maschinellen Dekors führte schon vor 1914 zu nie übertroffenen Lösungen für Gebrauchsgeräte, die vielfach über 20 Jahre lang unverändert produziert wurden und heute noch zeitlos funktional erscheinen.

4. Die Erfahrung des Ersten Weltkrieges erschütterte den Glauben an den industriellen Fortschritt, an die Technik als rationaler Organisationsform der modernen Welt und an den Welthandel als Brücke zwischen den Völkern. Walter Gropius wollte sich in der »Baulust« architektonischer Utopien und Kathedralvisionen von dem »abgestandenen Krämergeist einer vergangenen Epoche« erholen.[16] Sozialistische Ideen vermischten sich mit Träumen von der Wiederkehr der mittelalterlichen Bauhütten, Kathedralvisionen als Stadtkronen neuer Gartenstädte ersetzten die Werkbundkoalition aus Kunst und Industrie. Die Rückkehr zum Handwerk und zur Kollektivarbeit unter der Führung der Architektur vereinten Künstler der »Novembergruppe«, des »Ring« und der »Gläsernen Kette«. Zeichnungen der »Gläsernen Kette«, zu der Gropius, die Brüder Taut und Luckhardt, Scharoun, Gösch, Finsterlin, Hablik und Krayl gehörten, erinnern an die Ausstellung »Unbekannte Architekten« in der Galerie J. B. Neumann im Jahre 1919. Hier haben auch die wohlbekannten Glastürme und -kuben von Mies van der Rohe ihren Platz.

5. Schon ab 1923 widersprach vor allem Mies diesen rückwärts gewandten Utopien. Es ist erstaunlich, wie aus den Utopisten der »Gläsernen Kette« buchstäblich über Nacht die Baumeister des Neuen Bauens wurden, die im Bunde mit der osteuropäischen und holländischen Avantgarde aus Berlin in den 20er Jahren ein »Laboratorium« der Umformung der »stofflichen Realität« und der Lebenswelt des Menschen schufen.

In den Berliner Siedlungen für die Arbeiterbevölkerung fanden fast alle großen Berliner Architekten dieser Jahre ein ruhmreiches Arbeitsfeld. Die Hufeisensiedlung in Berlin-Britz *(Abb. 11, 44, 108–109)*, 1926 von dem sozialdemokratischen Stadtbaurat Martin Wagner organisiert und gemeinsam mit Bruno Taut gebaut, ist die bedeutendste Leistung. Außerordentlich produktiv erwies sich hier ein stimulierendes Milieu, in dem auch Architekten der zweiten Reihe, wie Erwin Gutkind und Fred Forbat, die erst neuerdings erschlossenen Bauten von Martin Punitzer den hohen Standard auch weniger bekannter Berliner Architekten dieser Jahre erweisen.

form, materials, and unassuming machine-made ornament, saw results even before 1914. Many of Behrens's designs were manufactured unchanged for over twenty years, and even today they appear timelessly functional. This was the realization of Werkbund ideals.

4. The devastation of the First World War shook the country's faith in industrial progress, in technology as a form of rational organization for the modern world, and in world trade as a bridge between nations. Walter Gropius fled from the "stale shopkeeping mentality of a bygone era" to indulge his "craving to build" in architectural utopias and visions of cathedrals.[16] Socialist ideas mingled with dreams of a revival of medieval craft guilds, and imaginary cathedrals loomed as the crowns of projected garden cities, replacing the Werkbund coalition of art and industry. The return to handcrafts and to collective endeavor under the aegis of architecture brought artists together into associations such as the Novembergruppe, the Ring, and the Gläserne Kette. Drawings by the architects of the Gläserne Kette – Gropius, the Taut and Luckhardt brothers, Hans Scharoun, Paul Gösch, Hermann Finsterlin, Wenzel August Hablik, and Karl Krayl – evoke the spirit of the 1919 exhibition *Unbekannte Architekten (Unknown Architects)* at the J. B. Neumann Gallery in Berlin.

5. Yet as early as 1923, Mies rejected these retrograde utopias, and in common with the Eastern European and Dutch vanguards, set up a unique laboratory of design that aimed at reshaping "material reality." It is astonishing how, literally overnight, so many of the utopians of the Gläserne Kette metamorphosed into masters of a new, functionalist architecture. Almost all of the famous Berlin architects made their reputations with the Berlin housing developments that were thrown up to meet the needs of the working population. The outstanding achievement is the Horseshoe Development in Berlin-Britz *(figs. 10, 44, 108–109)*, supervised by Martin Wagner, City Architect and a Social Democrat, and built together with Bruno Taut. This stimulating atmosphere was even good for lesser-known architects like Erwin Gutkind, Fred Forbat, and Martin Punitzer, whose buildings, which have only recently been recognized, demonstrate extraordinarily high standards.

6. The printing trades, graphic design, advertising, fashion, and photography all experienced a heyday during the 1920s, along with architecture. In these fields, too, designers aimed at lucidity and effectiveness, at the prototypical and matter-of-fact.

Useful ceramic goods, industrially produced and decorated, revealed the astonishing artistic standards

6. Wie die Architektur stand das graphische Gewerbe, die Buchproduktion, die Werbung, die Photographie und die Mode *(Abb. 10)* in hoher Blüte, gerade in der einfachen, wirksamen, das Typische und das Selbstverständliche suchenden Gestaltung. Das keramische Gebrauchsgeschirr der Weimarer Zeit *(Abb. 12–16)* zeigt den hohen künstlerischen Standard auch der billigsten Produkte. Der Zusammenhang mit den Formen der technischen Welt und den Formexperimenten der Maler führte in diesen Jahren zu der seltenen Gleichung, daß das Billigste auch das Beste sein kann und daß das Gute für jedermann erreichbar ist. Nur ein Großstadtmarkt wie Berlin ermöglichte die Produktion etwa einer Kaffeekanne aus Steingut um 1930 zum Kaufpreis von 2–3 Reichsmark. Die Porzellankanne der KPM von Marguerite Friedlaender-Wildenhain *(Abb. 77)* kostete 1930 13 Reichsmark, ein elektrischer Wasserkessel der AEG *(Abb. 133–134)* 1912 um 25 Goldmark. Das war der Wochenlohn eines Facharbeiters.

Die Leistungen der Berliner Filmkunst verdanken ihren unverwechselbaren Stil teilweise der zeitgenössischen Entwicklung der Architektur. Dies ist in der expressionistischen Phantasiewelt Hans Poelzigs ebenso offensichtlich wie in Erich Kettelhuts und Franz Schroedters präzisen Analogie zur Gegenstandsarchitektur.

7. Den Höhepunkt und zugleich den Endpunkt findet unser Überblick im »Internationalen Stil«, verkörpert in der legendären Deutschen Bauausstellung in Berlin 1931. Hier berührten sich die Großstadtarchitektur Erich Mendelsohns, Mies van der Rohes und der Brüder Luckhardt mit der Ausgestaltung des modernen Wohnhauses und der Organisation des Massenwohnungsbaus aller bekannten Berliner Architekten.

Den klaren und leichten, scharfen und runden Formen der Architektur entsprechen die strahlend weißen Porzellangefäße von Friedlaender-Wildenhain *(Abb. 75–77)* und Petri, die farbig leuchtenden Steingut-Geräte, die blanken Stahlrohrsessel von Mies *(Abb. 1)* und Marcel Breuer *(Abb. 96–97)*, die schwerelose Transparenz der Jenaer Glasgefäße von Wilhelm Wagenfeld *(Abb. 78–80)*. Dieses apollinische Licht der Vernunft und der Schönheit war dem Tumult politischer Zerrissenheit, wirtschaftlicher Depression und sozialer Verzweiflung abgerungen.

Keine zwei Jahre später zerbrach diese Vision des Gesamtkunstwerks eines modernen und internationalen Lebensstiles in Stadt, Haus und Siedlung. Ein Ideologe der konservativen Revolution, Oswald Spengler, hatte schon 1920 den expressionistischen Utopien der Nachkriegszeit »jenes triviale Kosmopolitentum und Schwärmen für Völkerfreundschaften und Mensch-

Fig. 18 *Hans and Wassili Luckhardt, Alfons Anker. Residence of Fritz Lang and Thea von Harbou, 1930. Berlin-Dahlem, Schorlemer Allee (early photo).*
A number of important film stars such as Brigitte Helm lived in this neighborhood before it was heavily damaged during the war.

Abb. 18 *Hans und Wassili Luckhardt, Alfons Anker. Wohnhaus Fritz Lang und Thea von Harbou, 1930. Berlin-Dahlem, Schorlemer Allee.*
In der Nachbarschaft wohnten einige der Stars der UFA wie Brigitte Helm. Im letzten Krieg stark beschädigt.

applied to even the most mundane products of the Weimar period. They demonstrated that the inexpensive product could very well be the best and that quality could be put within everyone's reach. Only a metropolitan marketplace like Berlin could have made possible such products as the 1930 earthenware coffeepot at a price of 2 to 3 Reichsmarks. Marguerite Friedlaender-Wildenhain's porcelain coffeepot *(fig. 77)* for KPM cost 13 Reichsmarks in 1930, and an AEG electric kettle *(figs. 133–134)* was to be had in 1912 for about 25 Goldmarks, the equivalent of a skilled worker's weekly earnings.

The achievements of the Berlin film arts owe their distinct style, in part, to contemporary developments in architecture. This is apparent in the expressionistic fantasy world created by Hans Poelzig as well as in Erich Kettelhut's and Franz Schroedter's precise references to the architecture of the time.

7. The style with which the period culminated is the so-called International Style, which was presented to the world in the legendary German Building

heitsziele« vorgeworfen. Seine Diagnose, »der Fehler aller Wollenden ist, daß sie das, was sein sollte, mit dem verwechseln, was sein wird«[17], sollte sich in einer Katastrophe erfüllen.

In der Internationalen Handwerksausstellung in Berlin 1934, deren Katalogumschlag von Herbert Bayer noch in bester Bauhaustradition entworfen werden konnte, machen sich die neuen Manifeste eines deutschen Nationalismus, der Germanischen Rasse und eines Volkes der Bauern und Handwerker breit.

Die Münchner Ausstellung »Entartete Kunst« von 1937 ist die düstere Konsequenz.

In dem geschichtlichen Zeitraum zwischen Kaiser und Führer vollzog sich die künstlerische Arbeit der Avantgarde im Klima eines ästhetischen Kulturkampfes, einer ästhetischen Opposition gegen die offizielle und die traditionelle Kunst im Kaiserreich, anfangs getragen hauptsächlich von den Schriftstellern und Malern, vor 1933 konzentriert auf die Architekten und die Maler.

Die Losung war am Anfang und blieb bis zum brau-

Fig. 19   *Peter Behrens. Kurt Lewin Residence, 1929. Berlin-Schlachtensee, Waldsängerpfad 3 (1986 photo).*
The world-famous psychologist Kurt Lewin (1890–1947) lived in this house until 1933. After difficulties with Behrens, Kurt Lewin commissioned the young Marcel Breuer to complete the interior design.

Abb. 19   *Peter Behrens. Wohnhaus Kurt Lewin, 1929. Berlin-Schlachtensee, Waldsängerpfad 3 (Zustand 1986).*
Hier wohnte bis 1933 der weltberühmte Sozial- und Kinderpsychologe Kurt Lewin (1890–1947). Nach Schwierigkeiten mit Behrens wurde der junge Marcel Breuer mit der Innenausstattung beauftragt.

Exhibition of 1931 in Berlin. There the streams converged – the big-city architecture of Erich Mendelsohn, Mies van der Rohe, and the Luckhardt brothers, with designs for modern private residences and mass public housing by all the better-known Berlin architects. The lucid contours of the architecture corresponded perfectly with the brilliant white porcelain vessels by Marguerite Friedlaender-Wildenhain *(figs. 75–77)* and Trude Petri, with the polished tubular steel chairs by Mies *(fig. 1)* and Marcel Breuer *(figs. 96–97),* and with the weightless transparency of Wilhelm Wagenfeld's glassware *(figs. 78–80).* This Apollonian light of reason and beauty was wrested from amid political chaos, economic depression, and social despair.

Not two years later, this vision of a comprehensive design for modern, international living in city, home, and apartment was shattered. As early as 1920, Oswald Spengler, an exponent of the conservative revolution, referred to the Expressionist utopias of the postwar period as "trivial cosmopolitanism" and derided fuzzy notions of friendship between all man-

nen Ende Nietzsches Gründerzeit-Kritik, seine Absage an den Wilhelminischen Staat: »Die Kultur und der Staat . . . sind Antagonismen«[18]. Fundamentaler noch wirkte vermutlich seine Vorstellung, daß nur »die Denkend-Empfindenden« es sind, »die wirklich und immerfort etwas *machen,* das noch nicht da ist: die ganze ewig wachsende Welt von Schätzungen, Farben, Akzenten, Perspektiven, Stufenleitern, Bejahungen und Verneinungen«. Diese Denkend-Empfindenden »erst haben die Welt, die den Menschen etwas angeht, geschaffen«. Diese »vis creativa« fehle dem »handelnden Menschen«, dem »sogenannten praktischen Menschen«[19].

Solche Gedanken übertrugen auf die Künstler der Wilhelminischen und Weimarer Zeit die Last und die Mission des »großen Veränderungswunsches«, die »Arbeit an der Umschaffung der Überzeugungen« in einem umfassend verstandenen ästhetischen Zugriff. Die Neue Kunst wollte den Neuen Menschen »nicht ausdrücken, sondern schaffen« (W. J. Siedler). Diese Vision einer »Umformung der Welt«, die nur als

kind. "The mistake of all of those who long for something is to confuse what should be with what will be," Spengler declared.[17] The tragedy was that his assessment was fulfilled with a catastrophe.

At the International Crafts Exhibition held in Berlin in 1934, for which Herbert Bayer was still able to design a catalogue cover in the best Bauhaus tradition, new manifestations of German nationalism, racial presumption, and self-definition as a people of farmers and artisans, consigned the Modern movement to obscurity. The 1937 Munich exhibition *Entartete Kunst (Degenerate Art)* was the sinister consequence.

In the period between the Kaiser and the Führer, the artistic accomplishments of the avant-garde grew out of an aesthetic rebellion against the official and traditional arts of the empire. At first this struggle was conducted primarily by writers and painters, but before 1933, architects had joined painters as the lead standard-bearers. From the beginning of the battle until its "brown" end, the battle cry was Nietzsche's critique of the *Gründerzeit:* "Culture and State are antagonisms."[18]

Probably even more fundamental was Nietzsche's conviction that "only those who think and feel" can "really and constantly produce things that do not yet exist: the whole continuously growing world of new values, colors, accents, perspectives, scales, agreements, and negations." Only the thinking and feeling "have created the world that is relevant to mankind." This *"vis creativa,"* Nietzsche concluded, is lacking in "matter-of-fact" men.[19]

The "great desire for change" that Nietzsche's ideas spawned, and the attempt to "transform these convictions into comprehensive aesthetic action," became a burden as well as a mission for Wilhelminian and Weimar artists. The New Art not only wanted to "express the New Man, but to create him."

This vision of a "transformation of the world" that could only occur in the form of an "aesthetic phenomenon" led to a shaped and formed world in which was sought and found the "unity of beauty and material reality"[20]: steel tubing, nickel, aluminum, glass, stoneware, porcelain, concrete, plaster, plastics, rayon, and wool were transformed into the elements of a previously unknown world of suspended transparency, elastic weightlessness, rhythmic geometries, brilliant colors, and radiant whites.

Was the power of the arts to reshape not only material but also social reality exaggerated? Were even "political" artists bound to fail? Was the growing hostility that critics on both the extreme right and the extreme left felt toward Weimar culture only the brutal reaction to a utopian claim?

»ästhetisches Phänomen« »auszuhalten« sei, führte zu jenem Glanz einer geformten Welt, in der »Die Einheit des Schönheitsideals und der stofflichen Realität«[20] gesucht und gefunden wurde: Stahl, Stahlrohr, Nickel, Aluminium, Glas, Steingut, Porzellan, Zement, Kalk, Kunststoff, Kunstseide und Wolle wurden in die Elemente einer bis dahin unbekannten Lebenswelt schwebender Transparenz, rhythmischer Stereometrie, federnder Schwerelosigkeit, eines strahlenden Weiß und leuchtender Farben umgeformt.

Wurde die Überzeugungskraft der Kunst zur Veränderung nicht nur der stofflichen, sondern auch der gesellschaftlichen Realität überanstrengt? Müssen auch »politische« Künstler hier scheitern? War die wachsende Feindseligkeit der rechts- und linksextremen Kritik an diesem Weimarer Weltmodell nur die brutale Reaktion auf einen utopischen Ganzheitsanspruch, der alle und alles kritisierte und zu Spießern verhöhnte, was nicht »elementar« reduziert, nicht als Einheit geplant, nach Oberflächenstrukturen und Millimeterdifferenzen beurteilt, wie eine Maschine geformt, als Genossenschaft gruppiert, als Sozialdemokratie orientiert werden wollte, – das alles in einer Großstadt ohne Geschichte? Durfte man, nach Meinung der Künstler, die Welt noch anders denn unter den ästhetischen Kategorien der »Elementaren Gestaltung« betrachten?

Diese Fragen standen im Zentrum der Avantgarde selbst, seit 1930. Sie fanden Ausdruck in Adolf Behnes scharfer Kritik an der Siedlung Dammerstock bei Karlsruhe von Gropius und Haesler, in Bruno Tauts Sorge vor einem leeren Formalismus der Avantgarde, in Werner Hegemanns Parteinahme für das spitze Dach im Zehlendorfer »Dächerkrieg« gegen die flachen Dächer der Onkel Tom-Siedlung oder in Ernst Blochs Bauhauskritik. Diese breite Selbstkritik mündete in eine verbreitete Sehnsucht des Neuen Bauens nach einer neuen »Ganzheit«, heraus aus der Extremität und Exzentrizität des anderen, des immer und nur »Neuen«. Für die neue Kritik der nachwachsenden Schüler der Protagonisten war die Zeit zu kurz. Diese Diskussion wurde 1933 beendet.

Derzeit werden diese Fragen erneut aufgegriffen und, man staune, wieder als Schuldzuweis gegen die Weimarer Avantgarde gewendet[21]. »Schuld« ist nicht die nationalsozialistische Reaktion und deren gewaltsamer Abbruch eines in Gang befindlichen Entwicklungsprozesses der Avantgarde, sondern das Werk, ja die Personen selbst, sowie das Werk der wenigen der Überlebenden, die wieder ein Wirkungsfeld in der Bundesrepublik fanden.

Es waren die Künstler nicht zuletzt, die Modernisierungskräfte der immobilen Wilhelminischen Macht-

Weimar artists did criticize everybody and everything. They ridiculed as Philistines those who were opposed to "elementary reduction"; they rejected whatever couldn't be totally designed; they judged everything according to surface appearances and millimeter differences; they ignored what couldn't be formed by a machine, grouped in cooperative societies, or oriented according to Social Democratic convictions. They attempted to achieve a city of the future by deleting history.

Was it still permissible, according to their philosophy, to look at the world in aesthetic categories other than those of "elementary design"? Such questions were asked at the center of the avant-garde itself. They found expression in Adolf Behne's severe criticism of the Dammerstock housing project near Karlsruhe that had been designed by Gropius and Haesler. Similarly, Bruno Taut was concerned that the ideas of the avant-garde might develop into an empty formalism. Werner Hegemann violently defended the pitched roof in the so-called Zehlendorf roof war and opposed Bruno Taut's flat-roofed Onkel-Tom Development. The Bauhaus criticism of Ernst Bloch fits in here, too. This widespread self-criticism led to the search for the "Neues Bauen," for a new "unity," that would lead away from the extremes and eccentricities of the perpetually "new" and totally different. But time was too short for the younger generation to develop a fresh approach. The discussion was abruptly ended on January 30, 1933.

Currently these issues are being discussed again in light of the widespread, international dissatisfaction with the architecture of the last decades. Surprisingly, the critics are turning against the Weimar avant-garde once again.[21] Their "guilty" verdict is not applied to the Nazis and their suppression of the avant-garde, but to individual artists and architects themselves, even against those few survivors who decided to work again in the Federal Republic.

In the final analysis, it must be remembered that it was the avant-garde who pitted their visions of modernization against the immobility of the Wilhelminian power elite; who spiritually conceived the revolutionary beginning, before and after the defeat of 1918; and who at the very least painted and drew the tribunal to convict those who were responsible for the war. For this they paid heavily under Germany's brown dictatorship – with the material destruction of their works, expatriation, suppression, and isolation. Yet in the end, it is the achievements of these artists and intellectuals that has provided the Weimar Republic with its fame and lasting fascination. Once again, Nietzsche may be right, "All great periods of culture are times of political decline."[22]

elite entgegenstemmten. Die Künstler lieferten den revolutionären Neuanfang, wenigstens im Geiste, vor und nach der Niederlage 1918. Es waren die Künstler, die das Tribunal der Abrechnung mit den Schuldigen an der Katastrophe wenigstens zeichneten. Später hatten diese Künstler aufgrund ihrer Opposition zur Nazidiktatur mit der materiellen Vernichtung ihrer Werke, mit Vertreibung, Unterdrückung oder dem einspurigen Weiterleben in der Sackgasse zu bezahlen. Und es waren schließlich die Künstler und Intellektuellen, die der Weimarer Republik ihren unvergänglichen Ruhm schufen, weil »alle großen Zeiten der Kultur politische Niedergangszeiten« sind[22].

Anmerkungen

1 Ch.-E. Jeanneret, *Etude sur le mouvement d'Art Décoratif en Allemagne* (La Chaux-de-Fonds, 1912, Nachdruck New York, 1968), S. 74 »Si Paris est le foyer de l'Art, l'Allemagne demure le grand chantier de production«.

2 Lothar Bucher, zitiert in Heinrich Waentig, *Wirtschaft und Kunst* (Jena, 1909), S. 258. Auf S. 250f. die folgenden Zitate.

3 Franz Reuleaux, *Briefe aus Philadelphia* (Braunschweig, 1877).

4 Wolf Jobst Siedler, »Der Traum der Vernunft gebar Ungeheuer«, *Der Tagesspiegel* (Berlin, 13. 11. 1986)

5 Karl Scheffler, *Berlin, ein Stadtschicksal* (Berlin, 1910), S. 169f.

6 Zitiert in: Tilmann Buddensieg, *Keramik in der Weimarer Republik 1919–1933* (Nürnberg: Germanisches Nationalmuseum: 1985), S. 11. (vorher: *Ceramiche della Repubblica di Weimar* (Mailand: Padiglione d'Arte Contemporanea: 1984), S. 12).

7 Cf. Kirk Varnedoe, *Vienna 1900 Art, Architecture and Design* (New York: The Museum of Modern Art 1986), Fig. S. 88.

8 Wilhelm Wagenfeld, »Jenaer Glas«, *Die Form* 6 (Dez. 1931), S. 461ff.

9 Theo van Doesburg, »Was ist angewandte Kunst?«, *Wohnungskultur* 1 (1924–25), S. 22f.

10 Walter Curt Behrendt, *Alfred Messel* (Berlin, 1911), S. 125.

11 Max Osborn, »Die modernen Wohnräume im Warenhaus von A. Wertheim zu Berlin«, *Deutsche Kunst und Dekoration* (1902–03), S. 159ff.

12 Karl Ernst Osthaus, »Ein Fabrikbau von Peter Behrens«, *Frankfurter Zeitung* (10. 2. 1910), nachgedruckt in: Tilmann Buddensieg unter Mitarbeit von Henning Rogge, *Industriekultur, Peter Behrens und die AEG, 1907–1914* (Berlin), S. D 298 ff.

13 Golo Mann, »Der letzte Großherzog«, *Ein Dokument deutscher Kunst. Darmstadt, 1901–1976*, 1 (Darmstadt: Hessisches Landesmuseum: 1976), S. 29.

Footnotes

1 Ch. – E. Jeanneret, *Étude sur le mouvement d'Art Décoratif en Allemagne* (La Chaux-de-Fonds, 1912, reprinted, New York, 1968), p. 74. "Si Paris est le foyer de l'Art, l'Allemagne demure le grand chantier de production."

2 Lothar Bucher, quoted in Heinrich Waentig, *Wirtschaft und Kunst* (Jena, 1909), p. 258. The quotes that follow are on pp. 250–251.

3 Franz Reuleaux, *Briefe aus Philadelphia* (Brunswick, 1877).

4 Wolf Jobst Siedler, "Der Traum der Vernunft gebar Ungeheuer," *Der Tagesspiegel* (Berlin, Nov. 13, 1986).

5 Karl Scheffler, *Berlin, ein Stadtschicksal* (Berlin, 1910), pp. 169–170.

6 Quoted in Tilmann Buddensieg, *Keramik in der Weimarer Republik 1919–1933* (Nuremberg: Germanisches Nationalmuseum, 1985), p. 11. (First published as *Ceramiche della Repubblica di Weimar* [Milan: Padiglione d'Arte Contemporanea, 1984], p. 12).

7 Cf. Kirk Varnedoe, *Vienna 1900: Art, Architecture and Design* (New York: The Museum of Modern Art, 1986), p. 88 (fig.).

8 Wilhelm Wagenfeld, "Jenaer Glas," *Die Form,* 6 (December, 1931), pp. 461ff.

9 Theo van Doesburg, "Was ist angewandte Kunst?" *Wohnungskultur,* 1 (1924–25), pp. 22–23.

10 Walter Curt Behrendt, *Alfred Messel* (Berlin, 1911), p. 125.

11 Max Osborn, "Die modernen Wohnräume im Warenhaus von A. Wertheim zu Berlin," *Deutsche Kunst und Dekoration* (1902/03), pp. 159ff.

12 Karl Ernst Osthaus, "Ein Fabrikbau von Peter Behrens," *Frankfurter Zeitung,* Feb. 10, 1918, reprinted in Tilmann Buddensieg, in collaboration with Henning Rogge, *Industriekultur: Peter Behrens and the AEG, 1907–1914* (Cambridge, Mass., 1984), pp. 238ff.

13 Golo Mann, "Der letzte Großherzog," *Ein Dokument deutscher Kunst: Darmstadt, 1901–1976,* 1 (Darmstadt: Hessisches Landesmuseum, 1976), p. 29.

14 Tilmann Buddensieg, "Die Kaiserlich Deutsche Botschaft in Petersburg von Peter Behrens," in Martin Warnke, ed., *Politische Architektur in Europa* (Cologne, 1984), pp. 380 ff.

15 Adolf Behne, "Der Kaiser und die Kunst," *Die Tat,* 5 (1913–14), pp. 576ff. For the Kaiser's policy in matters of the arts, see Peter Paret, *The Berlin Secession: Modern Art and Its Enemies in Imperial Germany* (Berlin, 1980). Nicolaas Teeuwisse, *Vom Salon zur Secession* (Berlin, 1986).

16 Walter Gropius, in *Wohnungskultur,* 1 (1924–25), p. 8.

17 Oswald Spengler, *Preussentum und Sozialismus* (Munich, 1920), p. 20, 3.

18 Friedrich Nietzsche, *Götzen-Dämmerung,* "Was den Deutschen abgeht," no. 4.

19 Friedrich Nietzsche, *Die fröhliche Wissenschaft:* IV, *Sanctus Januarius,* Aph. 301. On this problem, see the important book by Otto Westphal, *Die Feinde Bismarcks: Geistige Grundlagen der deutschen Opposition, 1848–1918* (Munich and Berlin, 1930).

20 Van Doesburg, "Was ist angewandte Kunst?," *loc. cit.*

21 Wolf Jobst Siedler, see footnote 4.

22 Nietzsche, *Götzen-Dämmerung, loc. cit.*

14 Tilmann Buddensieg, »Die Kaiserlich Deutsche Botschaft in Petersburg von Peter Behrens«, Martin Warnke, Hrsg., *Politische Architektur in Europa* (Köln, 1984), S. 380ff.

15 Adolf Behne, »Der Kaiser und die Kunst«, *Die Tat* 5 (1913–14), S. 576ff. Zur Kunstpolitik des Kaisers siehe Peter Paret, *Die Berliner Secession: Moderne Kunst und ihre Feinde im Kaiserlichen Deutschland* (Berlin, 1981). Nicolaas Teeuwisse, *Vom Salon zur Secession* (Berlin, 1986).

16 Walter Gropius, in: *Wohnungskultur* 1 (1924–25), S. 8.

17 Oswald Spengler, *Preußentum und Sozialismus* (München, 1920), S. 20, 3.

18 Friedrich Nietzsche, *Götzen-Dämmerung: Was den Deutschen abgeht,* Nr. 4.

19 Friedrich Nietzsche, *Die fröhliche Wissenschaft* IV, *Sanctus Januarius,* Aph. 301. Zu dem ganzen Problem siehe das bedeutende Buch von Otto Westphal, *Feinde Bismarcks. Geistige Grundlagen der Deutschen Opposition, 1848–1918.* München und Berlin 1930.

20 van Doesburg, siehe Anmerkung 9.

21 W. J. Siedler, siehe Anm. 4.

22 Friedrich Nietzsche, *Götzen-Dämmerung,* loc. cit.

Fig. 20 *Peter Behrens. Building application for the AEG Turbine Factory, 1908. Berlin-Moabit, Hutten- and Berlichingenstrasse. Blueprint, signed and dated. Bezirksamt Tiergarten, Abt. Bau- und Wohnungswesen.*
The design, developed in the fall of 1908, was received at Berlin's municipal building office on February 5, 1909. Actual work on the project began on March 30, 1909. When the structure was completed, it departed in several respects from this proposal, notably in the organization of windows on the facade and side elevation, the subdivision of the corner pillars, and the positioning and detailing of the small building to the left.

Abb. 20 *Peter Behrens. Entwurf für die Turbinenfabrik der AEG, 1908. Berlin-Moabit, Hutten- und Berlichingenstraße. Blaupause, signiert und datiert. Bezirksamt Tiergarten, Abt. Bau- und Wohnungswesen.*
Der Entwurf vom Herbst 1908, als Bauauftrag bearbeitet am 5. 2.1909, weicht in mehreren Details von der Ausführung seit 30. 3. 1909 ab: Das Seitengebäude, die Fenstergliederung der Stirn- und Seitenfront, die Untergliederung der Eckpylonen.

Fritz Neumeyer

Nexus of the Modern: The New Architecture in Berlin

Fritz Neumeyer

Aufbruch zur Moderne: Neues Bauen in Berlin

It is not historical simply to retain or repeat the past; history would cease if that were so. To act historically is to bring about the New and to ensure the continuation of history.

Karl Friedrich Schinkel

»Historisches ist nicht, das Alte allein festzuhalten oder zu wiederholen; dadurch würde die Historie zu Grunde gehen; historisch handeln ist das, welches das Neue herbeiführt und wodurch die Geschichte fortgesetzt wird.«   *Karl Friedrich Schinkel*

The Neoclassical Vanguard

"When you stand before the AEG Turbine Factory at the corner of Hutten and Berlichingen streets in Moabit, you gain one of the most remarkable impressions to be had in modern Berlin." Karl Scheffler, the influential art critic of the first two decades of this century, recorded this reaction of mingled praise and astonishment in his popular book *Die Architektur der Gross-Stadt (The Architecture of the Metropolis)* in 1913.[1] He was inspired by the work and personality of Peter Behrens, an architect who had risen to European rank about 1910, whom Scheffler moreover considered to be the creator of a new, "consciously metropolitan, functional architecture." This Behrens was, and his achievement finally put an end to the ban that narrowly historical thinking in the nineteenth century had laid upon industry.

The development of "functional architecture" – at that time still a term of approval – involved nothing less than a revolution in aesthetic values. The "new perception," as Josef August Lux called it in his *Ingenieur-Ästhetik (Engineering Aesthetics)* of 1910, followed a motto voiced in Nietzsche's statement: "I want to learn more and more to see as beautiful the necessary in things; then I shall be one of those who make things beautiful."[2] Peter Behrens's turbine factory *(figs. 20–21, 122–125)* in Berlin should not be neglected by anyone who undertakes a history of twentieth-century art and architecture, for it rang in a new era. It was the "manifesto of a young industrial art," which proclaimed its acceptance of the prevailing forces of the age, and which by so doing became "the creator of a new beauty and guide to a higher utility."[3]

In defiance of tradition and art history, said Lux, the "modern eye" was able to perceive in the contem-

Die klassizistische Avantgarde

»Steht man in Moabit vor der Turbinenfabrik der AEG, an der Ecke Hutten-/Berlichingenstraße, so hat man eine der merkwürdigsten Impressionen, die man im heutigen Berlin erleben kann.« – Diese von Staunen begleitete Bewunderung, niedergelegt von Karl Scheffler in seiner weitverbreiteten ›Architektur der Großstadt‹ von 1913[1], galt Werk und Person des Architekten Peter Behrens, der um 1910 in Europa zu einer einzigartigen Stellung aufgestiegen war. Ihn feierte Scheffler als den Schöpfer einer neuen, »bewußten großstädtischen Zweckarchitektur«. Von ihr wurde der Bannkreis, den das historisch befangene Denken des 19. Jahrhunderts um die Industrie gelegt hatte, endlich durchbrochen.

Unter der Signatur der »Zweckarchitektur« – einer um 1910 noch als Auszeichnung empfundenen Begrifflichkeit – vollzog sich eine ästhetische Umwertung der Anschauungen: das »neue Auge«, so wurde es 1910 in der ›Ingenieur-Ästhetik‹ von Josef August Lux charakterisiert, folgte einer Maxime, die mit dem Satz Friedrich Nietzsches umrissen war: »Ich will immer mehr lernen, das Notwendige an den Dingen als das Schöne sehen – so werde ich einer von denen sein, welche die Dinge schön machen.«[2] Mit der Turbinenhalle von Peter Behrens in Moabit *(Abb. 20–21, 122–125)*, die fortan in keiner Kunstgeschichte zum 20. Jahrhundert mehr fehlen sollte, begann eine neue Ära der Architektur. Dieses Bauwerk verkörperte das »Manifest der jungen Industriekunst«, die zu den Grundmächten der Zeit ihr ›Ja‹ gesprochen hatte, um sich »zugleich als Schöpferin neuer Schönheit und als Führerin zu höherer Zweckmäßigkeit« zu behaupten.[3]

Das moderne »Auge« stürzte die Tradition und sah, wie Lux es formulierte, »der Kunstgeschichte zum

porary constructions of the engineer "the secret of a new beauty revealed."[4] Behrens was among the first to discover this secret, an exhilarating moment that found its echo in the enthusiastic reception given to his turbine factory by critics of the day. His industrial architecture had at long last shown, declared Scheffler, that it was possible "to arrive by way of the harsh realities of a quite unsentimental age at new, expressive forms."[5]

Around the time of the Crystal Palace Exhibition in London, Gottfried Semper had decried iron as unsuitable for architectural purposes because of the dematerialized, apparently weightless appearance of its structures. Behrens came along, however, and demonstrated by means of the rhetorical fervor of lucid, classical form that iron could produce an effect of unexpected monumentality. He transformed the sheer, undecorated structures of contemporary engineers by potentiating these structures to produce a compelling architectural form that possessed dignity and sublimity, overwhelming intensity, even passion. Behrens had adopted his idealistic notion of a "will to form" from the aesthetic theory of Alois Riegl, an influential art historian at the turn of the century. This by definition excluded a materialist aesthetic. Technology, Behrens stated emphatically in 1910, could not be considered an "end in itself," but would become significant only when used as "the principal means to achieve *Kultur*." And a "mature culture," he did not forget to point out, could not express itself through the language of technology but "only through the language of art."[6]

The AEG buildings that went up among the endless blocks of working-class tenements in the Moabit and Wedding districts in the heart of Berlin in the five years before the First World War – self-confident and forceful in design, as indebted to the Prussian classical revival as to the abstractions of engineering – marked a new epoch in architecture. They achieved the convergence of technological and aesthetic modernism that was the prime goal of the manufacturers and artists who had founded the Deutsche Werkbund in 1907. This synthesis toward an "industrial culture" was accomplished by Peter Behrens, a painter, craftsman, and self-taught architect who was still very much an outsider in German art circles when he was nominated to the AEG design advisory committee in 1907.

In Behrens's hands lay the task of creating the artistic image of a corporate empire. The responsibilities of this pioneer of industrial design were unprecedented in scope, encompassing the entire range of the company's diverse production. Behrens's endeavor to create lasting form, understood as a unified style that would

Trotz« in den modernen technischen Konstruktionen »das Geheimnis einer neuen Schönheit aufgehen«.[4] Dieses Geheimnis neuer Schönheit zu lüften, war Behrens gelungen und das beglückende Gefühl der Erlösung konnte man in der enthusiastischen Aufnahme der Turbinenhalle in der zeitgenössischen Kritik nachhallen hören. Endlich war der sichtbare Beweis erbracht, daß jenes unmöglich Scheinende möglich werden konnte, nämlich, so Scheffler, »auf dem Wege über die harten Realitäten einer ganz unsentimental gesonnenen Zeit zu neuen ausdrucksvollen Formen« zu gelangen.[5]

Hatte Gottfried Semper dem Eisen wegen der filigranen, masselos erscheinenden konstruktiven Natur um 1850 prophezeit, daß es nur einen mageren Boden für die Baukunst abgeben werde, so demonstrierte Behrens jetzt mit dem rhetorischen Pathos einer klaren Antiqua unerwartet neue Monumentalität. Nicht die ungeschminkte Sachform, nicht der ontologische Befund der Konstruktion, sondern ihre Steigerung zur eindringlichen architektonischen Form, die von Ernst und Größe, vom Bewußtsein der Berufung, von überwältigender Intensität und Leidenschaft zeugte, war das künstlerische Ziel der Gestaltung. Das idealistische Konzept des ›Willens zur Form‹, dem Behrens unter Berufung auf die Kunsttheorien von Alois Riegl folgte, verweigerte sich einer materialistischen Ästhetik. Technik, so stellte es Behrens 1910 unmißverständlich klar, durfte nicht »als Selbstzweck« aufgefaßt werden, sondern sie gewann ihre Bedeutung erst, »als vornehmstes Mittel zu einer Kultur«. Und eine »reife Kultur«, so versäumte Behrens nicht hinzuzufügen, artikulierte sich nicht durch die Sprache der Technik, sondern »nur durch die Sprache der Kunst«.[6]

Die für die AEG errichteten Bauwerke, die sich mit selbstbewußter, kraftvoller Geste, gleichermaßen preußisch-klassizistisch wie industriell-abstrakt, in den proletarischen Vierteln Moabit und Wedding aus dem Häusermeer erhoben, waren Epochebauten. In ihnen fand die Konvergenz von technologischem und ästhetischem Modernismus, wie sie der 1907 im Zusammenschluß von Industriellen und Künstlern gegründete Deutsche Werkbund zum Programm erhob, ihren markanten Ausdruck. Ins Werk gesetzt hatte diese Synthese einer signifikanten ›Industriekultur‹ ein Maler, Kunstgewerbler und Architekturautodidakt, der im Jahr seiner Berufung zum künstlerischen Beirat der AEG 1907 in Kunstkreisen noch als Außenseiter gehandelt wurde.

In den Händen jenes Mannes lag die künstlerische Gestaltung eines industriellen Imperiums: das Arbeitsgebiet dieses Pioniers des ›industrial design‹ umfaßte in einzigartiger Vollständigkeit die universale Palette

suffuse all areas of life, amounted to a *Gesamtkunst-werk*, extending from the typography for advertising brochures to letterheads and logos, from the design of switches, fittings, arc lamps, and various types of electrical appliances, all the way to the designing of huge factories and housing for workmen and their families.[7]

No other single architect's office in Europe or perhaps even in the United States was entrusted with such a fascinating variety of tasks by any comparable industrial firm. This alone empowered Behrens's Berlin studio with magnetic attraction for the younger generation, who began flocking there around 1910. Almost overnight, the forty-year-old Behrens had become a pioneer and a father figure of modern architecture. Among those who converged on his office were the future "big three," Walter Gropius, Ludwig Mies van der Rohe, and for a short time, Le Corbusier (then still Charles-Eduard Jeanneret), each of whom assisted Behrens, to their benefit and his.

Structures like the turbine factory in Moabit and the plants for small electric motors *(figs. 22, 126–127)* and heavy machinery at Humboldthain, a rocky hill high above Wedding, crowned the industrial landscape of Berlin, forming a veritable Acropolis for the Industrial Age that rendered the city a must for everyone interested in modern architecture. At the center of this achievement stood, in the words of Jeanneret, "a powerful, incredibly serious genius, profoundly suffused by an urge to dominate, a man cut out for this challenge and this era."[8]

Behrens's industrial buildings rose with "heavy grace," wrote Scheffler, above "a confusion of shabby, balcony-adorned apartment houses . . . truly dominating them . . . as a landmark not only of the AEG but of modern industrial labor itself."[9] The attraction of these monuments of the Modern movement, which to contemporaries embodied the promise of a culture suited to the age, was extraordinary. The young Walter Gropius saw in this synthesis of far-sighted organization and great artistic gifts "the strongest and clearest evidence of a new, European architectural thinking," for "with the simple means of elementary tectonics . . . structures of truly classsical grandeur" had been created, "which sovereignly dominated their surroundings."

Behrens had produced "monuments of nobility and force that no one could pass by unaffected."[10] As if to confirm Gropius's words, Edmund Schüler later recalled in his obituary for Behrens, "We went on a pilgrimage to the gigantic AEG buildings on Brunnenstrasse, and to the turbine plant. And when one of us

der Produkte des Unternehmens. Der Wille zur großen Form, die als einheitliche Stiläußerung in allen Lebenserscheinungen herbeigesehnt wurde, umspannte das Universum eines ›Gesamtkunstwerks‹, welches von der Typographie der Werbebroschüren, dem Entwurf von Briefkopf und Firmen-Signet über die Gestaltung von Schaltern, Armaturen, Bogenlampen und diversem elektrischen Gerät schließlich bis zur Planung der gewaltigen Fabriken nebst dazugehörigen Arbeitersiedlungen reichte.[7]

Kein anderes europäisches Architekturbüro dieser Zeit konnte eine solche faszinierende Fülle der Aufgaben, die den Nerv des modernen Industriezeitalters berührten, auf sich vereinen. Allein dieser Umstand mußte das Berliner Atelier von Peter Behrens gleichsam zu einem magischen Anziehungspunkt für die jüngere Generation verwandeln, die sich um 1910 hier einfand. Fast über Nacht war der vierzigjährige Behrens zum bedeutendsten Baukünstler aufgestiegen, den seine künstlerische Leistung als Bahnbrecher und Vaterfigur der modernen Architektur auszeichnete. In seinem Atelier trafen zu dieser Zeit die kommenden ›Großen Drei‹ der modernen Architektur zusammen: Walter Gropius, Ludwig Mies van der Rohe und kurzzeitig auch Le Corbusier (damals noch Charles Eduard Jeanneret) schauten Behrens als Mitarbeiter seines Büros über die Schultern.

Bauwerke wie die Turbinenhalle in Moabit, die Kleinmotorenfabrik *(Abb. 22, 126–127)* und Schwermaschinenhalle auf dem Humboldthain im Wedding bereicherten die Industrielandschaft der Metropole Berlin um eine moderne Stadtkrone, die als eine Art ›Akropolis des Industriezeitalters‹ Berlin zu einer Pilgerstätte der modernen Architektur verwandelte. »Deutschland ist ein Aktualitätenbuch«, so berichtete Jeanneret 1911, der aus der Schweiz angereist war, von seinen Eindrücken: »Behrens ist der kraftvolle, abgründig ernste Genius, zutiefst erfaßt von einem Drang nach Beherrschung, wie geschaffen für diese Aufgabe und diese Zeit.«[8]

Mit »schwerer Grazie« erhoben sich nach den Worten von Scheffler die Industriebauten von Behrens, »in einer wirren Umgebung von ärmlichen, balkongeschmückten Mietshäusern . . . wahrhaft beherrschend . . . als ein Wahrzeichen nicht nur der AEG, sondern der modernen Industriearbeit überhaupt«.[9] Die Ausstrahlung dieser Monumente der Moderne, die als Verheißung zeitgemäßer ›Kultur‹ die Zeitgenossen in Bann schlug, war außerordentlich. Der junge Walter Gropius erblickte in dieser Synthese von großzügiger Organisation und großem Künstlertum »die stärksten und reinsten Zeugen eines neuen europäischen Baugedankens, denn hier waren mit »den einfachen Mit-

Fig. 21 *Peter Behrens. AEG Turbine Factory, 1908–09. Berlin-Moabit, Hutten- and Berlichingenstrasse (1986 photo).*

Abb. 21 *Peter Behrens. Turbinenhalle der AEG, 1908–09. Berlin-Moabit, Hutten- und Berlichingenstraße (Zustand 1986).*

began to sing the praises of the 'affinities' between new industrial architecture and Hellenic antiquity, the gates seemed to open on a new heaven, a long-awaited heaven of our own."[11]

In the hands of an artist, nineteenth-century fears of the industrial method, of the moral and aesthetic consequences of building with iron, had been transmuted into hopes and thus into new values. Behrens's interpretation of the classical canon, encouraged by his confrontation with the buildings of Karl Friedrich Schinkel in Berlin and Potsdam, aimed at a merger of functional with noble form, of contemporary requirements with classical ideals. The evocative formal syntax of his industrial structures proclaimed that Behrens indeed possessed the energy and capacity, as Gropius said, to "revaluate" architectural tradition.[12]

Behrens's instinct for analogy brought about a synthesis between the classical canon and the requirements of the modern age – mass production and standardization. His industrial classicism revealed an

teln elementarer Tektonik Baugebilde von wahrhaft klassischer Gebärde« entstanden, »die souverän ihre Umgebung beherrschen«. Behrens hatte Denkmäler »von Adel und Kraft gesetzt, an denen keiner mehr empfindungslos vorüberwandelt«.[10] Wie eine Bestätigung dieser Worte von Gropius liest sich die Schilderung, die Edmund Schüler in seinem Nachruf auf Peter Behrens von der Wirkung der AEG-Bauten überlieferte: »Wir pilgerten zu den Riesenbauten der AEG, in der Brunnenstraße und zur Turbinenhalle. Und als jemand die nahe Wahlverwandtschaft zwischen neuer Industriearchitektur und früher hellenischer Antike besang, da schien uns das Tor geöffnet zu einem neuen Himmel, zu einem ersehnten eigenen.«[11]

Die Ängste des 19. Jahrhunderts vor der industriellen Praxis, vor den moralischen und ästhetischen Konsequenzen des Eisens, hatten sich unter den Händen des Künstlers Behrens in Hoffnungen und somit in neue Werte verwandelt. Seine moderne Interpretation des Klassizismus, bekräftigt durch die Begegnung mit den Bauten von Karl Friedrich Schinkel in Berlin und

independent appreciation of tradition that was entirely new. The values of Greek and Roman architecture found their confirmation in a revival of a new kind, a rebirth that at the same time revolutionized classical forms by subjecting them to the abstract principles of engineering and industry.

With his recourse to the classical tradition, Behrens intended not so much to revive as to infuse new life into the spirit of the classical age, in the hope of finding a language to express the spirit of his own. To him, the paradigm of classical art, compressed into an aphorism by Hölderlin in 1801, still held valid: "But what is our own must be learned as well as what is alien. That is why the Greeks are indispensable to us."[13] It was not until the 1920s, when a younger generation claimed to express the abstract spirit of the age directly, without recourse to analogy, that this path was rejected as a detour.

Potsdam, zielte auf die Verschmelzung von Zweck- und Würdeform, auf die Synthese von zeitgemäßen Erfordernissen und klassischen Idealen. Die suggestive Formensprache der industriellen Großbauten kündete von jener »Fähigkeit der Umwertung«, die Walter Gropius der künstlerischen Energie von Behrens attestierte,[12] und die vor ihm Nietzsche zur kulturellen Kraft schlechthin erklärt hatte.

Das Behrenssche Analogie-Wollen synthetisierte antike Gesetzmäßigkeit und den Takt der modernen Zeit mit ihren seriellen Erfordernissen von Standardisierung und Typisierung. Sein industrialistischer Klassizismus offenbarte eine Freiheit und Verbindlichkeit des Umgangs mit der Tradition, deren Selbständigkeit neuartig war. Hier fand die Antike ihre Bestätigung in der Wiedergeburt unter neuen Vorzeichen, zugleich aber auch ihre Revolutionierung im Zeichen industriell-abstrakter Prinzipien.

Fig. 22 *Peter Behrens. AEG Small Motor Factory, 1910–13. Berlin-Wedding, AEG complex at Humboldthain, Voltastrasse facade (1984 photo).*

Abb. 22 *Peter Behrens. Kleinmotorenfabrik der AEG, 1910–13. Berlin-Wedding, AEG-Komplex am Humboldthain, Fassade an der Voltastraße (Zustand 1984).*

Fig. 23   *Walter Gropius and Adolf Meyer. Fagus Shoe-Last Factory, 1910–11. Alfeld an der Leine (early photo).*
Abb. 23   *Walter Gropius und Adolf Meyer. Faguswerk, Schuhleistenfabrik, 1910–11. Alfeld an der Leine (ursprünglicher Zustand).*

The "plastic force" of revaluation ensured that the obligation of carrying on the great tradition would find convincing, contemporary form. To Nietzsche, the "philosopher of culture" whose influence on the artistic and intellectual life of the prewar period was decisive,[14] this force represented the first criterion of all cultural achievement. It was man's ability to reevaluate all values that made him human in the first place; and it was his task and duty "to use the past to live, and to remake what has been into history."[15]

Thanks to a powerful creative will, which as early as 1901 led art critics to call his a "Zarathustra style,"[16] Peter Behrens succeeded in spanning past and present aesthetically. Those who saw his factory buildings and the appliances he designed, noted Robert Breuer in 1910, clearly perceived "the arch stretching back to the classical codex"; but they also just as clearly sensed the presence of the modern Iron Age, for they "expected and looked for machinery."[17]

Modern industrial classicism became the symbol of a new identity. The stream of historical significance

Behrens hatte einen Zugriff auf die antike Tradition unternommen, der nicht die eigentliche Form, sondern den Geist der Epoche zum Leben erwecken wollte, um auf diesem Weg den Geist der eigenen Zeit zur Sprache zu bringen. Das Paradigma des Klassizismus, wie es der Dichter Friedrich Hölderlin 1801 in einen Aphorismus gekleidet hatte, behielt noch für Behrens seine Gültigkeit: »Aber das Eigene muß so gut gelernt sein, wie das Fremde. Deswegen sind uns die Griechen unentbehrlich.«[13] Erst die kommende Generation, die in den zwanziger Jahren für sich in Anspruch nahm, den abstrakten Geist der Zeit direkt, d.h. ohne Analogien zum Sprechen zu bringen, sollte diesen Weg als Umweg ablehnen.

Die »plastische Kraft« zur Umwertung war die Voraussetzung, um der Verbindlichkeit und Kontinuität des großen Formengedankens Gegenwärtigkeit und Überzeugungskraft zu verleihen. Dem ›Philosophen der Kultur‹ Friedrich Nietzsche, der auf Kunst- und Geistesleben der Vorkriegszeit entscheidenden Einfluß ausübte,[14] galt jene Kraft als Kriterium von Kulturleistung schlechthin. Erst durch die Fähigkeit zur Umwertung der Werte wurde der Mensch zum Menschen, denn es war seine vornehme Aufgabe und Verpflichtung, »das Vergangene zum Leben zu gebrauchen und aus dem Geschehenen wieder Geschichte zu machen«.[15]

Das Formwollen des Peter Behrens, dem die Kunstkritik bereits um 1901 einen »Zarathustra-Stil« attestierte,[16] verschränkte Vergangenheit und Gegenwart im ästhetischen Brückenschlag. Im Angesicht der Industriebauten und der von Behrens gestalteten technischen Geräte ließ sich, wie es Robert Breuer 1910 treffend registrierte – zwar der »Bogen rückwärts zum klassischen Kodex« eindeutig empfinden, aber man spürte ebenso bewußt den Geist der eisernen Gegenwart: »Man erwartet und sucht die Maschinen.«[17]

Der moderne Industrieklassizismus wurde zum Sinnbild neuer Identität. Der im 19. Jahrhundert versiegte Fluß des Bedeutungsstromes überhistorischer Werte war über eine »kulturvolle Verbindung«, wie Behrens sie konzipierte, wiederhergestellt. Jetzt konnte über ein verlorenes Jahrhundert hinweg Karl Friedrich Schinkel die Hand gereicht werden, denn er war es, der im Sinne jenes läuternden Vorbildes ›Um 1800‹[18] bezeichnenderweise von der Zeit ›Um 1910‹ als Vorläufer einer modernen Bauweise entdeckt wurde. Technizismus und Klassizismus waren nicht länger Feinde; im Gegenteil, sie schienen einander gegenseitig zu bedingen.[19] Was die Zeit suchte, durfte sie sich durch Schinkel bestätigen lassen, enthielt doch sein Werk bereits »schon entschieden moderne Elemente im Sinne der heutigen Nutzbaukünstler…, leise

Fig. 24   *Ludwig Mies van der Rohe. Perls Residence, 1910–11.*
Berlin-Zehlendorf, Hermannstrasse 20 (early photo).

Abb. 24   *Ludwig Mies van der Rohe. Haus Perls, 1910–11.*
Berlin-Zehlendorf, Hermannstraße 20 (ursprünglicher
Zustand).

Fig. 25   *Ludwig Mies van der Rohe. Werner Residence,*
1912–13. Design for street facade, Berlin-Zehlendorf, Quer-
matenweg 4. Watercolor. Bauhaus-Archiv, Berlin.

Abb. 25   *Ludwig Mies van der Rohe. Haus Werner, 1912–13.*
Entwurf für die Straßenfassade, Berlin-Zehlendorf, Quer-
matenweg 4. Aquarell. Bauhaus-Archiv, Berlin.

Fig. 26 *Peter Behrens. Wiegand Residence, 1911–12. Garden facade, Berlin-Dahlem, Peter-Lenné-Strasse (early photo).*

Abb. 26 *Peter Behrens. Haus Wiegand, 1911–12. Gartenfassade, Berlin-Dahlem, Peter-Lenné-Straße (ursprünglicher Zustand).*

and values that the nineteenth century had diverted into countless backwaters now flowed again, thanks to what Behrens called a "deep cultural connection." Across the wasteland of a century, architects could again stretch out a hand to Karl Friedrich Schinkel. The modern architects of 1910 rediscovered him as the central figure of the newly admired period, "around 1800."[18] Suddenly classical form and the rational structures calculated by the engineer's mind no longer seemed antagonistic but positively interdependent.[19] What the age was searching for could certainly be found in Schinkel, for his work already contained "decidedly modern elements of the kind today's utilitarian architects employ . . . faint beginnings of a consciously metropolitan, functional architecture."[20]

As early as 1905, when he noted the first signs of Greek influence and formal borrowings from antiquity in the work of Behrens, the eminent art critic Julius Meier-Graefe suggested that behind the veil of classical form lay a contemporary beauty that was merely waiting to be revealed. Meier-Graefe formulated an issue for which the time was apparently ripe, an issue that was raised by Behrens's sense of aesthetic anal-

Ansätze zu einer bewußten großstädtischen Zweckarchitektur«.[20]

Bereits 1905, angesichts der ersten Anzeichen griechischen Kunsteinflusses und antikisierender Formensprache im Werk von Peter Behrens, deutete der bekannte Kunstkritiker Julius Meier-Graefe die präexistente, durchschimmernde Möglichkeit zeitgemäßer Schönheit an, die hinter der antikisierenden Folie klassischer Formen ihr verborgenes Dasein führte und darauf wartete, freigelegt zu werden. Meier-Graefe formulierte eine Fragestellung, für die die Zeit reif geworden zu sein schien – eine Frage, die Behrens durch sein Analogiewollen aufwarf und auf die sein Schüler Mies van der Rohe erst zwei Jahrzehnte später eine definitive Antwort geben sollte: »Wäre es nicht möglich, so zu bauen, daß nichts von der Form, nur dieser anbetungswürdige kühle Geist der Griechen auferstünde?«[21]

Die prinzipielle Analogiemöglichkeit zwischen Antike und Moderne rückte den befreienden Schritt aus dem Bann des Historischen in greifbare Nähe. »Der Weg zur Antike«, so führte Meier-Graefe seinen Gedanken fort, »liegt in unserem Bereich. Er darf nicht

ogy but would not in fact be resolved until two decades later, by his student, Mies van der Rohe. "Might it not be possible," asked Meier-Graefe, "to build in such a way that nothing of the form of the Greeks is resurrected, but only that splendid, cool spirit of theirs?"[21]

The very possibility of drawing an analogy between antiquity and the modern age rendered liberation from the historical ban imminent. "The path to antiquity," Meier-Graefe declared, "runs through our own territory. It should not end in Greece, but must bring Hellenic clarity, Hellenic reason, or let us say instead beauty pure and simple, into contemporary forms."[22] The path sketched here has a vanishing point at which – beyond mere history – past and future, source and utopia, coincide. Modernism and classicism merge, as timeless, suprahistorical values.

The neoclassical vanguard nourished a notion of modern art that would distill "beauty pure and simple" into an essence in which ancient and modern beauty would mingle indistinguishably. The abstract classicism of the industrial age heralded an architecture that, as the Dutch architect J. J. P. Oud put it in 1921,

Fig. 28   *Bruno Taut. Glass Pavilion at the Werkbund Exhibition, Cologne, 1914. Staircase in the waterfall room.*
Abb. 28   *Bruno Taut. Glaspavillon auf der Werkbundausstellung, Köln, 1914. Treppe im Kaskadenraum.*

Fig. 27   *Bruno Taut. Glass Pavilion at the Werkbund Exhibition, Cologne, 1914 (destroyed).*
Abb. 27   *Glaspavillon auf der Werkbundausstellung, Köln 1914 (Zerstört).*

in Griechenland enden, sondern muß hellenische Klarheit, hellenische Vernunft, oder sagen wir statt dessen schlechtweg das Schöne in unsere Formen tragen.«[22] Der hier skizzierte Weg in die Antike fluchtete in einem Punkt, in dem – jenseits des Historischen – Vergangenheit und Zukunft, Ursprung und Utopie zusammenfielen. Modernität und Klassizität verschmolzen miteinander als überhistorische Werte.

Die klassizistische Avantgarde nährte die Vision einer Moderne, die das »schlechtweg Schöne« als Essenz einlösen wollte. In ihr gingen ursprüngliche und neue Schönheit nahtlos ineinander auf. Der überhistorische, abstrakte Klassizismus des Industriezeitalters verhieß eine Baukunst, die sich, nach den Worten des holländischen Architekten J. J. P. Oud von 1921, »frei von aller impressionistischen Stimmungsgestaltung, in der Fülle des Lichtes entwickelt zu einer Reinheit des Verhältnisses, einer Blankheit der Farbe und einer organischen Klarheit der Form, welche durch das Fehlen jedes Nebensächlichen die klassische Reinheit wird übertreffen können.«[23]

would be able to "shed all impressionistic evocation of mood, developing in broad daylight to a purity of proportion, a brilliance of color, and an organic lucidity of form that, stripped of all irrelevancies, will be able to surpass classical purity."[23]

The factory buildings Peter Behrens designed for the AEG in Berlin were superb illustrations of modern industrial potential. And, as Walter Gropius noted, they showed that industrial architecture in Germany was far in advance of that in other European nations. Furthermore, they articulated an essentially modern attitude to life, an optimism and self-confidence that led architects to compare the new functional architecture of America and Europe, "in terms of the monumental force of its impact . . . with the buildings of ancient Egypt."[24]

These "structures of truly classical grandeur" were felt to exemplify a new intellectual discipline, valid not

Die Industriebauten von Peter Behrens, die in Berlin dem Boden entwachsen waren, lieferten den schlagenden Beweis moderner großindustrieller Leistungsfähigkeit. An ihnen, so Walter Gropius, ließ sich beispielhaft der Vorsprung, den Deutschland auf dem Gebiet der modernen Industriebaukunst im Vergleich zu den übrigen Ländern Europas gewonnen hatte, ablesen. Diese Bauwerke artikulierten das Lebensgefühl der neuen Zeit, die sich in ihrem optimistischen Selbstverständnis dazu ermutigt sah, die Schöpfungen des modernen Zweckbaus, die in Amerika und Europa entstanden, »hinsichtlich der monumentalen Gewalt des Eindrucks . . . mit den Bauten des alten Ägypten« zu messen.[24]

Jene »Baugebilde von wahrhaft klassischer Gebärde« exemplifizierten eine neue – nicht allein im Künstlerischen als gültig anzuerkennende – geistige Disziplin, die zu der »knappen Straffheit unseres tech-

Fig. 29 *Bruno Taut. Glass Pavilion at the Werkbund Exhibition, Cologne, 1914. Waterfall room.*

Abb. 29 *Bruno Taut. Glaspavillon auf der Werkbundausstellung, Köln, 1914. Kaskadenraum.*

solely in art and architecture, that suited "the austerity of our technical and economic affairs, our exploitation of resources, financial means, labor and time." Modern organization and mastery required that art, too, be fundamentally modernized. "The modern age," wrote Gropius, "dictates its own significances: precisely delineated form divested of everything accidental, clear contrasts, regular articulation, a sequential arrangement of identical parts, and unity of form and color." These qualities were to characterize the design of the future and provide "the aesthetic tools of the modern artist-builder."[25]

The truth of Gropius's prophecy of 1913 was confirmed in 1927 by Ludwig Hilberseimer, in the epilogue to his book *Gross-Stadt-Architektur (Metropolitan Architecture).* Starting from Nietzsche's concept of style, Hilberseimer defined the modern "will to form," and the ardor for abstraction that marked it, by saying that it "reveres and glorifies the general case, the principle, while on the contrary discarding the exception and slurring the nuance. Moderation reigns; chaos is compelled into form: logical, unambiguous, a Mathematics, a Law."[26]

Fantastic Intermezzo:
The Cathedral of the Future

Only a few years later the high hopes of 1910 had been shattered, seemingly for good. The optimistic attempt to refine industrial civilization into an "industrial culture" by merging art with technology had succumbed to the first war in history to be waged with the full force and logic of industrialism. Between 1914 and 1918, the veil of humanism so carefully contrived by the reform movements was torn from the face of the new Iron Age. This St. Bartholomew's Day Massacre of technology was conducted with the entire repertoire of progress, including for the first time submarines, tanks, airplanes, and poison gas, at the cost of millions of human lives. The destruction unleashed by "modern" war seemed a reply on the part of the military machine to Nietzsche's "God is dead! We have killed him!" – the death knell of a European culture that had "long been veering . . . toward catastrophe."[27]

More than a few German intellectuals had welcomed the war as patriotically as most of their countrymen, hoping that it would be an antidote to bourgeois repletion and a turning point for German society and culture. By 1918 at the latest, this mood had turned into its opposite. Expressionist architects began to enthuse over peace and have visionary dreams of redemption. Bruno Taut – like many others a victim

Fig. 30 *Lyonel Feininger. Cover design for "Ja. Stimmen des Arbeitsrates für Kunst in Berlin," 1919. Private collection.*
Abb. 30 *Lyonel Feininger. Holzschnitt für »Ja! Stimmen des Arbeitsrates für Kunst in Berlin,« 1919. Privatbesitz.*

nischen und wirtschaftlichen Lebens, zu der Ausnutzung von Material, Geldmitteln, Arbeitskräften und Zeit« paßte. Im Zeichen neuen Ordnens und Herrschens bedurften auch die »Richtlinien« künstlerischer Praxis entsprechend grundlegender Modernisierung: »Die neue Zeit fordert den eigenen Sinn. Exakt geprägte Form, jeder Zufälligkeit bar, klare Kontraste, Ordnen der Glieder, Reihung gleicher Teile und Einheit von Form und Farbe« – so lautete die Gestaltcharakteristik der Zukunft, die nach Walter Gropius »das ästhetische Rüstzeug des modernen Baukünstlers« ausmachen würde.[25]

1927 sollte Ludwig Hilberseimer im Schlußwort seiner ›Großstadtarchitektur‹ diese Prophezeiung aus dem Jahr 1913 nachdrücklich bestätigen. Unter Berufung auf Nietzsches Verständnis vom Stil, definierte Hilberseimer den modernen, vom Pathos der Abstraktion geprägten Formwillen: »... der allgemeine Fall, das Gesetz wird verehrt und herausgehoben, die Ausnahme umgekehrt beiseitegestellt, die Nuance weggewischt, das Maß wird Herr, das Chaos gezwungen Form zu werden: logisch, unzweideutig, Mathematik, Gesetz.«[26]

of war fever in 1914 – wrote a manifesto to introduce the first issue of his magazine *Frühlicht (Dawn)* in January 1920, in which he castigated all "worshippers of violence" and cried out: "Their blood-swilling makes us sick – morning-after hangover. Our dawn gleams on the horizon. Long live our realm of non-violence!"[28]

War and revolution forced artists to search in new directions. Their values completely disoriented, many prewar leaders of the Modern movement turned penitently back to a medieval mystique of builders' guilds, with the aid of which Expressionism would erect a Cathedral of the Future. Peter Behrens was among them. In 1920, as if to punish himself for complicity in the carnage, he looked back on the preceding years and the hubris of *Gesamtkunstwerk* and "will to form," passing judgment on them in the devastating verdict: "Monumental art – aesthetic imperialism."[29]

The debris of values and vacuum of meaning that the war had left in its wake made utopian visions almost a matter of mental survival. Disgusted at the decline of their materialistic society, creative minds took refuge in an ideal realm of crystalline purity, from the vantage point of which they could dream, like Bruno Taut, of becoming a "master builder of the universe."[30] With his *Alpine Architektur (Alpine Architecture),* begun as early as 1917, Taut followed Zarathustra into the mountains.[31] In that rarefied air, far from the sloughs of human existence, his imagination raised crystal edifices dedicated to a universal religion in which the pure spirit, exiled, could find a new home.

The crystal, the high mountain – both symbols of primal innocence and favorite landmarks of Zarathustran topography – illustrate the themes and locale of Expressionist architectural reveries. Taut had already given an impressive tangible example of this otherworldliness in the pavilion that he designed for the glass industry for the Cologne Werkbund Exhibition of 1914 *(figs. 27–29).* The shell was built entirely of glass and let light flood into the interior space; yet for all its insubstantiality, the material of the walls cut off all visual connection with the outside world. As in Gothic cathedrals with their stained-glass windows, the real world was excluded from the interior, whose atmosphere of unreality transported the spectator into the depths of a crystal. *Crystal House, Cathedral Star, House of Heaven, Mountain Cathedral, Cosmic Edifice, Museum in the High Mountains* – such were the titles of the drawings that emerged in 1919 and 1920 from the Gläserne Kette circle in which the Taut brothers had joined with Wassili Luckhardt and his brother Hans, Wenzel August Hablik and Paul Gösch, Carl Krayl, Hans Scharoun and Walter Gropius, to renew architecture *(figs. 33–39).*

Intermezzo des Phantastischen: Die Kathedrale der Zukunft

Die großen Hoffnungen von 1910 hatten sich schon wenige Jahre später, wie es schien, für immer zerschlagen. Der optimistische Versuch, die industrielle Zivilisation durch eine Synthese von Kunst und Technik zur ›Industriekultur‹ zu veredeln, war zwischen 1914 und 1918 auf ganzer Linie gescheitert. In den Materialschlachten des ersten, mit industrieller Konsequenz geführten Weltkriegs zerriß die humanistische Folie, welche die Reformbestrebungen der eisernen Gegenwart mühsam abgerungen hatten. Die Bluthochzeit industrieller Technik mit dem Kosmos, die mit dem ganzen Repertoire des Fortschritts inszeniert wurde und erstmals U-Boote, Tanks, Flugzeuge und Giftgase zum Einsatz kommen ließ, mußte mit dem Preis von Millionen Menschenleben bezahlt werden. Das Ausmaß der Vernichtung durch den ›modernen‹ Krieg lieferte gleichsam den militärischen Kommentar zu jenem »Gott ist tot! Wir haben ihn umgebracht!«, das Nietzsche wie ein Menetekel über die europäische Kultur gesetzt hatte, die für ihn »seit langem schon« auf einen Abgrund, »auf eine Katastrophe« zusteuerte.[27]

In dieser ›Katastrophe‹ des Weltkrieges erlebte die technische und wirtschaftliche Zivilisation ihren totalen Zusammenbruch. Unter dem Stigma dieses Zeitgeschehens stand die junge Kunst der Nachkriegszeit, aus der die tiefgreifende moralische Erschütterung mit Vehemenz hervorbrach. Voller Empörung gegen die geglättete, beruhigte Linie einer unmenschlichen Sachlichkeit und voller Verachtung gegenüber dem trügerischen Harmoniebegriff der alten Welt, richtete eine berstende und splitternde Formenwelt im Expressionismus ihre Stacheln gegen alle Konventionen und klassische Schönheitsregeln auf, um mit neuen, unbefleckten Formen ein ideales Reich der Gegenwirklichkeit zu errichten.

Hatten nicht wenige Intellektuelle im Zuge der allgemeinen nationalen Hurra-Stimmung den Krieg zunächst noch als Reinigungsfaktor gegen bürgerliche Übersättigung und als Wendepunkt für die deutsche Gesellschaft und Kultur emphatisch begrüßt, so war diese Euphorie spätestens 1918 in ihr Gegenteil umgeschlagen. Verzweiflung und Friedensbegeisterung nährten jetzt die expressionistischen Architektenträume und Erlösungsvisionen. Bruno Taut, 1914 ebenfalls von der allgemeinen Hochstimmung angesteckt, verdammte in seinem Eröffnungsmanifest des ›Frühlicht‹ vom Januar 1920 die »Anbeter der Gewalt«: »Uns ist übel von ihrem Blutsaufen – Katzenjammer im Frühlicht. In der Ferne glänzt unser Morgen. Hoch, dreimal hoch unser Reich der Gewaltlosigkeit!«[28]

Fig. 31 *Hermann Finsterlin. Architectural Fantasy, 1917. Pencil and watercolor. SMPK Kunstbibliothek, Berlin.*

Abb. 31 *Hermann Finsterlin. Architektonische Phantasie, 1917. Bleistift und Aquarell. SMPK Kunstbibliothek, Berlin.*

These glass cathedrals for "the Spirit," the crystal domes of Expressionism, remained disassociated from the profane depths of human society both theoretically and in actuality, announcing with prophetic pathos that rationalism and materialism – the principles on which Taut, for one, blamed the war – had been overcome. It was only logical that Taut should go on to challenge bourgeois architecture and its norms with the battle cry, "Tear down those limestone columns in Doric, Ionic, and Corinthian, smash the whole Punch and Judy show! Down with the 'dignity' of sandstone and plate glass, rip out the marble and fine woods, throw all that rubbish on the junk pile!"[32]

This iconoclasm stopped short only at the Gothic. Medieval churches and cathedrals towered above the

Krieg und Revolution drängten den Blick in eine andere Richtung. Zutiefst verunsichert zogen sich bedeutende Künstler der Vorkriegszeit bußfertig in den mittelalterlichen Mystizismus einer expressionistischen ›Dombauhütte‹ oder ›Kathedrale der Zukunft‹ zurück. Auch Peter Behrens wandelte als Pilger unter ihnen. Wie ein Akt der Selbstbestrafung nach dem Eingeständnis der Schuld klingt sein Urteil, das er 1920 mit Seitenblick auf die Vorkriegszeit über die Anmaßung von Gesamtkunstwerk und Kunstwollen fällt, die er unter das vernichtende Satzkürzel stellt »Monumentalkunst, ästhetischer Imperialismus.«[29]

Das Vakuum der Werte und die Wirklichkeitsleere, die der Krieg hinterlassen hatte, verlangte fast lebensnotwendig danach, mit Visionen und Utopien gefüllt zu

Fig. 32   *Erich Mendelsohn. Sketch for the Einstein Tower,*
Potsdam-Neubabelsberg, 1917. Graphite and colored chalk.
SMPK Kunstbibliothek, Berlin.
Abb. 32   *Erich Mendelsohn. Entwurfskizze zum Einstein-*
turm, Potsdam-Neubabelsberg, 1917. Graphit und farbige
Kreide. SMPK Kunstbibliothek, Berlin.

centuries, shining ideals whose refulgence illuminated a drab present. The "Spirit of the Gothic" – the title of a book published by Karl Scheffler in 1917 – could certainly be seen to bear a family resemblance to the mood of the years immediately following the First World War. The community spirit to which the cathedrals owed their existence, and the broad and solid emotional foundation on which they were thought to have rested, rendered these buildings vehicles of hope to a disillusioned vanguard, perfect manifestations of that unity of social idea and religious energy for which postwar architects longed. Surveying the entire history of art from this viewpoint, they concluded, like Adolf Behne writing in Bruno Taut's *Die Stadtkrone (The City Crown),* that, "In the Gothic, Europe possessed a visual art for the last time."[33]

Associated with the monopoly on greatness enjoyed by the Gothic style was the notion of a new *Dombauhütte,* a guild of artisans and artists for the modern age. Once again, the myth of the power of

werden. Angewidert von der Verfallsgeschichte und ihrer materialistischen Kultur zog sich die tief erschütterte Künstlerseele in ein idealistisches Reich kristalliner Reinheit zurück, um aus diesem utopischen Refugium heraus, wie Bruno Taut, als ›Weltbaumeister‹[30] tätig zu werden. Mit seiner bereits 1917 begonnenen ›Alpinen Architektur‹[31] war Taut dem Weg Zarathustras in die Berge gefolgt. Fernab von den Niederungen menschlicher Existenz errichtete die Phantasie auf den Gipfeln der Alpen Kristallhäuser der heiligen Weltverehrung, in denen der reine Geist ein Exil finden konnte.

Der Kristall und das Hochgebirge – beides Symbole ursprünglicher Unschuld und Lieblingsmotive aus der Topographie des Zarathustra – bezeichneten Thema und Vorzugsort expressionistischer Architekturträume. Mit seinem Pavillon für die Glasindustrie auf der Kölner Werkbundausstellung von 1914 *(Abb. 27– 29)* hatte Taut ein solches Exempel entrückter Innerlichkeit bereits gegeben. Der ganz in Glas erstellte diaphane Baukörper umhüllte einen lichterfüllten Raum, verweigerte aber trotz seiner Immaterialität den Sichtbezug zur Außenwelt. Diese blieb wie in der gotischen Kathedrale mit ihren farbigen Fenstern aus dem Innenraum ausgeschlossen, dessen Atmosphäre der Unwirklichkeit den Besucher in das Innere eines Kristalls versetzte. ›Kristallhaus‹, ›Domstern‹, ›Haus des Himmels‹, ›Berg-Dom‹, ›Kosmischer Bau‹, ›Museum im Hochgebirge‹ – so oder ähnlich lauteten vorzugsweise die Titel von Zeichnungen, die 1919/20 als Variationen über das Thema Kristall aus dem Kreis der ›Gläsernen Kette‹ hervorgingen, zu der sich u. a. die Gebrüder Taut und Luckhardt, Wenzel Hablik, Paul Gösch, Carl Crayl, Hans Scharoun und Walter Gropius zusammengeschlossen hatten *(Abb. 33–39).*

Die gläsernen Tempel des ›Geistes‹ und die Kristall-Dome des Expressionismus, die weltlichen Niederungen auch räumlich entrückt blieben, verkündeten mit prophetischem Pathos die Überwindung von Rationalismus und Materialismus – jenen Prinzipien, die nach Meinung von Taut, zum Krieg geführt hatten. Der bürgerlichen Architektur und ihren Normen wurde von Taut mit dem Schlachtruf der Kampf angesagt: »Zerschmeißt die Muschelkalksteinsäulen in Dorisch, Jonisch und Korinthisch, zertrümmert die Puppenwitze! Runter mit der ›Vornehmheit‹ der Sandsteine und Spiegelscheiben, in Scherben der Marmor- und Edelholzkram, auf den Müllhaufen mit dem Plunder!«[32]

Einzig vor dem Gotischen machte der ›Bildersturm‹ halt. Als leuchtendes Vorbild überragten die mittelalterlichen Dome und Kathedralen die Jahrhunderte und strahlten bis in die Gegenwart. Der Geist der Gotik – so der gleichlautende Titel einer Schrift, die Karl

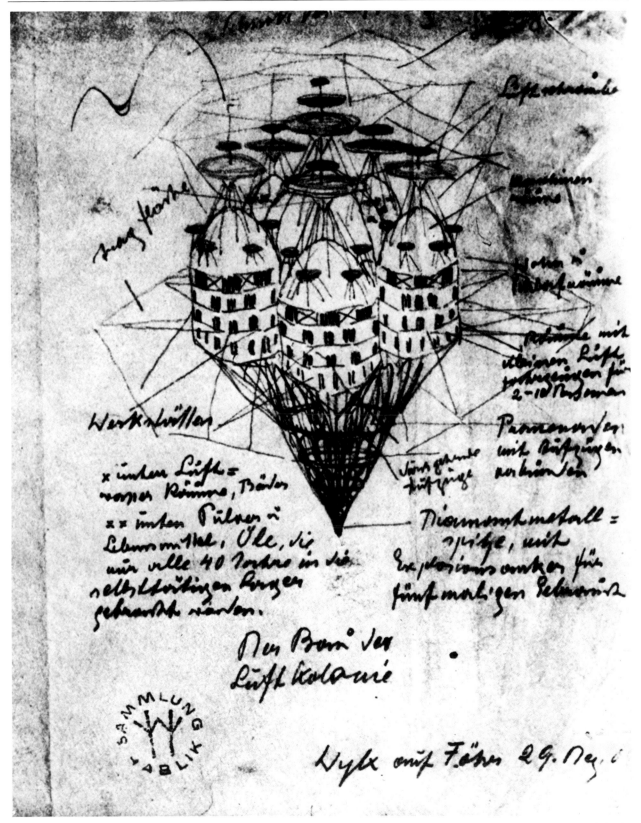

Fig. 33 *Wenzel August Hablik. Space Colony project, 1908. Pencil. Wenzel-Hablik-Stiftung, Itzehoe.*

Abb. 33 *Wenzel August Hablik. Der Bau der Luftkolonie, 1908. Bleistift. Wenzel-Hablik-Stiftung, Itzehoe.*

architecture to weld a community together was revived; but this time, the myth fed the idea of a "cathedral of socialism." The building of this cathedral would reunite the creative forces that the division of labor in the nineteenth century, with its separation of science from art, of engineering from architecture, had driven into isolation. The "creative conception of a cathedral of the future," which would once again make every creative person a "builder" of his own society, bridged a historical hiatus. Before the portals of this cathedral Walter Gropius founded the Bauhaus in 1919. The cathedral as a creative conception embodied the final and most sublime end of art: the splendid, daring, clairvoyant vision of "a happier age that must come."[34] This longing for redemption and salvation fed architectural dreams in which men's hopes and nostalgia for community would symbolically crystallize in a single great architectural idea. In this sense, not only the great buildings of the Middle Ages but also the romantic cathedral projects of Schinkel only a hundred years before might well have been taken as predecessors of such sanguine hope.

This recurrence of the medieval ideology, which found support in the work of Wilhelm Worringer and Karl Scheffler,[35] aimed at an artistic reflorescence whose dawn would coincide with a rebirth of the idea of community. An "ideal become building, bringing happiness," and making the people aware that "they are part of one great architecture, as it was long ago,"[36] – this shining future was the focus of Bruno Taut's architectural dreams. To the architect, Taut assigned the role of a Messiah, who was to meditate on his "high, gloriously priest-like, divine vocation," to immerse himself in the "great general soul" of his people, and to transmute dead material into the structural expression of the "soul forces" slumbering "in the depths of the human spirit." His mission was to overcome the constrictions of matter and infuse it with spiritual life. It was this longing for dematerialization that made the Gothic style appear to be the ideal solution. After all, art theory had attributed to the Gothic a "spiritualizing tendency," an essential aspect of a style that was diametrically opposed to the "sensualizing tendency" of Greek architecture.[37]

The rather presumptuous role of spiritual leader, in which the architect would voice the dark longings of his people for an ideal community, corresponded to the great social significance accorded to architecture as a shaping cultural force. The belief in the redemptive power of glass architecture that Bruno Taut shared with his comrades-in-arms came from Paul Scheerbart, the mentor of fantastic structures in glass. "Our culture is in a sense a product of our architecture,"

Scheffler 1917 publizierte – rückte aus der Perspektive von 1919 durchaus in eine bestimmte nachbarschaftliche Beziehung zum Geist der eigenen Zeit. Der Gemeinschaftsgeist, dem die Kathedralen ihre Entstehung verdankten, und die breite und starke Grundlage des Empfindens, das ihnen zugetragen wurde, machte aus diesen Bauwerken Hoffnungsträger ersten Ranges, in denen die ersehnte Verbindung von sozialer Idee und religiöser Energie in exemplarischer Weise zur Anschauung kam. Aus der Perspektive dieser Gesinnung wurde über die Geschichte geurteilt und – so Adolf Behne in Bruno Taut's ›Stadtkrone‹ – befunden: »In der Gotik hatte Europa zum letzten Male eine bildende Kunst.«[33]

An die Höhe der Monopolstellung dieser Kunst mochte eine neue ›Dombauhütte‹ anknüpfen. Sie erneuerte den Mythos von der gemeinschaftsstiftenden Macht der Architektur, der die Utopie der ›Kathedrale des Sozialismus‹ speiste. Ihr Bau würde die schaffenden Kräfte wiedervereinen, die das arbeitsteilige 19. Jahrhundert mit der Scheidung von Wissenschaft und Kunst, von Ingenieur und Architekt isoliert hatte. Die »schöpferische Konzeption der Zukunftskathedrale«, die alle Schaffenden wieder zu »Bauenden« werden ließ, schloß eine geschichtliche Kluft. Diese ›Zukunftskathedrale‹, vor deren Portalen Walter Gropius 1919 das ›Bauhaus‹ gründete, verkörperte das höchste und letzte Ziel der Kunst, denn sie lieferte die glühende, kühne, weitvorauseilende Bauidee für »eine glücklichere Zeit, die kommen muß«.[34] Erlösungssehnsucht und Heilserwartung nährten einen Architekturtraum, in dem das Sehnen und Hoffen der Menschen auf Gemeinschaft in einem großen Baugedanken symbolhaft kristallisieren würde. Doch nicht erst die großen Bauwerke des Mittelalters, auch die nur hundert Jahre zuvor von Karl Friedrich Schinkel entworfenen romantischen Dom-Projekte hätten in diesem Zusammenhang als kathedrale Vorläufer in Anspruch genommen werden dürfen.

Die kunsttheoretisch begleitete Perspektivwendung ins Mittelalter, die mit den Arbeiten Worringers und Schefflers legitimiert werden konnte,[35] galt der Wiedergeburt einer Kunst, die erst mit der Erneuerung der Idee der Gemeinschaft ans Licht wuchs: Ein »glückbringendes, baugewordenes Ideal«, das alle zum Bewußtsein führte, »daß sie Glieder einer großen Architektur sind, wie es einst war«,[36] stand im Orientierungszentrum Tautscher Architekturträume, die den Bau der Zukunft beschworen. Der Architekt, dem Taut die Rolle eines Messias zugedacht hatte, sollte sich auf seinen »hohen, priesterhaft herrlichen, göttlichen Beruf« besinnen, sich in die »Seele des Volksganzen« vertiefen, und den Materie gewordenen, baulichen

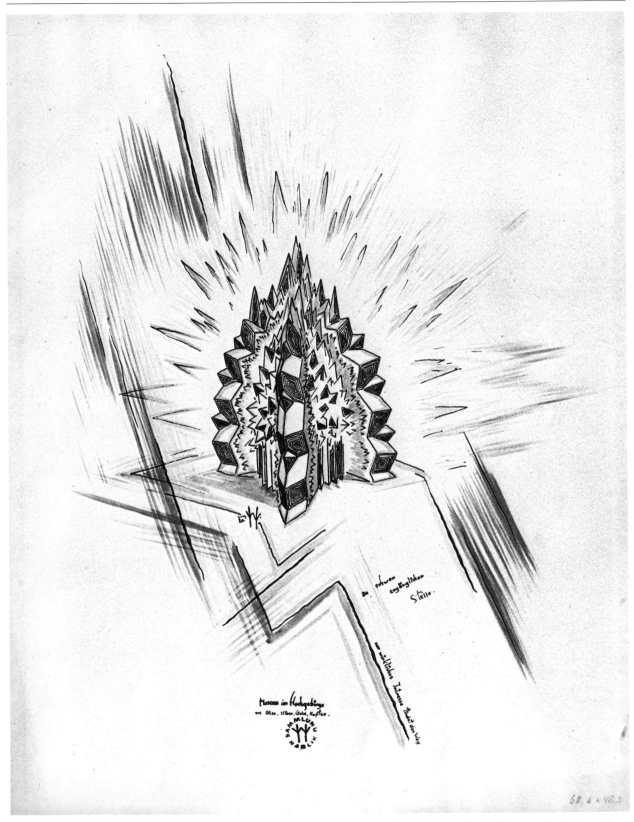

Fig. 34   *Wenzel August Hablik. Museum in the Mountains,*
c. 1920. Ink wash. Wenzel-Hablik-Stiftung, Itzehoe.

Abb. 34   *Wenzel August Hablik. Museum im Hochgebirge,*
um 1920. Zeichnung. Wenzel-Hablik-Stiftung, Itzehoe.

Fig. 35 *Paul Gösch. Fantasy Tabernacle, c. 1919. Watercolor and ink. Private collection.*

Abb. 35 *Paul Gösch. Phantastischer Tabernakelbau, um 1919. Aquarell und Tusche. Privatbesitz.*

begins the passage in Scheerbart's *Glasarchitektur (Glass Architecture)* of 1914, which architects after 1918 frequently cited as their credo.[38] They likewise followed Scheerbart's reversal of the proposition, which reads: "If we want to bring our culture to a higher level, we shall be compelled, like it or not, to transform our architecture.... But that can be done only by introducing glass architecture.... The new milieu we thereby create must bring us a new culture."[39]

Scheerbart, a humorously dogmatic poet of glass, and in Behne's affectionate term the "true patron saint" of the Gläserne Kette,[40] provided the main literary visions from which the Expressionists' crystal euphoria drew sustenance. They transmuted this insubstantial, inorganic material into a mythical substance, one of whose intrinsic qualities, it seemed, was an ability to purify and redeem. The moral force of glass would create a new paradise on earth. Indeed, its powers of healing were so strong that its advocates surmised it could transform even Europeans into human beings.[41]

In a glass architecture that would suspend the force of gravity and overcome the obstinate solidity of matter, the "new spirit" replaced religious faith in the Beyond with the idea of community, of a just society on

Ausdruck für die »in der Tiefe des Menschengemüts« schlummernden »Seelenkräfte des Volkes« schaffen. Seine Kunst war es, das Materielle zu überwinden und dem toten Stoff Geist einzuhauchen. Und es war dieser Drang nach Entmaterialisierung, der die gotische Architektur vorbildlich machte, denn ihr war von der Kunsttheorie jene ›Vergeistigungstendenz‹ als wesensgemäß zugeschrieben, die als Gegensatz zur ›Versinnlichungstendenz‹ der griechischen Architektur verstanden werden durfte.[37]

Dem nicht unbescheidenen Rollenverständnis des Architekten als dem geistigen Führer, der das Streben des Volkes nach der idealen Gemeinschaft artikulierte, entsprach die führende gesellschaftliche Bedeutung, die der Architektur kulturell beigemessen wurde. Von Paul Scheerbart, dem Mentor phantastischer Glasarchitektur, stammte der Glaube an die erlösende Macht der Glasarchitektur, in dem sich Bruno Taut und seine Mitstreiter eins wußten. »Unsre Kultur ist gewissermaßen ein Produkt unsrer Architektur«, so begann jene Passage aus Scheerbart's Glasarchitektur von 1914, die nach 1918 als Glaubensbekenntnis gerne zitiert wurde.[38] In ihm wurde auch der Umkehrschluß gezogen: »Wollen wir unsre Kultur auf ein höheres

Fig. 36 *Paul Gösch. Gate, undated. Watercolor with ink. Private collection.*

Abb. 36 *Paul Gösch. Tor, undatiert. Aquarell mit Tusche. Privatbesitz.*

earth. The glass temple was to be its consecrated place, emerging from the center of the great Garden City like a crown of multicolored glass, towering like a cathedral over a medieval town; and to this sacred symbol the inhabitants would climb, individuals longing to experience and be uplifted by the spirit of community. Chastened and blessed by the sacraments of the crystalline, they might well then join Bruno Taut in his paean: "Long live our realm of non-violence! Long live the transparent, the clear! Long live the crystal. And long and ever longer live the fluid, graceful, angular, brilliant, sparkling, light – eternal building, long may it live!"[42]

However, these dreams of a future architecture were not spared their "morning-after hangover" either. The retreat from the realm of the fantastic was not long in coming. In 1920, members of the Gläserne Kette ceased their correspondence, and Bruno Taut temporarily suspended publication of the *Frühlicht* series. A year later, the Berlin Arbeitsrat für Kunst (Working Council for Art) *(fig. 30)*, that most important of all associations of Expressionist artists, disbanded; they had overestimated their capacity to influence cultural policy in Germany. The reasons why leading agitators of the movement like Taut and Behne turned their backs on utopia were numerous enough. Criticism from outside their ranks, to which they had at first seemed impregnable, could not in the long run be pushed aside by yet another fervent confession of faith. Tensions and conflicts within, which could be ignored just as little, did the rest.

Particularly disillusioning was the co-optation of Expressionist forms by popularizers. During 1920 and 1921, the vanguard style became all the rage in Berlin. The interior design of the Berlin nightclub Skala Dance Casino, done in 1920 by Walter Würzbach and Rudolf Belling, and the expressionistic decoration in 1921 of a roller coaster at the popular amusement center, Lunapark, in Berlin-Halensee, were two of the more extreme instances of clever commercial exploitation of the revered symbols of purity. Even Wassili Luckhardt, the apostle of purism, thought it not beneath him to assist in the erection of a gigantic crystalline structure for advertising purposes at the Avus, Berlin's automobile racing track. Twenty-four-carat Expressionist buildings – assuming such heady conceptions were capable, technically, of being built at all – remained few and far between. The most impressive manifestations of the New Age, such as Erich Mendelsohn's Einstein Tower of 1917 *(fig. 32)*, or the auditorium of the Grosses Schauspielhaus built to Hans Poelzig's designs in 1919, whose ceiling recalled Islamic stucco arching like that of the Alhambra, could figure as programmatic struc-

Niveau bringen, so sind wir wohl oder übel gezwungen, unsre Architektur umzuwandeln...Das aber können wir nur durch die Einführung der Glasarchitektur... Das neue Milieu, das wir uns dadurch schaffen, muß uns eine neue Kultur bringen.«[39]

Der Glaspoet Scheerbart, den Behne liebevoll als »wahrhaftigen Schutzheiligen« der Gläsernen Kette titulierte,[40] hatte mit seinem literarischen Schaffen die entscheidenden Visionen geliefert, mit denen sich die Kristall-Euphorie der Expressionisten versorgte. Bei ihnen verwandelte sich dieses immaterielle, unorganische Material in einen mythischen Stoff, dem eine reinigende, erlösende Wirkung gleichsam als Substanzeigenschaft anhaftete. Die moralische Kraft des Glases erzeugte eine neue, paradiesische Welt, und diesem heilsbringenden Stoff durfte man sogar die bekehrende Macht zutrauen, selbst aus dem Europäer einen Menschen zu machen.[41]

In der Überwindung der Schwere und der Materie durch die Glasarchitektur triumphierte der neue ›Geist‹, der an die Stelle der alten Religion den sozialen Gedanken, die Idee der Gemeinschaft setzte. Ihr war der gläserne Tempel als Heiligtum geweiht, der als ›Stadtkrone‹ aus der Mitte der großen Gartenstadt herauswuchs. Zu diesem Kultbau aus farbigem Glas, der sich wie eine Kathedrale über der mittelalterlichen Stadt erhob, stieg der Mensch als einzelner empor, um den Geist der Gemeinschaft sinnhaft zu erleben und sich mit ihm zu durchdringen. Geläutert und durch die Sakramente des Kristallinen geweiht, mochte er dann ergriffen mit Bruno Taut emphatisch anstimmen: »Hoch, dreimal hoch unser Reich der Gewaltlosigkeit! Hoch das Durchsichtige, Klare! Hoch die Reinheit! Hoch der Kristall! und hoch und immer höher das Fließende, Grazile, Kantige, Funkelnde, Blitzende, Leichte – hoch das ewige Bauen!«[42]

Aber auch diesen Träumen vom Bau der Zukunft blieb der »Katzenjammer im Frühlicht« nicht erspart. Der Rückzug aus dem Reich des Phantastischen ließ nicht lange auf sich warten. 1920 stellte die ›Gläserne Kette‹ ihre Korrespondenz ein, im gleichen Jahr beendete Bruno Taut fürs erste die Herausgeberschaft der ›Frühlicht‹-Reihe. 1921 löste sich der Berliner ›Arbeitsrat für Kunst‹ *(Abb. 30)* auf, der wichtigste Zusammenschluß expressionistischer Künstler, der seine Einflußnahme auf die Kulturpolitik als Organisation überschätzt hatte. Gründe dafür, weshalb führende Agitatoren der Bewegung wie Taut und Behne der utopischen Welt den Rücken kehrten, gab es genug. Die Kritik von außen, gegenüber der man bisher regelrecht imprägniert zu sein schien, ließ sich auf die Dauer nicht allein mit pathetischen Bekenntnissen vom Tisch wischen. Widersprüche und Spannungen im Inneren,

Fig. 37   *Carl Krayl. Cosmic Building, c. 1919–20. Graphite, ink and watercolor. Private collection.*

Abb. 37   *Carl Krayl. Kosmischer Bau, um 1919–20. Graphit, Tusche und Aquarell. Privatbesitz.*

tures only with reservations. In Berlin, too, such clients as the owner of the Villa Buchthal in Berlin-Westend, who permitted his architects, the Luckhardts, and his landscape architect, Eryk Pepinski, to carry the jagged lines of the furniture on through the outline of the house and all the way to the shape of the flower beds, remained, emphatically, exceptions.

Such less stringent confessions of faith in crystalline form as the Otte Residence of 1921 prove that Expressionist exuberance had by no means deprived the prewar canon of all validity. In the neoclassical axiality of the Otte House, Gropius paid homage to his teacher – the same Peter Behrens whom in 1919 he could still call an "architectural confidence man"[43] – by quite obviously updating Behrens's 1908 Cuno Residence in Hagen. There is an oblique tension created, however, by the layout of the entry path and garden walls, which, too, may well owe less to Expressionism than to the influence of Frank Lloyd Wright, whose idea of diagonal composition would certainly have been

die gleichermaßen nicht zu ignorieren waren, traten hinzu.

In besonderem Maße desillusionierend wirkte die Vereinnahmung expressionistischer Formen durch den Alltag. Der Stil der Avantgarde wurde 1920/21 in Berlin zur populären Mode. Der Innenausbau des Berliner Nachtclubs des Skala-Tanzkasinos 1920 durch Walter Würzbach und Rudolf Belling, die expressionistische Außendekoration einer Achterbahn auf dem bekannten Rummelplatz ›Lunapark‹ in Berlin-Halensee 1921 zeigten extreme Beispiele geschickter kommerzieller Verwertung der ehernen Symbole der Reinheit. Selbst Wassili Luckhardt, der Apostel des Purismus, war sich 1922 nicht zu schade, an der Errichtung einer gigantischen Kristallform für Reklamezwecke an Berlins Autorennstrecke, der Avus, mitzuwirken. Lupenreine expressionistische Bauwerke waren, sofern sich die eigenwilligen Gebilde im technischen Sinn überhaupt ›bauen‹ ließen, kaum auszumachen. Die eindrucksvollen Manifestationen der neuen Zeit,

Fig. 38   *Hans Scharoun. Untitled, 1919. Watercolor. Akademie der Künste, Berlin.*

Abb. 38   *Hans Scharoun. Ohne Titel, 1919. Aquarell. Akademie der Künste, Berlin.*

Fig. 39 *Hans Scharoun House of the Dead, 1919. Water-color. Akademie der Künste, Berlin.*

Abb. 39 *Hans Scharoun. Haus der Toten, 1919. Aquarell. Akademie der Künste, Berlin.*

familiar to Gropius from the famous Wasmuth publication of Wright's work in 1911. Though it would be going too far to interpret the Otte Residence as a sign of transition, the time for rethinking had evidently arrived by 1921. "Watered-down Expressionism,"[44] which by that time was masquerading as the real thing even in "racketeers' dives," caused even those who had still hotly defended the phantasms of the Gläserne Kette in 1920 to break out in a cold sweat. The return to the here and now, which architects had believed they must sacrifice in order to devote themselves to "working for the future,"[45] had begun.

Building Contemporary Reality: "Architecture and the Demands of the Age"

"No one can shape the past or the future, only the present. This is true, creative building – creating form

wie der 1917 durch Erich Mendelsohn errichtete Einsteinturm *(Abb. 32)* oder der 1919 nach dem Entwurf von Hans Poelzig entstandene Saal des Großen Schauspielhauses, der an islamische Stuckgewölbe wie die der Alhambra erinnerte, durften nur bedingt als programmatische Bauwerke gelten. Auch in Berlin blieben Bauherrn, wie jener der ›Villa Buchthal‹ in Berlin-Westend, der es seinen Architekten Luckhardt und dem Gartenarchitekten Pepinski gestattete, die kantige Linie des kristallinen Design vom Möbel über den Baukörper bis in die Blumenrabatten des Gartenplans hinauszutragen, eine ausgesprochene Seltenheit.

Weniger formenstrenge Bekenntnisse zum Kristallinen, wie das Haus Otte von 1921, belegten, daß das expressionistische Pathos die Ordnungsmächte von einst keineswegs entwertet hatte. In der neoklassizistischen Axialität des Hauses Otte erwies Gropius seinem 1919 noch »Architektenhochstapler«[43] geziehenen Lehrer Peter Behrens Reverenz, dessen Haus Cuno

Fig. 40   *Fritz Höger. Perspective view of Evangelical Church on Hohenzollernplatz, c. 1928. Graphite. SMPK Kunstbibliothek, Berlin.*
Abb. 40   *Fritz Höger. Perspektive der Evangelischen Kirche am Hohenzollernplatz, um 1928. Graphit. SMPK Kunstbibliothek, Berlin.*

Fig. 41   *Ludwig Mies van der Rohe. Design for a skyscraper at the Friedrichstrasse Station, 1922. Charcoal and pencil. Museum of Modern Art, New York.*
Abb. 41   *Ludwig Mies van der Rohe. Entwurf für ein Hochhaus am Bahnhof Friedrichstraße, 1922. Bleistift und Kohle. Museum of Modern Art, New York.*

out of the nature of the task and with present-day means. *That is our work.*"[46] This recall to order, a demand that architects concentrate on the job at hand, heralded a new appoach. Its most outspoken advocate, Mies van der Rohe, confident of being in possession of an objective truth, relegated all high-flown utopias to the realm of illusion. Not until the fundamental relationships governing all architecture past and present were determined, Mies proclaimed, would true renewal become a possibility.

"The art of building is the will of the time translated into space. Vital – changing – new."[47] This universal definition of architecture claimed validity beyond historical vicissitude. It was a typically Miesian formula that raised contemporaneity to a vital principle, a truth relevant not solely to architecture, whose objective character seemed undeniable. The laws governing contemporary design, Mies thought, must be derived not from subjective artistic imagination, nor from aesthetic tradition, but only from contemporary life itself, its given conditions and requirements.

in Hagen von 1908 hier sichtlich erneuert wurde. Auch die Über-Eck-Verspannung des Baukörpers durch die Wegeführung des Zugangs mochte weniger auf den Expressionismus, als vielmehr auf den Einfluß von Frank Lloyd Wright zurückzuführen sein, dessen Idee der Diagonalkomposition Gropius durch die berühmte Wasmuth-Publikation von 1911 selbstverständlich bekannt war. Man greift vermutlich zu hoch, wollte man das Haus Otte als ein Signal der Umkehr interpretieren, doch die Zeit der Besinnung schien 1921 gekommen. Der »heutige Allerweltsexpressionismus«,[44] der sich als Maskerade sogar in »Schieberlokalen« breit gemacht hatte, löste selbst bei denen, die die Phantastizismen der ›Gläsernen Kette‹ noch 1920 glühend verteidigt hatten, nur blankes Entsetzen aus. Die Rückkehr in die Gegenwart, die man zugunsten der »Zukunftsarbeit« glaubte preisgeben zu müssen,[45] hatte begonnen.

Once again architectural priorities were reordered. Instead of escaping from reality into fantastic utopias and visionary dreams, architects rediscovered their enthusiasm for the here and now. The focus shifted from the imaginary realm of cathedrals for the future to the concrete world of a mechanized present that required direction and order. The subjectivity of Expressionism was supplanted with equal passion by the objectivity of rationalism.

To seize utopia – no less an aim impelled the reorientation of German art and architecture that set in after 1922, affecting even Expressionism. The same Adolf Behne who in 1920 had staunchly defended the crystalline visions against the critics, now, in 1921, introduced readers of Bruno Taut's new *Frühlicht* series to the ideas of Dutch de Stijl and French L'Esprit Nouveau. Hans Poelzig's expressive naturalism was an intellectual misunderstanding – declared the changed Behne – who turned his sympathies to J. J. P. Oud and Le Corbusier, architects who accepted the machine as a means to liberate the spirit, who instead of fleeing the present affirmed its significance.[48]

Others, such as Mies, laconically dismissed the efforts of the Expressionists as futile, laying them to rest once and for all:

Die Konstruktion zeitgemäßer Wirklichkeit: ›Baukunst und Zeitwille‹

»Nicht das Gestern, nicht das Morgen, nur das Heute ist formbar. Nur dieses Bauen gestaltet. Gestaltet die Form aus dem Wesen der Aufgabe mit den Mitteln unserer Zeit. *Das ist unsere Arbeit*«[46] – Aus diesem ›Rappel à l'Ordre‹, das zur Besinnung auf die eigentliche Sache drängte, tönte der Geist der neuen Zeit. In der Person von Mies van der Rohe hatte er den entschlossenen Fürsprecher gefunden, der mit der Selbstsicherheit eines jenen, der sich im engen Kontakt mit der objektiven Wahrheit wähnte, die hochfliegenden utopischen Scheinwelten ins Abseits stellte. Erst die Klärung grundlegender Zusammenhänge, die für das Wesen des Bauens allgemeine Verbindlichkeit besaßen, so betonte Mies, eröffnete die Möglichkeiten zu einer wirklichen Erneuerung.

»Baukunst ist raumgefasster Zeitwille. Lebendig. Wechselnd. Neu.«[47] – Nicht anders lautete die universale Definition der Baukunst, die über den historischen Wechsel hinaus Gültigkeit beanspruchen durfte. Diese Miessche Formel proklamierte den Willen zum Zeitgemäßen als Lebensprinzip und eine Wahrheit jenseits der Architektur, deren objektiver Charakter bejaht wer-

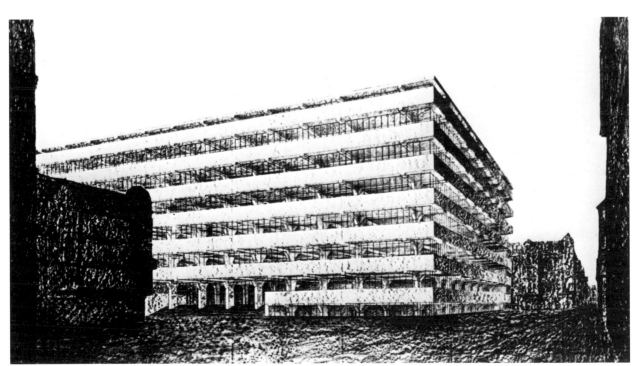

Fig. 42 *Ludwig Mies van der Rohe. Design for a concrete office building, 1923. Charcoal and pencil. Museum of Modern Art, New York.*

Abb. 42 *Ludwig Mies van der Rohe. Entwurf für ein Bürohaus in Beton, 1923. Bleistift und Kohle. Museum of Modern Art, New York.*

Present-day aspirations are secularly oriented. The mystics' efforts will remain an episode. Despite a greater profundity in our conception of life, we shall build no cathedrals. That is not the will of our time; we value not the grand gesture but reason and the real. The demands of the age for utility and functionality must be fulfilled. If this is done with compassion, contemporary buildings will carry the greatness of which the age is capable, and only a fool will be able to maintain that they are without greatness.[49]

In 1922 Mies had already given a convincing demonstration that truth to materials and functionality, without relying on historically derived form of any kind, could indeed produce a great building design: his competition entry for a high-rise office block at Fried-

den mußte. Nicht aus subjektiver ästhetischer Phantasie noch aus der ästhetischen Tradition, sondern allein aus dem Leben selbst und seinen vorgegebenen Notwendigkeiten waren die Gesetze des Zeitgemäßen herzuleiten.

Eine Ablösung wurde vollzogen: An die Stelle der Wirklichkeitsflucht in phantastische Utopien und der Sehnsucht nach wirklichkeitsentrückten Bildern trat ein neuer Enthusiasmus für die unmittelbare Realität. Der Fluchtpunkt des Utopischen wanderte von der imaginären Welt der ›Kathedrale der Zukunft‹ herüber in die dinglich-konkrete Welt der maschinellen Gegenwart, die nach einer neuen Definition der Ordnung und nach einer Vision für die Strukturierung der sichtbaren Realität verlangte. Das kühle Pathos der Sachlichkeit löste das schwärmerische Pathos des Subjektivismus ab.

Fig. 43 *Erich Mendelsohn. Redesigned facade of the Mosse commercial premises, Berlin, 1922.*

Abb. 43 *Erich Mendelsohn. Umbau des Geschäftshauses Mosse, Berlin, 1922.*

Fig. 44   *Bruno Taut and Martin Wagner. Horseshoe Development, 1925–31. Berlin-Britz, view of the horseshoe curve (1986 photo).*

Abb. 44   *Bruno Taut und Martin Wagner. Hufeisensiedlung, 1925–31. Berlin-Britz, Blick in das Hufeisen (Zustand 1986).*

richstrasse Station *(fig. 41)* in Berlin. Mies's daring studies of glass-walled skyscrapers were unparalleled at the time in terms of structural logic, radical concept, and perfection of form. They had a definitiveness, a poetic precision, that made them seem at once wildly utopian and solidly realistic; they were designs of absolute maturity that nevertheless marked only the beginning of a new departure.

The critics of the day, impressed by the "towering Gothic force" of these prisms and polygons of glass, announced a breakthrough for the architecture of the future, a new "architecture in the highest sense," for which Mies's designs were to provide the prototype. Impersonal and timeless, abjuring every ornamental idiosyncrasy, they embodied the spirit of a new age. "In their unheard-of monumentality, which scorns traditional ideas of scale," wrote Carl Gottfried, "they speak a new language – the language of our era."[50]

This vision of a coming architecture was not without its links to the crystalline visions of Expressionism. A dematerialization of architectural volume could hardly be carried further than in Mies's pure skin-and-bones designs. The steel skeleton was enveloped in an

Die Eroberung der Utopie durch die Realität – nichts Geringeres stand über der Neuorientierung der deutschen Kunst nach 1922, von der auch der Expressionismus nicht unberührt blieb. Derselbe Adolf Behne, der 1920 noch mutig die Luftschlösser gegen die Stimmen der Kritiker verteidigte, führte 1921 die Leser von Bruno Tauts neuer Folge des ›Frühlicht‹ in die Ideenwelt der holländischen ›De-Stijl‹ Bewegung und des französischen ›L' Esprit Nouveau‹ ein. Den expressiven Naturalismus eines Hans Poelzig stempelte Behne jetzt als geistiges Mißverständnis ab, um im Kontrast dazu die Gedanken von J. J. Oud und Le Corbusier zu präsentieren. Ihnen galt jetzt seine Sympathie, weil sie die Maschine als ein Mittel zur Freiheit des Geistes akzeptierten, weil sie nicht aus der Gegenwart flohen, sondern ihren Sinn bejahten.[48]

Andere, wie Mies, zogen in lapidarer Diagnose einen Schlußstrich unter das aussichtslose Bemühen der Expressionisten: »Das Streben unserer Zeit ist auf das Profane gerichtet. Die Bemühungen der Mystiker werden Episode bleiben. Trotz einer Vertiefung unserer Lebensbegriffe werden wir keine Kathedralen bauen. Unsere Zeit ist unpathetisch, wir schätzen nicht den

uninterrupted surface of glass, as in a transparent veil; the traditional facade dissolved into a fascinating play of reflected light. A majestic, sharp-edged, glittering crystal cliff rose into the air, overtopping the mundane bustle of the historical city with the power of a cathedral. It was probably this "near-Expressionism" of Mies's version of the Cathedral of the Future, in which glass architecture reached its culmination, that prompted Taut to publish it in his *Frühlicht* – which, with this issue, finally ceased publication altogether.[51]

Berlin's pervasive optimism between 1922 and 1924 made the city an intellectual focus and gathering place for the European vanguard. A long list of exhibitions and publications reveals the active role Berlin played in the dissemination of 1920s art, with its broad spectrum of approaches and stylistic pluralism. The Novembergruppe in particular, founded in 1918 with a membership that included important Berlin artists of all persuasions, manifested the European breadth of the Modern movement. It was from this group that the initiators of the journal *G* emerged, the European organ of *Elementare Gestaltung (Elementary Design)* published in Berlin by Hans Richter, Werner Graeff, Mies van der Rohe, Theo van Doesburg, El Lissitzky, and Ludwig Hilberseimer. Its contributing authors included, among others, Piet Mondrian, Kasimir Malevich, Naum Gabo, Antoine Pevsner, Viking Eggeling, George Grosz, John Heartfield, Tristan Tzara, Man Ray, Raoul Hausmann, and Hans Arp.

großen Schwung, sondern die Vernunft und das Reale. Die Forderungen der Zeit nach Sachlichkeit und Zweckmäßigkeit sind zu erfüllen. Geschieht das großen Sinnes, dann werden die Bauten unserer Tage die Größe tragen, deren die Zeit fähig ist, und nur ein Narr kann behaupten, daß sie ohne Größe sind.«[49]

Ein schlagendes Beispiel für die beeindruckende Größe, die sich gewinnen ließ, wenn man Bauten unter Verzicht auf jede historisch ableitbare Form allein nach den Bedingungen der Zweckmäßigkeit und Materialgerechtigkeit entwarf, hatte Mies 1922 mit seinem Beitrag zum Wettbewerb für ein Hochhaus am Bahnhof Friedrichstraße *(Abb. 41)* gegeben. In der prinzipiellen Durchdachtheit, in der radikalen Konzeption und formalen Vollendung zeigten sich die kühnen Glashochhaus-Studien von Mies ohne jeden Vergleich. Exemplarisch in ihrem definitorischen Charakter, phantastisch in ihrer präzisen Poesie, wirkten diese neuartigen gläsernen Gebilde realistisch und utopisch zugleich, erschienen sie ausgereift und zu Ende gedacht und standen doch erst am Beginn der Entwicklung.

Die zeitgenössische Kritik, die den Prismen und Polygonen aus Glas »turmhaft, gotische Kraft« attestierte, erblickte in ihnen den Durchbruch der Gestaltcharakteristik kommender Architektur. Die Prototypen einer neuen »Baukunst im höchsten Sinne« waren geboren: unpersönlich und zeitlos, konträr jedem ornamentalen Individualismus vergegenwärtigten sie

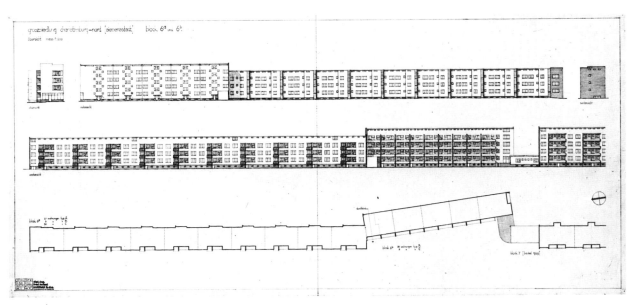

Fig. 45 *Alfred Forbat. Preliminary drawing for Siemensstadt housing project, 1929–30. Berlin-Charlottenburg, Geisslerpfad 1–29, elevation of the east and west facades of block 6a, b. Pencil. Bauhaus-Archiv, Berlin.*

Abb. 45 *Alfred Forbat. Vorentwurf für die Großsiedlung Siemensstadt, 1929–30. Berlin-Charlottenburg, Geißlerpfad 1–29, Aufrisse der Ost- und Westfassade, Block 6a, b. Bleistift. Bauhaus-Archiv, Berlin.*

Fig. 46   *Erwin Gutkind. Living quarters for the Gruppe Nord, 1927–28. Berlin-Reinickendorf, Ollenhauerstrasse at the corner of Pfahlerstrasse (early photo).*

Abb. 46   *Erwin Gutkind. Wohnanlage für die Gruppe Nord, 1927–28. Berlin-Reinickendorf, Ollenhauerstraße, Ecke Pfahlerstraße (ursprünglicher Zustand).*

Fig. 47 *Walter Gropius. Project for a high-rise apartment house with steel skeleton construction, 1929–30. Perspective of the "Green City." Ink and colored washes. Busch-Reisinger Museum, Harvard University.*

Abb. 47 *Walter Gropius. Projekt Wohnhochhaus mit Stahlskelettkonstruktion, 1929–30. Perspektive der »Stadt im Grünen«. Tusche, farbig laviert, gespritzt. Busch-Reisinger Museum, Harvard University.*

To create form on an objective, contemporary basis – that was the common denominator that united representatives of elementary design, Dutch Neo-Plasticism, and Russian Contructivism. This modern Constructivist connection believed that art and life could no longer exist side by side as separate phenomena, that the old forms and concepts that smothered reality must be brushed aside in order to shape the real world by constructive instead of imitative principles, by producing rather than reproducing what had gone before. Only laws derived from the generative principles of life itself would guarantee artistic originality, integrity, and authenticity. An art that opened itself to

den Geist der neuen Epoche: »In ihrer unerhörten Monumentalität, jedem überlieferten Maßstab höhnend, reden sie eine neue Sprache: Die Sprache unserer Zeit.«[50]

In diesem architektonischen Zukunftsbild erfüllte sich eine Vision, die zu der Kristall-Vision der Expressionisten nicht ohne Beziehung blieb. Bis auf ein nicht weiter reduzierbares Maß war die Dematerialisierung des Baukörpers zu einer reinen Haut-und-Knochen-Architektur gelungen. Eine ununterbrochene gläserne Außenhaut hüllte das Skelett der Konstruktion in einen transparenten Schleier, und die herkömmliche Fassade löste sich in ein einzigartiges Spiel von Lichtreflexen

Fig. 48 *Ludwig Mies van der Rohe. German Pavilion at the Barcelona Exposition, 1929. Sketch of exterior. Graphite. SMPK Kunstbibliothek, Berlin.*

Abb. 48 *Ludwig Mies van der Rohe. Deutscher Pavillon auf der Internationalen Ausstellung, Barcelona, 1929. Skizze zur äußeren Gestalt. Graphit. SMPK Kunstbibliothek, Berlin.*

Fig. 49 *Ludwig Mies van der Rohe. German Pavilion at the Barcelona Exposition, 1929. Sketch of entrance. Graphite. SMPK Kunstbibliothek, Berlin.*

Abb. 49 *Ludwig Mies van der Rohe. Deutscher Pavillon auf der Internationalen Ausstellung, Barcelona, 1929. Skizze zum Eingangsbereich. Graphit. SMPK Kunstbibliothek, Berlin.*

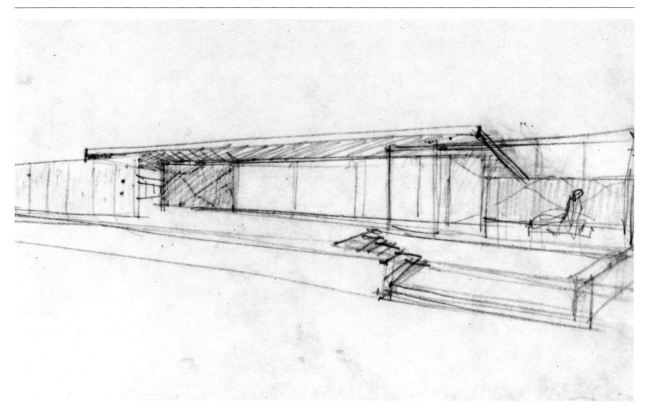

Fig. 48 / Abb. 48

Fig. 49 / Abb. 49

Fig. 50 *Ludwig Mies van der Rohe. German Pavilion at the Barcelona Exposition, 1929. View of the sculpture garden, sculpture by Georg Kolbe (early photo).*

Abb. 50 *Ludwig Mies van der Rohe. Deutscher Pavillon auf der Internationalen Ausstellung in Barcelona, 1929. Blick in den Skulpturenhof, Plastik von Georg Kolbe (ursprünglicher Zustand).*

modern life would become a tool in the general labor process and hence an expression of the creative energy that ensures human progress. Modern artists could compliment themselves on being "constructors of a new life."[52]

The identification of construction with form became the premise on which "objective" architectural design was based; the proponents of elementary design raised this premise to their first principle, indeed, the first principle of *all* architecture. From this viewpoint, even the Greek temple was retroactively transformed into "a perfectly engineered structure in stone."[53] The technical products of the Machine Age, the automobiles, aircraft, and ocean liners that Le Corbusier proudly christened the "splendid firstborn of a New Era,"[54] became icons for a new architecture. Photographs of American grain silos and industrial

auf. Unerschrocken wuchs die mächtig aufragende, scharfkantig-glitzernde Kristallklippe aus dem Boden und setzte sich mit kathedralem Pathos über das kleinliche Gewirr der historischen Stadt hinweg. Diesem ›Beinahe-Expressionismus‹ darf man es zuschreiben, daß die Miessche Version der Zukunftskathedrale, in der die Glasarchitektur ihren Höhepunkt feierte, in der neuen Folge von Tauts ›Frühlicht‹ veröffentlicht wurde; in einer Zeitschrift, die ihr Erscheinen – was im Nachhinein geradezu logisch anmuten will – mit dieser Ausgabe endgültig einstellte.[51]

In der Aufbruchsstimmung zwischen 1922 und 1924 wurde die Metropole Berlin geistiger Mittelpunkt und Drehscheibe der europäischen Avantgarde. Eine Fülle von Ausstellungen und Publikationen belegt die aktive Rolle, die Berlin in der Auseinandersetzung mit dem breiten Spektrum der Konzepte und dem Stil-Plu-

plants, already discovered by the Werkbund about 1910, again began to grace the pinboards in architects' offices. Le Corbusier or Oud, Gropius, Taut, Mendelsohn or Hilberseimer – no one who published on modern architecture would dream of passing over these glorious forerunners of a new architectural aesthetic. Engineering structure, which had made such modern building types as the skyscraper possible and thus contributed to the rise of a "consciously urban architecture" (as Hilberseimer put it), was destined to become the principal model for objective design.[55]

"Naked structure compels truthfulness." This dictum of Erich Mendelsohn's[56] compressed into its shortest form the architectural theory of elementary design, which intended to create form by objective analysis rather than by mirroring visual appearances. The promise of a new art lay – so Mies claimed – not in applying "aesthetic speculations" to architecture but in systematically analyzing architectural conditions, defined by the materials used and the most functional and economic methods of using them. As Mendelsohn clearly realized, in view of the Gothic ornament applied on American skyscrapers, there were only two paths of development open to modern architects: "Either you swear by the eternal validity of historical forms, or you cease casting an awed glance back at history and attempt to find a formal expression fitting to the purposes and materials of our own times."[57]

"What the age demanded" was a clear, objective eye, and an architecture that answered to practical and commercial needs, technically, structurally, and aesthetically. The attempt to find a common denominator for these qualities is recorded in the fundamental studies of metropolitan architecture by Mies and Hilberseimer. The concrete results, the completed buildings of these two in particular, uncompromisingly radical in both concept and quality of design, exemplify the "square built body and soul" by which Nietzsche characterized modern man, and which certainly by implication perfectly describes the Neues Bauen.[58]

Clarity, logic, simplicity, straightforwardness, regularity – these were the hallmarks of the "rational style." With it, architecture submitted to the Machine Age, whose technological optimism had led to the suffusion of virtually every area of life with the principles of industrial production. In Germany, this faith in the universal beneficence of rational methods was bolstered by the economic upswing that followed the currency reforms of 1924. Henry Ford's autobiography, the German edition of which appeared in 1923 with the inspiring subtitle "The Great Present and the Greater Future," became a Bible for the new era, selling out thirteen

ralismus der zwanziger Jahre zukam. Insbesondere die 1918 gegründete Novembergruppe, der zahlreiche bedeutende Berliner Künstler aller Richtungen angehörten, vergegenwärtigte den europäischen Horizont der Moderne. Aus den Reihen ihrer Mitglieder stammten auch die Initiatoren der 1923 gegründeten Zeitschrift ›G‹, die sich als europäisches Organ für ›Elementare Gestaltung‹ präsentierte und von Hans Richter, Werner Graeff, Mies van der Rohe, Theo van Doesburg, El Lissitzky und Ludwig Hilberseimer in Berlin herausgegeben wurde. Zu ihren Autoren zählten Künstler wie Piet Mondrian, Kasimir Malewitsch, Naum Gabo, Antoine Pevsner, Viking Eggeling, George Grosz, John Heartfield, Tristan Tzara und Man Ray, Raoul Hausmann, Hans Arp u.a.

Der Wille zur Form auf objektiver, zeitgemäßer Grundlage war der gemeinsame Nenner, der die Vertreter der elementaren Gestaltung, des holländischen Neoplastizismus und des russischen Konstruktivismus miteinander verband. Im Selbstverständnis der konstruktivistischen Moderne durften Kunst und Leben nicht länger als isolierte Phänomene nebeneinander existieren. Die alten Formen und Begriffe, die sich über die Wirklichkeit gelegt hatten, mußten zertrümmert werden, um Wirklichkeit ›selbst‹ nach konstruktiven und nicht imitativen, nach bildenden und nicht abbildenden Prinzipien zu gestalten. Allein Gesetze, die aus den schöpferischen Prinzipien des Lebens hergeleitet waren, garantierten Ursprünglichkeit, Echtheit und damit Authentizität. Die Kunst, die sich dem modernen Leben öffnete, verwandelte sich in ein Werkzeug des allgemeinen Arbeitsprozesses und wurde somit Ausdruck der schöpferischen Energie, die den Fortschritt der Menschheit organisierte. Und der moderne Künstler durfte sich selbst das Kompliment machen: »Man kann heute nur noch von den Konstrukteuren des neuen Lebens sprechen.«[52]

Die Identität von Konstruktion und Form wurde zur Prämisse ›sachlicher‹ Gestaltung im Bauen. Die elementare Gestaltung erklärte die konstruktive Grundidee zum Primat aller Architektur. Selbst der griechische Tempel verwandelte sich aus dieser Perspektive rückwirkend in »ein vollkommenes Ingenieurwerk in Stein«.[53] Die technischen Gebilde des Maschinenzeitalters, die Automobile, Flugzeuge und Ozeandampfer, die Le Corbusier stolz als »prachtvolle Erstgeburten einer neuen Zeit« präsentierte,[54] verwandelten sich zu Ikonen der neuen Architektur. Abbildungen amerikanischer Großsilos und Industrieanlagen, die der Deutsche Werkbund bereits um 1910 entdeckt hatte, wanderten ein zweites Mal als ›Pin-up-Photos‹ an die Wände der Ateliers von modernen Architekten. Ob Le Corbusier, Oud oder Gropius, ob Taut, Mendel-

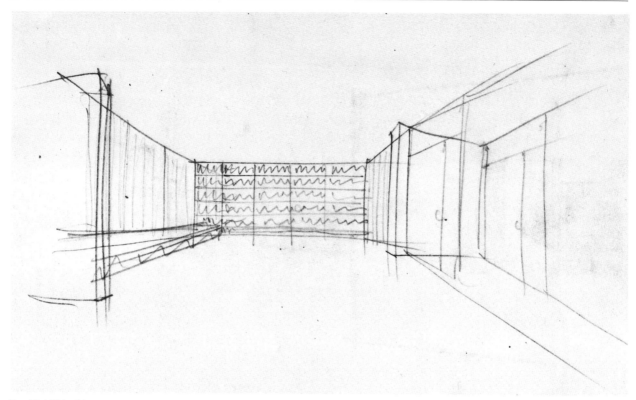

Fig. 51 / Abb. 51

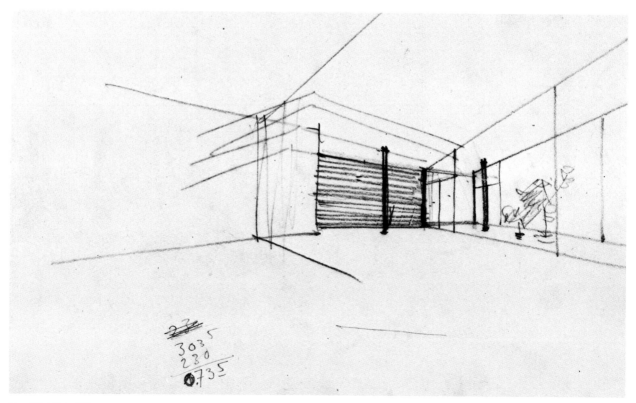

Fig. 52 / Abb. 52

Fig. 53   *Hans and Wassili Luckhardt. Residence am Rupen-horn, 1929. Berlin-Charlottenburg, Heerstrasse 161 (formerly 55), corner of Am Rupenhorn.*

Abb. 53   *Hans und Wassili Luckhardt. Haus am Rupenhorn, 1929. Berlin-Charlottenburg, Heerstraße 161 (früher 55), Ecke Am Rupenhorn.*

printings in its first year of publication alone, and going through thirty further printings by 1930.

The Cartesian thinking of the engineer, who, unfettered by tradition and unhampered by bias, seeks the logical, economic solution to every problem, became the new architects' discipline. To alleviate a pressing, war-exacerbated housing shortage, they believed apartments must be mass-produced and building methods industrialized à la Henry Ford. The euphoria of mechanization raised expectations whose honorable naiveté was almost a match for the Expressionists' utopian irrationality. "If we succeed in implementing this industrialization," as Mies still confident of its blessings wrote in 1924, "then the social, economic, technical, and even artistic problems will be easily solved."[59]

sohn oder Hilberseimer – keiner von ihnen mochte in seinen Publikationen auf diese prägnanten Exemplare neuer architektonischer Wesensschönheit verzichten. Der Ingenieurbau, der erst moderne Bautypen wie das Hochhaus ermöglichte und damit für eine »bewußte großstädtische Architektur« (Hilberseimer) konstitutiv war, sollte das entschiedene Leitbild sachlicher Gestaltung werden.[55]

»Die nackte Konstruktion zwingt zur Wahrheit« – dieser Satz von Erich Mendelsohn[56] komprimierte die Architekturtheorie der elementaren Gestaltung – die Kunst nach objektiven Methoden, nicht aber als Spiegelbild der Erscheinungen schaffen wollte –, zur prägnanten Formel. Nicht in »ästhetischen Spekulationen« (Mies), die von außen mehr oder minder geistvoll

---

Fig. 51   *Ludwig Mies van der Rohe. Library of the Tugend-hat Residence, Brünn, Czechoslovakia, 1929–30. Graphite. SMPK Kunstbibliothek, Berlin.*

Abb. 51   *Ludwig Mies van der Rohe. Bibliothek des Hauses Tugendhat, Brünn, Tschechoslowakei, 1929–30. Graphit. SMPK Kunstbibliothek, Berlin.*

Fig. 52   *Ludwig Mies van der Rohe. Conservatory wall of the Tugendhat Residence, Brünn, Czechoslovakia, 1929–30. Graphite. SMPK Kunstbibliothek, Berlin.*

Abb. 52   *Ludwig Mies van der Rohe. Wintergartenwand des Hauses Tugendhat, Brünn, Tschechoslowakei, 1929-30. Graphit. SMPK Kunstbibliothek, Berlin.*

Fig. 54 *Hans and Wassili Luckhardt. Row houses, 1928.*
Berlin-Dahlem, Schorlemer Allee.

Abb. 54 *Hans und Wassili Luckhardt. Reihenhäuser, 1928.*
Berlin-Dahlem, Schorlemer Allee.

Fig. 55 *Hans and Wassili Luckhardt. Competition entry for the redesign of Alexanderplatz, Berlin, 1928. Chalk. Whereabouts unknown.*

Abb. 55 *Hans und Wassili Luckhardt. Entwurf für die Umgestaltung des Alexanderplatzes, Berlin, 1928. Kreide. Verbleib unbekannt.*

In this case, too, disenchantment was not long in coming. Just three years later, in 1927, the prophet had become an admonisher, one of the first in the new school to criticize his colleagues for relying too exclusively on "mathematical means." In his comments on the Weissenhof Development in Stuttgart, Mies hammered it into his readers that "the battle cry of 'rationalization and standardization'" touched only on "partial problems" of architecture, and that therefore it would be "not entirely irrelevant expressly to emphasize at this time that the problem of modern housing is a problem of the art of building, despite its technical and economic aspects."[60]

Mass housing, probably the most important social and artistic challenge faced by Weimar architects, became the proving ground for Neues Bauen. No other field of modern architecture was so closely bound up with the special conditions of the Republic. In designing and building huge public housing projects, the utopian reforming zeal of the early twenties could enter a fruitful liaison with the rationalist ethic of organization, for to build a better world, imagination was required – not only architectural but social, technical, and organizational imagination. New contracting

an das Bauen herangetragen wurden, sondern in der systematischen Erschließung der architektonischen Bedingungen des Materials, in den Methoden seiner zweckmäßigen und ökonomischen Verwendung lag das Versprechen einer neuen Kunst verborgen. Es gab – das wurde Erich Mendelsohn beim Anblick des mit gotischen Formen dekorierten amerikanischen Wolkenkratzers in aller Schärfe deutlich –, im Grunde nur zwei Möglichkeiten der architektonischen Entwicklung: »Entweder man schwört auf die Immergültigkeit der historischen Formen, oder man lehnt den Angstblick auf die Historie ab und versucht aus Zweck und Material den unserer Zeit entsprechenden Formausdruck zu finden.«[57]

Der ›Zeitwille‹ verlangte Sachlichkeit und Objektivität und eine Architektur, die den praktischen und ökonomischen Bedürfnissen technisch, konstruktiv und ästhetisch antwortete. Von der Suche nach der Übereinkunft dieser Bedingungen zeugen die prinzipiellen Studien zur Großstadtarchitektur von Mies und Hilberseimer. Vor allem ihre Arbeiten vermittelten in der kompromißlosen Radikalität ihrer konzeptuellen und gestalterischen Qualität jene ›Rechtwinkligkeit an Leib und Seele‹, die mit Nietzsche den modernen Men-

Fig. 56 *Hans and Wassili Luckhardt. Competition entry for the redesign of Alexanderplatz, Berlin, 1928. Model, Königsstrasse axis. Whereabouts unknown.*

Abb. 56 *Hans und Wassili Luckhardt. Entwurf für die Umgestaltung des Alexanderplatzes, Berlin, 1928. Modellbild, Achse der Königsstraße. Verbleib unbekannt.*

arrangements, new financing methods made possible by tax reforms and better credit conditions, the introduction of new manufacturing methods into construction, and finally, a new image of the modern city – these were the constituent parts of a model known as *Neues Wohnen* (New Living), which found its most significant architectural expression in the large housing development.

Bruno Taut and Martin Wagner embodied in almost pure form the two main architectural tendencies of the 1920s. Taut, concerned to define "the artist's socialism,"[61] sought to realize the community building of the future; Wagner, likewise a socialist, had exhaustively studied the "American building industry"[62] and harbored the ambitious aim of achieving in the field of minimal housing "what Ford succeeded in doing for the automotive industry."

The joint efforts of Taut and Wagner, who was

schen, und im übertragenen Sinn jetzt auch das ›Neue Bauen‹ auszeichnete.[58]

Klarheit, Logik, Einfachheit, Unzweideutigkeit, Gesetzmäßigkeit – dies waren die Kennzeichen für den ›Stil‹ des Rationalismus. Ihm unterwarf sich die Baukunst eines Maschinenzeitalters, dessen technologischer Optimismus die Prinzipien der Industrieproduktion auf nahezu alle Lebensbereiche übertrug. Der 1924 mit der Stabilisierung der Währung einsetzende wirtschaftliche Aufschwung bestätigte den Glauben an die Universalität rationaler Methoden. In dem Buch des amerikanischen Automobilherstellers Henry Ford ›Mein Leben und Werk‹, das 1923 in deutscher Sprache mit dem verheißungsvollen Untertitel ›Das große Heute und das größere Morgen‹ erschien, fand die neue Zeit ihre Bibel, die allein 13 Auflagen im Erscheinungsjahr und weitere 20 Auflagen bis 1930 erreichte.

architect for the city of Berlin, were more than successful. Their Gross-Siedlung Britz *(figs. 11, 44, 108–109)*, soon to be internationally known as the Horseshoe Development, became a landmark of Social Democratic housing policy in the Weimar Republic. The democratic demand that every tenant had a right to his share of light, air, and sun – a garden city idea that inspired a reduction in urban density, achieved in this case by strict row construction – and the economic postulate of seriality, which meant lines of identical apartments whose inhabitants were to enjoy a corresponding social equality, could hardly have been more convincingly fulfilled than in Wagner and Taut's Horseshoe Development.

Symbolically, this project lent concrete form to the premises of mass housing. It amounted to a monumental expression of the collective principle which had been central to its planning, both as an architectural structure and as a part of the larger urban context. The great sweep of its arc, conceivably a free translation of the crescents of Bath or London, or even of Bernini's colonnades at St. Peter's, at last provided a salient symbol of the social commitment of the Neues Bauen.

Die cartesianische Denkweise des Ingenieurs, der ohne traditionelle Bindungen vorurteilslos und zielstrebig die ökonomische und logische Lösung suchte, wurde zur Disziplin des neuen Architekten. Allein durch Massenherstellung von billigem Wohnraum und durch die Industrialisierung der Bauproduktion nach Fordschem Muster konnte auf die allgemeine Wohnungsnot, die sich durch den Krieg verschärft hatte, eine überzeugende Antwort gefunden werden. Die Mechanisierungseuphorie erzeugte Erwartungen, deren ehrenvolle Naivität dem utopischen Irrationalismus der Expressionisten kaum nachstand: »Gelingt es uns, diese Industrialisierung durchzuführen«, so äußerte sich Mies 1924 noch überzeugt vom Segen einer solchen Maßnahme im Bauwesen, »dann werden sich die sozialen, wirtschaftlichen, technischen und auch künstlerischen Fragen leicht lösen lassen.«[59]

Auch in diesem Fall ließ die Ernüchterung nicht lange auf sich warten. Bereits 1927 war aus dem Rufer ein Warnender geworden, der als einer der ersten kritisch die Stimme gegen die Überbetonung der »rechnerischen Mittel« erhob. In seinen Stellungnahmen zur Stuttgarter Weißenhofsiedlung wurde Mies

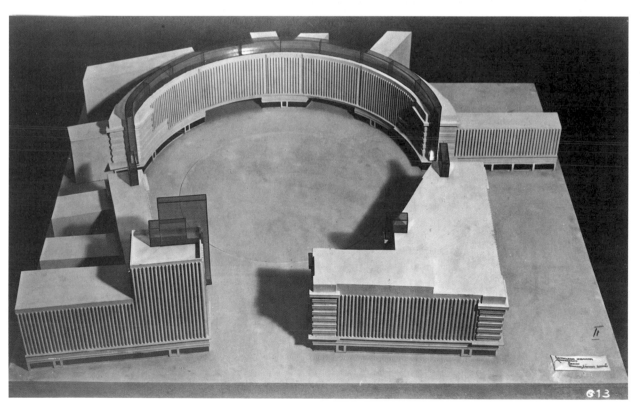

Fig. 57 *Peter Behrens. Competition entry for the redesign of Alexanderplatz, Berlin, 1928. Model, Königsstrasse axis. Whereabouts unknown.*

Abb. 57 *Peter Behrens. Entwurf für die Umgestaltung des Alexanderplatzes, Berlin, 1928. Modellbild, Achse der Königsstraße. Verbleib unbekannt.*

The Cathedral of the Future had fulfilled its mission as precursor of a coming social order; visibly embodied in this new configuration, its metamorphosis into reality had been accomplished.

During the latter half of the 1920s Berlin was a single great laboratory for public housing. No other city achieved such architectural quality in its housing developments, experimented in such variety, or could match Berlin's figures for housing volume. On this proving ground the new architectural elite united forces to create, besides the Horseshoe Development, the Waldsiedlung Zehlendorf *(figs. 111–114)* by Taut, Häring, Salvisberg), Siemensstadt housing in Charlottenburg *(fig. 45)* (Wagner, Scharoun, Gropius, Häring, Forbat, Henning, Bartning), and Weisse Stadt *(fig. 118)* in Reinickendorf (Salvisberg, Ahrends, Büning).[63] The new developments encircled the metropolis like a belt – green satellites with buildings set in open rows were a conscious reaction to the closed blocks of the existing city – and did their part to realize Taut's vision of "dispersing the cities," which he believed would at last make the earth a good place to live.[64]

Because the modern dogma of the green city could only be realized where property values were low, developments of this kind remained the exception in central city locations. Bruno Taut's Wohnstadt Carl Legien in Berlin-Weissensee, the apartment complex on Kurfürstendamm designed by Erich Mendelsohn in conjunction with the Universum Cinema, and Mies van der Rohe's blocks of flats on Afrikanische Strasse, all departed from the pattern of dispersed developments. Instead, they returned to the much-maligned tradition of high-density housing, and managed to beat it at its own game. Precisely by not adhering to the concept of urban dispersal, and by seeking a metropolitan alternative to the tenement-block style, they proved how effective the principles of the Neues Bauen could be, by showing that modern planning approaches could contribute to amenable living in downtown areas.

Yet living was not the central concern of metropolitan architecture as such. Its true domain remained the commercial and office building, which, as old city centers were rapidly transformed into bustling downtowns, became the characteristic building type. The 1929 competition for a redesign of Alexanderplatz *(figs. 55–59)*, in the heart of old Berlin, typically envisioned a transformation of the historical space into a modern square whose wide streets and traffic flow seemed themselves to have determined the shape of the surrounding structures. In the prize-winning design by the Luckhardt brothers *(figs. 55–56)*, facades sweep around the square in great streamlined arcs, like cliffs

nicht müde zu betonen, daß das »Feldgeschrei ›Rationalisierung und Typisierung‹« nur »Teilprobleme« des Bauens betraf, und es erschien daher »nicht ganz zwecklos, heute ausdrücklich hervorzuheben, daß das Problem der neuen Wohnung ein baukünstlerisches Problem ist, trotz seiner technischen und wirtschaftlichen Seite.«[60]

Der Massenwohnungsbau, der für den Architekten der Weimarer Republik die wohl bedeutendste soziale und künstlerische Aufgabe darstellte, wurde zum Hauptschlachtfeld des ›Neuen Bauens‹. Keine andere Aufgabe der modernen Architektur war so eng an die besonderen Verhältnisse der Weimarer Republik gebunden, wie jene der Großsiedlungen. Hier konnte sich der sozialutopische Reformeifer der aktivistischen Phase mit dem modernen Rationalismus des entschlossenen Organisierens fruchtbar paaren, denn soziale, technische, organisatorische und architektonische Phantasie war zum Bau einer besseren Welt erforderlich. Neue Organisationsformen der Bauträgerschaft, neue Finanzierungsmodelle durch staatliche Steuergesetzgebung und Kreditvergabe, die Einführung neuer Herstellungsmethoden in der Bauproduktion und schließlich ein neues Bild von der modernen Großstadt – aus diesen Bestandteilen setzte sich das Modell ›Neues Wohnen‹ zusammen, das in der Großsiedlung seinen signifikanten baulichen Ausdruck fand.

Durch die Architekten Bruno Taut und Martin Wagner waren die beiden bedeutenden Strömungen der zwanziger Jahre geradezu idealtypisch vertreten: Der eine, der sich mit dem ›Sozialismus des Künstlers‹[61] auseinandergesetzt hatte, suchte den Gemeinschaftsbau der Zukunft, – der andere, ebenfalls ein Sozialist, hatte die ›Amerikanische Bauwirtschaft‹[62] intensiv studiert und sich das ehrgeizige Ziel gesteckt, »das, was Ford in der Automobilindustrie gelang«, auf dem Feld des Kleinwohnungsbaus zu verwirklichen.

Die gemeinsame Arbeit von Bruno Taut und dem Berliner Stadtbaurat Martin Wagner war mehr als erfolgreich. Ihre ›Großsiedlung Britz‹ *(Abb. 11, 44, 108–109)*, die als ›Hufeisensiedlung‹ weit über Berlin hinaus bekannt wurde, verkörpert gleichsam im Wahrzeichen den sozialdemokratischen Wohnungsbau der Weimarer Republik: Überzeugender als in diesem Beispiel konnten die soziale Forderung nach Licht, Luft und Sonne – die im Sinne der Gartenstadtidee zu einer Auflösung des urbanen Zusammenhangs führen mußte, wie es bei konsequenter Zeilenbauweise der Fall war – und das ökonomische Postulat des Seriellen, das sich in der Reihung von gleichen Wohnungen und auch in der Gleichheit der Bewohner wiederholte, nicht erfüllt werden.

Fig. 58 *Ludwig Mies van der Rohe. Competition entry for the redesign of Alexanderplatz, Berlin, 1928. Model, general view. Whereabouts unknown.*

Abb. 58 *Ludwig Mies van der Rohe. Entwurf für die Umgestaltung des Alexanderplatzes, Berlin, 1928. Modellbild, Gesamtansicht. Verbleib unbekannt.*

left standing by a roaring river of traffic as it cut its bed. This direct adaptation of frontages to traffic needs prompted Ludwig Hilberseimer, an apologist for functional urban architecture, to make the acerbic comment: "It used to be architecture that did violence to transport. Now the opposite seems to be the case."[65]

In the commercial and office buildings of the late 1920s, rationalist architecture had its finest hour. It was in this field that the neoclassicism of structural skeletons derived from engineering and the austere language dictated by new materials was architecturally polished and rhetorically refined into the International Style. This cultivation of skeleton construction – the fundamental innovation from which Le Corbusier had derived his domino principle in 1914 and Mies his skin-and-bones style in 1922 – culminated in Berlin around 1930 in such structures as Bruno Paul's Kathreiner Building, Erich Mendelsohn's Trade Union Building, the

Im ›Hufeisen‹ waren die Prämissen des Massenwohnungsbaus zur sinnlich einleuchtenden Form überführt: Das Prinzip der Kollektivität, das für die architektonische und städtebauliche Komposition bestimmend war, fand zur monumentalen Gestalt. Die einprägsame Großform des Hufeisens, die den Crescents von Bath oder London, aber auch Berninis Kolonnaden am Petersdom in freier Übersetzung nachempfunden sein konnte, lieferte der sozialen Idee des Neuen Bauens das eigentliche Symbol. Die ›Kathedrale der Zukunft‹ hatte ihre Mission als Vorstadium einer zukünftig sich erst ordnenden Welt erfüllt. Mit ihrer Wiederkehr in neuer Erscheinung war ihre Metamorphose zur Realität vollendet.

In der zweiten Hälfte der zwanziger Jahre bildete Berlin ein Großlaboratorium für die Volkswohnung. Keine andere Großstadt erreichte im Bau von Großsiedlungen die gleiche architektonische Qualität, die

Fig. 59   *Ludwig Mies van der Rohe. Competition entry for the redesign of Alexanderplatz, Berlin, 1928. Photo-collage. Whereabouts unknown.*

Abb. 59   *Ludwig Mies van der Rohe. Entwurf für die Umgestaltung des Alexanderplatzes, Berlin, 1928. Photocollage. Verbleib unbekannt.*

Shell Building by Emil Fahrenkamp, and the new office block on Alexanderplatz by Peter Behrens.

The private housing designs of these years likewise depended largely on a sophisticated skeleton structure to express a modern lifestyle by means of transparency and the interpenetration of interior and exterior space. In the houses of Erich Mendelsohn, the villas of the Luckhardt brothers *(fig. 53)*, and above all the model house designed by Mies van der Rohe for the 1931 Building Exhibition in Berlin *(fig. 98)*, space expanded with an unprecedented freedom evocative of a new quality of life.

Mies's 1931 exhibition house was the last opportunity he or any other German architect would have to practice the liberty-within-order manifested to perfection by his Tugendhat House *(figs. 51–52)* of 1929 or his Barcelona Pavilion *(figs. 48–50)*. As economic and political conditions worsened after the crisis of 1929, pressures on the Modern movement increased, and, as its publications reveal, the Neues Bauen was forced into the defensive. If in 1927 its advocates could still prematurely revel in the "victory of the new architectural style,"[66] by 1930 they were not only defending themselves against reactionary polemics that accused

gleiche Vielseitigkeit im Experimentellen und das Volumen an geschaffenem Wohnraum. Auf diesem Schlachtfeld wurde die Elite des Neuen Bauens mit vereinten Kräften tätig, und aus diesem Zusammenwirken entstanden neben der ›Hufeisensiedlung‹ die ›Waldsiedlung Zehlendorf‹ *(Abb. 111–114)* durch Taut, Häring und Salvisberg, die ›Großsiedlung Siemensstadt‹ *(Abb. 45)* in Charlottenburg durch Wagner, Scharoun, Gropius, Häring, Forbat, Henning und Bartning, oder die ›Weiße Stadt‹ *(Abb. 118)* in Reinickendorf durch Salvisberg, Ahrends und Büning.[63] Wie ein Gürtel legten sich die Siedlungen um die Großstadt. Als grüne Satelliten, die ihre offenen Zeilen bewußt gegen die geschlossene Blockstruktur der Mietskasernen-Stadt richteten, trugen sie auf ihre Weise dazu bei, die Tautsche Vision von der ›Auflösung der Städte‹ näherzurücken, durch die erst sich die Erde in eine gute Wohnung verwandelte.[64]

Das moderne Dogma von der durchgrünten Stadt, aber auch die Höhe der Bodenpreise machten innerstädtische Wohnanlagen zur Ausnahme. Bruno Tauts ›Wohnstadt Carl Legien‹ in Berlin-Weißensee, die Wohnhausanlage von Erich Mendelsohn am Kurfürstendamm, die in Verbindung mit dem Bau des Univer-

Fig. 60   *Felix Jacob. Study of a reinforced concrete tower for the German Building Exhibition, Berlin, 1931. Interior view. Pencil and gouache. SMPK Kunstbibliothek, Berlin.*

Abb. 60   *Felix Jacob. Entwurf für einen Eisenbetonturm für die Deutsche Bauausstellung Berlin, 1931. Stereometrische Ansicht des Innern. Bleistift und Deckfarben. SMPK Kunstbibliothek, Berlin.*

them of cultural bolshevism or racial degeneration; they were beginning to fear for the survival of culture itself in Germany.

When the Republic fell, the fate of the Neues Bauen was sealed. The Bauhaus crisis was indicative in its way of the demise of Weimar. After the Dessau Bauhaus was closed by the city administration in 1932, its last director, Mies van der Rohe, rented a factory loft in Berlin and attempted to continue the school's work on a private basis. In July 1933, a few months after Hitler's takeover in March, the Berlin Bauhaus, too, was closed down by the new regime. The darkest chapter of modern German history had begun.

Footnotes

1 Karl Scheffler, *Die Architektur der Gross-Stadt* (Berlin, 1913), p. 158. See also the influential publication by the same author, *Moderne Baukunst* (Leipzig, 1908).

2 Friedrich Nietzsche, *Die fröhliche Wissenschaft* (Book 4, Aphorism 276); English edn. *The Gay Science*, translated with commentary by Walter Kaufmann, New York, p. 223.

3 Franz Mannheimer, "A.E.G.-Bauten," in *Die Kunst in Industrie und Handel* (yearbook of the Deutsche Werkbund), (Jena, 1913), pp. 35, 37.

4 Josef August Lux, *Ingenieur-Ästhetik* (Munich, 1910), p. 8.

5 Scheffler, *op. cit.,* p. 155.

6 Peter Behrens, *Kunst und Technik.* Lecture held on May 26, 1910; reprinted in Tilmann Buddensieg and Henning Rogge, *Industriekultur: Peter Behrens und die AEG, 1907–1914* (Berlin, 1979), p. D 281.

7 On this question, see Buddensieg and Rogge, *ibid.*

8 Quoted in *Peter Behrens 1888–1940.* Memorial publication with catalogue (Kaiserslautern, Hagen, Darmstadt, and Vienna, 1966–67), p. 21.

9 Scheffler, *op. cit.,* p. 157.

10 Walter Gropius, "Die Entwicklung moderner Industriebaukunst," in *Die Kunst in Industrie und Handel,* p. 21.

11 Edmund Schüler, "Peter Behrens (Nachruf)," *Kunst im Deutschen Reich,* ed. B, ser. 4 (April 1940), p. 65.

12 Gropius, *loc. cit.*

13 Friedrich Hölderlin to Casimir Ulrich Böhlendorff, in Hölderlin, *Sämtliche Werke und Briefe,* ed. Günter Mieth (Munich, 1970), vol. 2, p. 927.

14 Cf. Jürgen Krause, *"Märtyrer" und "Prophet." Studien zum Nietzsche-Kult in der bildenden Kunst der Jahrhundertwende* (Berlin and New York, 1984).

15 Friedrich Nietzsche, "Vom Nutzen und Nachteil der Historie," in *Werke in drei Bänden,* ed. Karl Schlechta (Munich, 1982), vol. 1, pp. 214–215.

16 For the influence of Nietzsche on the early work of Peter Behrens, see Tilmann Buddensieg, "Das Wohnhaus als Kultbau. Zum Darmstädter Haus von Behrens", in *Peter Behrens und Nürnberg. Geschmackswandel in*

sum-Kinos entstand, und die Wohnblöcke von Mies van der Rohe in der Afrikanischen Straße unterschieden sich von dem herkömmlichen Muster räumlich aufgelockerter Siedlungen. Sie setzten sich mit dem vielgeschmähten Mietskasernen-Städtebau auseinander, um ihn auf eigenem Terrain zu schlagen. Gerade indem diese Beispiele nicht dem Konzept der Auflösung der Stadt folgten, sondern nach einer großstädtischen Alternative zur Mietskaserne suchten, stellten sie die Überlegenheit der Prinzipien des Neuen Bauens unter Beweis, weil sie zeigten, daß mit den Grundsätzen moderner Planung auch eine bessere innerstädtische Wohnform möglich werden konnte.

Doch das Wohnen wurde kein Thema der eigentlichen Großstadtarchitektur. Deren Domäne blieb das Büro- und Geschäftshaus, das mit der beschleunigten Verwandlung der Innenstadt zur City zum charakteristischen Bautypus aufstieg. Der 1929 ausgeschriebene Wettbewerb zur Umgestaltung des Alexanderplatzes *(Abb. 55–59)* im Herzen vom alten Berlin, zeigte die zeittypische Verwandlung der historischen Stadträume zum modernen Verkehrsplatz. Selbst die Architektur des Platzes schien vom Verkehrsfluß die Kontur gewonnen zu haben. Der mit dem 1. Preis ausgezeichnete Entwurf der Gebrüder Luckhardt *(Abb. 55–56)* zeigte Baukörper, deren Fassaden mit großen, schwungvollen Gesten den Platz umgaben, als habe der Verkehrsfluß sich an dieser Stelle sein tiefes Bett gegraben. Diese direkte Anpassung der Bauflucht an den Verkehr veranlaßte Ludwig Hilberseimer, den Apologeten der funktionalen Großstadtarchitektur, zu dem ebenso treffenden wie bissigen Kommentar: »Früher vergewaltigte die Architektur den Verkehr. Heute scheint das Umgekehrte der Fall zu sein.«[65]

In den Büro- und Geschäftshäusern der späten zwanziger Jahre feierte die rationalistische Architektur ihre Triumphe. Hier wurden der Rohbauklassizismus der modernen Ingenieurskonstruktion und die Sprache der neuen Materialien zum ›International Style‹ architektonisch kultiviert und rhetorisch verfeinert. Die Kultivierung des Skelettbaus – jener grundlegenden konstruktiven Neuerung in der modernen Architektur, von der Le Corbusier 1914 sein Domino-Prinzip und Mies 1922 seine Haut-und-Knochen-Architektur ableiteten – fand um 1930 ihren Höhepunkt. Bauwerke wie das Kathreiner-Hochhaus von Bruno Paul, das Gewerkschaftshaus von Erich Mendelsohn, das Shell-Haus von Emil Fahrenkamp, die Geschäftshäuser am Alexanderplatz von Peter Behrens gaben dem Stadtbild neue Akzente.

Auch die Villen- und Landhausbauten dieser Jahre, die im Typus des Pavillons den modernen Lebensstil mit einem neuen Maß an Transparenz und räumlicher

Deutschland; Historismus, Jugendstil und die Anfänge der Industriereform (Munich, 1980), pp. 37–48.

17 Robert Breuer, "Kleine Kunstnachrichten," Deutsche Kunst und Dekoration, 17 (1910–11), p. 492.

18 See the influential publication by Paul Mebes, Um 1800. Architektur und Handwerk im letzten Jahrhundert ihrer traditionellen Entwicklung, 2 vols. (Munich, 1908).

19 Cf. Adolf Behne, Die Wiederkehr der Kunst (Munich, n. d. [1920]), p. 73. There Behne writes: "Technicism is the intellectual attitude, classicism its artistic expression."

20 Scheffler, op. cit., p. 97.

21 Julius Meier-Graefe, "Peter Behrens – Düsseldorf," Dekorative Kunst, 8 (1905), p. 389.

22 Ibid.

23 J. J. P. Oud, "Über die zukünftige Baukunst und ihre architektonischen Möglichkeiten," Frühlicht (ed. Bruno Taut) 1, no. 4 (1921–22). Quoted from the reprint, Bruno Taut. Frühlicht 1920–1922. Eine Folge für die Verwirklichung des neuen Baugedankens (Berlin, Frankfurt, and Vienna, 1965), p. 208.

24 Gropius, "Die Entwicklung moderner Industriebaukunst," op. cit., p. 21.

25 Ibid., p. 19.

26 Ludwig Hilberseimer, Gross-Stadtarchitektur (Stuttgart, 1927); quoted from the 2nd edn. (1978), p. 103.

27 Friedrich Nietzsche, "Aus dem Nachlass der Achtziger Jahre," Werke in drei Bänden, ed. Karl Schlechta (Munich, 1966), vol. 3, p. 634: "Our entire European culture has long been moving, with a tortuous tension that increases from decade to decade, as if toward a catastrophe – restless, violent, precipitous like a current desiring only to reach the end, no longer stopping to think, afraid to stop and think."

28 Bruno Taut, "Nieder mit dem Seriosismus!" Frühlicht, January 1920; quoted in Bruno Taut, 1920–22, p. 11. For statements made by Taut during the war years, see Iain Boyd Whyte, Bruno Taut, and the Architecture of Activism (Cambridge, 1982), especially the letter of October 1914, p. 41.

29 Peter Behrens, "Das Ethos und die Umlagerung der künstlerischen Probleme," in Graf H. Keyserling, ed. Der Leuchter. Jahrbuch der Schule der Weisheit, (Darmstadt, 1920), p. 324.

30 Bruno Taut, Der Weltbaumeister. Architekturschauspiel für symphonische Musik (Hagen, 1920).

31 Bruno Taut, Alpine Architektur (Hagen, 1919). See also, by the same author, Die Auflösung der Städte oder Die Erde eine gute Wohnung oder auch: Der Weg zur Alpinen Architektur (Hagen, 1920), p. 63, with a passage from Nietzsche's Thus Spoke Zarathustra ("Vom neuen Götzen").

32 Taut, "Nieder mit dem Seriosismus!," op. cit., p. 11.

33 Adolf Behne, "Wiedergeburt der Baukunst," in Bruno Taut, Die Stadtkrone, with contributions by Paul Scheerbart, Erich Baron, and Adolf Behne (Jena, 1919), p. 130.

34 Walter Gropius, flyer for the exhibition Für unbekannte Architekten, organized by the Arbeitsrat für Kunst, April 1919. Reprinted in Arbeitsrat für Kunst: Berlin 1918–1921,

Beziehung nachzeichneten, stehen im Zeichen der Verfeinerung des Skelettbaus. In den Häusern von Erich Mendelsohn, den Villen der Gebrüder Luckhardt (Abb. 53), noch eindeutiger in dem 1931 für die Berliner Bauausstellung von Mies van der Rohe errichteten Musterhaus (Abb. 98), wurde ein neues Maß an räumlicher Freiheit etabliert, das eine bestimmte Qualität des Lebens repräsentierte.

Das Haus auf der Berliner Bauausstellung von 1931 war nicht nur für Mies die letzte Gelegenheit, im Wohnungsbau jenes Maß an Freiheit und Ordnung zu realisieren, das 1929 im Haus Tugendhat (Abb. 51–52) und im Barcelona Pavillon (Abb. 48–50) zur Vollendung gelangt war. Mit der Verschärfung der wirtschaftlichen und politischen Verhältnisse seit der Weltwirtschaftskrise von 1930 geriet die Moderne zunehmend unter Druck. Auch publizistisch befand sich das Neue Bauen um 1930 in der Defensive. War 1927 bereits voreilig der ›Sieg des neuen Baustils‹[66] proklamiert worden, so ging es jetzt nicht allein darum, sich gegen reaktionäre Polemik zu verteidigen, die von Kulturbolschewismus oder gar rassischer Entartung sprach, sondern um den Fortbestand der Kultur in Deutschland überhaupt.

Mit dem Ende der Republik war auch das Ende des Neuen Bauens gekommen. Die Krise um das Bauhaus kommentierte auf ihre Art den Niedergang der Weimarer Republik. Nach der Schließung des Bauhaus in Dessau im Frühjahr 1932 durch die dortige Regierung versuchte sein letzter Direktor Mies van der Rohe die Schule auf privater Basis in einem Berliner Fabrikhof fortzuführen. Im Juli 1933, wenige Monate nach der Machtübernahme durch Hitler im März 1933, wurde auch das Berliner Bauhaus von den neuen Machthabern geschlossen. Das düstere Kapitel aus der deutschen Geschichte, das jetzt folgte, warf seinen Schatten voraus.

Anmerkungen

1 Karl Scheffler, Die Architektur der Großstadt, Berlin 1913, S. 158. – Vgl. auch die einflußreiche Publikation von Karl Scheffler, Moderne Baukunst, Leipzig 1908.

2 Friedrich Nietzsche, Die fröhliche Wissenschaft, 4. Buch, Aphor. 276, zit. nach Werke in drei Bänden, hrsg. von Karl Schlechta, München 1966, Bd. II, S. 161.

3 Franz Mannheimer, A.E.G.-Bauten, in: Die Kunst in Industrie und Handel, Jahrbuch des Deutschen Werkbundes, Jena 1913, S. 35, 37.

4 Josef August Lux, Ingenieur-Ästhetik, München 1910, S. 8.

5 Karl Scheffler, Die Architektur der Großstadt, a.a.O., S. 155.

6 Peter Behrens, Kunst und Technik, Vortrag gehalten am 26.5.1910, nachgedruckt in: Tilmann Buddensieg/

exhibition catalogue, Akademie der Künste (Berlin, 1980), p. 90.

35 Karl Scheffler, *Der Geist der Gotik* (Leipzig, 1917). A full five years before Scheffler, Wilhelm Worringer published his seminal study, *Formprobleme der Gotik* (Munich, 1912).

36 Taut, *Die Stadtkrone,* pp. 59–60.

37 Worringer, *Formprobleme der Gothik.*

38 See, e. g., Adolf Behne, *Ruf zum Bauen. Zweite Buchpublikation des Arbeiterrats für Kunst* (Berlin, 1920); quoted in *Arbeitsrat für Kunst . . . 1918–1921,* p. 78.

39 Paul Scheerbart, *Glasarchitektur* (Berlin: Verlag "Der Sturm," 1914); quoted in the new edition of the same title, with an afterword by Wolfgang Pehnt (Munich, 1971).

40 Cf. Adolf Behne, *Die Wiederkehr der Kunst* (1919); quoted in Scheerbart, *Glasarchitektur,* p. 155.

41 Cf. Adolf Behne, "Glasarchitektur," *Frühlicht,* (January 1920); quoted in *Bruno Taut, 1920–1922,* pp. 12 ff. On the link between glass architecture and social utopia, see Iain Boyd Whyte, *Bruno Taut and the Architecture of Activism,* Whyte, "Bruno Taut und die sozialistischen und weniger sozialistischen Wurzeln des sozialen Wohnungsbaues," *Neue Heimat Monatshefte,* 5, no. 27 (1980), pp. 28–37; Whyte, Expressionistische Architektur – der philosophische Kontext," *Das Abenteuer der Ideen: Architektur und Philosophie seit der industriellen Revolution,* exhibition catalogue, Internationale Bauausstellung Berlin (Berlin, 1987), pp. 167–184; and Wolfgang Pehnt, *Die Architektur des Expressionismus* (Stuttgart, 1973).

42 Taut, "Nieder mit dem Seriosismus!," p. 11.

43 Walter Gropius, letter to Karl-Ernst Osthaus on February 2, 1919. "Dear Osthaus, I'm very glad to hear that you are beginning to really appreciate Taut. I consider him exceptionally able, and also as a person so far beyond the sadly so numerous architectural confidence-men (Behrens, Paul, Muthesius, etc.) that I expect great things from him . . . ." Quoted in *Arbeitsrat für Kunst 1918–1921,* p. 117.

44 Adolf Behne, "Die Zukunft unsere Architektur," *Sozialistische Monatshefte,* 27, Jan. 31, 1931, pp. 90–94; quoted in Whyte, *Bruno Taut, Baumeister einer neuen Welt,* p. 178. See particularly chapter 23 of this book, "Das Ende einer Avantgarde," from which these references were taken.

45 "When the world comes to be guided by insight and goodness, we shall help build it. And until then we will protect the pure flame . . . . We are working for the future. We have to sacrifice the present . . . ," Behne, *Ruf zum Bauen,* p. 78.

46 Mies van der Rohe, "Bürohaus," *G,* 1, July 1923, p. 3.

47 *Ibid.*

48 Cf. Adolf Behne, "Architekten," *Frühlicht,* new series, 2, 1921; quoted in *Bruno Taut. Frühlicht 1920–1922,* pp. 126 ff.

49 Mies van der Rohe, "Baukunst und Zeitwille," *Der Querschnitt,* 4, no. 1, (1924), pp. 31–32.

50 Carl Gottfried, "Hochhäuser," *Qualität. Internationale Pro-*

Henning Rogge, Industriekultur. Peter Behrens und die AEG, 1907–1914, Berlin 1979, S. D 281.

7 Siehe hierzu Buddensieg/Rogge, Industriekultur, a.a.O.

8 Zitiert nach Peter Behrens 1888–1940, Gedenkschrift mit Katalog, Kaiserslautern, Hagen, Darmstadt, Wien 1966/1967, S. 21.

9 Karl Scheffler, Die Architektur der Großstadt, Berlin 1913, S. 157.

10 Walter Gropius, Die Entwicklung moderner Industriebaukunst, in: Die Kunst in Industrie und Handel, Jahrbuch des Deutschen Werkbundes 1913, Jena 1914, S. 21.

11 Edmund Schüler, Peter Behrens (Nachruf), in: Kunst im Deutschen Reich, Ausgabe B, 4. 1940, Folge 4, S. 65.

12 Walter Gropius, Die Entwicklung moderner Industriebaukunst, a. a. O.

13 Friedrich Hölderlin an Casimir Ulrich Böhlendorff, in: Friedrich Hölderlin. Sämtliche Werke und Briefe, hrsg. von Günter Mieth, München 1970, Band 2, S. 927.

14 Vgl. Jürgen Krause, ›Märtyrer‹ und ›Prophet‹. Studien zum Nietzsche-Kult in der bildenden Kunst der Jahrhundertwende, Berlin/New York 1984.

15 Friedrich Nietzsche, Vom Nutzen und Nachteil der Historie, in: Werke in drei Bänden, Hrsg. Karl Schlechta, Bd. 1 München 1982, S. 214f.

16 Zur Nietzsche-Rezeption im Frühwerk von Peter Behrens siehe Tilmann Buddensieg, Das Wohnhaus als Kultbau. Zum Darmstädter Haus von Behrens, in: Peter Behrens und Nürnberg. Geschmackswandel in Deutschland; Historismus, Jugendstil und die Anfänge der Industriereform, München 1980, S. 37–48.

17 Robert Breuer, Kleine Kunstnachrichten, in: Deutsche Kunst und Dekoration, 17. 1910/11, S. 492.

18 Siehe die einflußreiche Veröffentlichung von Paul Mebes, Um 1800. Architektur und Handwerk im letzten Jahrhundert ihrer traditionellen Entwicklung, 2 Bde., München 1908.

19 Vgl. Adolf Behne, Die Wiederkehr der Kunst, München o. J. (1920), S. 73: »Der Technizismus ist die geistige Verfassung, der Klassizismus sein künstlerischer Ausdruck.«

20 Karl Scheffler, 1913, a.a.O., S. 97.

21 Julius Meier-Graefe, Peter Behrens – Düsseldorf, in: Dekorative Kunst, 8. 1905, S. 389.

22 Julius Meier-Graefe, ebenda.

23 J. J. P. Oud, Über die zukünftige Baukunst und ihre architektonischen Möglichkeiten, in: Frühlicht, hrsg. von Bruno Taut, 1. 1921/22, Heft 4, zitiert nach der Neuausgabe: Bruno Taut. Frühlicht 1920–1922. Eine Folge für die Verwirklichung des neuen Baugedankens, Berlin, Frankfurt, Wien 1965, S. 208.

24 Walter Gropius, Die Entwicklung moderner Industriebaukunst, a.a.O., S. 21.

25 Walter Gropius, Die Entwicklung moderner Industriebaukunst, a.a.O., S. 19. Ebenda auch die vorhergehenden Zitate.

26 Ludwig Hilberseimer, Großstadtarchitektur, Stuttgart 1927, zit. nach der 2. Auflage 1978, S. 103.

27 Friedrich Nietzsche, Aus dem Nachlaß der Achtziger Jahre, in: Werke a.a.O., Bd. III, S. 634: »Unsere ganze euro-

paganda für Qualitätserzeugnisse, 3, no. 5, (1922), pp. 63–64.

51 *Frühlicht,* new series, 4, 1922, pp. 122–124, which includes the contribution referred to by Mies. On Mies's relationship to Expressionism, see Wolfgang Pehnt, "Wall and Crystal: Mies van der Rohe and German Expressionism," *Inland Architect,* March-April, 1986, pp. 20–27.

52 Theo van Doesburg and Cornelius van Eesteren, "Auf dem Weg zu einer kollektiven Konstruktion," *De Stijl,* 6/7, 1923–1925, pp. 89–90. See also in this context Werner Gräff, "Es kommt der neue Ingenieur," *G,* 1, July 1923, p. 4.

53 Ludwig Hilberseimer, "Konstruktion und Form," *G,* 3, June 1924, p. 14; and *Gross-Stadtarchitektur,* p. 101–102.

54 Le Corbusier, *Kommende Baukunst* (Stuttgart, 1926); quoted in the new German edition entitled *Ausblick auf eine Architektur* (Berlin, 1963), p. 40.

55 See a Wasmuth publication that was very widespread among architects of the 1920s, Werner Lindner, *Die Ingenieurbauten in ihrer guten Gestaltung* (Berlin, 1923).

56 Erich Mendelsohn, *Amerika, Bilderbuch eines Architekten* (Berlin, 1926), p. 13.

57 *Ibid.*

58 Hilberseimer, in *Berliner Architektur der 20er Jahre* (Berlin, 1967), p. 61, uses this Nietzsche aphorism to characterize Mies's famous project for an office building in concrete.

59 Mies van der Rohe, "Industrielles Bauen," *G,* 3, June 1924, p. 8.

60 Preface to the book *Bau und Wohnung,* Stuttgart: Deutscher Werkbund, 1927. On Mies's changing position during the 1920s, see my own *Mies van der Rohe: Das kunstlose Wort. Gedanken zur Baukunst* (Berlin, 1986).

61 Bruno Taut, "Der Sozialismus des Künstlers," *Sozialistische Monatshefte,* 25, no. 52 (1919), pp. 259–262.

62 Martin Wagner, *Amerikanische Bauwirtschaft* (Berlin, 1925).

63 *Siedlungen der zwanziger Jahre – heute. Vier Berliner Gross-Siedlungen 1924–1984* (Berlin: Bauhaus Archiv, 1985); Liselotte Ungers, *Die Suche nach einer neuen Wohnform. Siedlungen der zwanziger Jahre damals und heute* (Stuttgart, 1983).

64 Bruno Taut, *Die Auflösung der Städte oder Die Erde eine gute Wohnung* (Hagen, 1920).

65 Ludwig Hilberseimer, "Das Formproblem eines Weltstadtplatzes," *Das Neue Berlin: Monatshefte für Probleme der Gross-Stadt,* 2, Feb. 1929, p. 39; also, by the same author, "Entwicklungstendenzen des Städtebaus," *Die Form,* 4, pp. 209–211.

66 Walter Curt Behrendt, *Der Sieg des neuen "Baustils"* (Stuttgart, 1927).

päische Kultur bewegt sich seit langem schon mit einer Tortur der Spannung, die von Jahrzehnt zu Jahrzehnt wächst, wie auf eine Katastrophe los: unruhig, gewaltsam, überstürzt: einem Strom ähnlich, der ans *Ende* will, der sich nicht mehr besinnt, der Furcht davor hat sich zu besinnen.«

28 Bruno Taut, Nieder der Seriosismus!, in: Frühlicht, Januar 1920, zit. nach Bruno Taut 1920–1922. Frühlicht. Eine Folge für die Verwirklichung des neuen Baugedankens, Berlin, Frankfurt, Wien 1963, S. 11. – Zu Äußerungen von Taut aus den Kriegsjahren, siehe: Iain Boyd Whyte, Bruno Taut, Baumeister einer neuen Welt. Architektur und Aktivismus 1914–1920, Stuttgart 1981, insbes. S. 41 Brief vom Oktober 1914.

29 Peter Behrens, Das Ethos und die Umlagerung der künstlerischen Probleme, in: Der Leuchter. Jahrbuch der Schule der Weisheit. Hrsg. Graf H. Keyserling, Darmstadt 1920, S. 324.

30 Bruno Taut, Der Weltbaumeister. Architekturschauspiel für symphonische Musik, Hagen 1920.

31 Bruno Taut, Alpine Architektur, Hagen 1919. Vgl. auch Bruno Taut, Die Auflösung der Städte oder Die Erde eine gute Wohnung oder auch: Der Weg zur Alpinen Architektur, Hagen 1920, S. 63 mit Wiedergabe einer Passage aus Nietzsches Zarathustra (›Vom neuen Götzen‹).

32 Bruno Taut, Nieder mit dem Seriosismus!, a.a.O., S. 11.

33 Adolf Behne, Wiedergeburt der Baukunst, in: Bruno Taut, Die Stadtkrone. Mit Beiträgen von Paul Scheerbart, Erich Baron, Adolf Behne, Jena 1919, S. 130.

34 Walter Gropius, Flugblatt zur Ausstellung ›Für unbekannte Architekten‹, veranstaltet vom Arbeitsrat für Kunst, April 1919, wiedergegeben in: Arbeitsrat für Kunst. Berlin 1918–1921, Ausstellungskatalog, Berlin 1980, S. 90.

35 Karl Scheffler, Der Geist der Gotik, Leipzig 1917; bereits fünf Jahre vor Scheffler veröffentlichte Wilhelm Worringer die einflußreiche Studie über Formprobleme der Gotik, München 1912.

36 Bruno Taut, Die Stadtkrone, a.a.O., S. 59 f.

37 Wilhelm Worringer, Formprobleme der Gotik, München 1912

38 Vgl. z. B. Adolf Behne, Ruf zum Bauen. Zweite Buchpublikation des Arbeitsrats für Kunst, Berlin 1920, zit. nach: Arbeitsrat für Kunst 1918. 1921, a.a.O., S. 78.

39 Paul Scheerbart, Glasarchitektur, Berlin (Verlag ›Der Sturm‹) 1914, zit. nach der gleichnamigen Neuausgabe, mit einem Nachwort von Wolfgang Pehnt, München 1971, S. 25.

40 Vgl. Adolf Behne, Die Wiederkehr der Kunst, 1919, zitiert nach Paul Scheerbart, Glasarchitektur, a.a.O., S. 155.

41 Vgl. Adolf Behne, Glasarchitektur, in: Bruno Taut, Frühlicht, Januar 1920, nach: Bruno Taut 1920–1922, a.a.O., S. 12 ff. – Zum Zusammenhang von sozialer Utopie und Glasarchitektur siehe: Iain Boyd Whyte, Bruno Taut. Baumeister einer neuen Welt, a.O.; ders., Bruno Taut und die sozialistischen und weniger sozialistischen Wurzeln des sozialen Wohnungsbaues, in: Neue Heimat Monatshefte, 27. 1980, Heft 5, S. 28–37; ders., Expressionistische Architektur – der philosophische Kontext, in: Das Aben-

teuer der Ideen. Architektur und Philosophie seit der industriellen Revolution, Katalog der Internationalen Bauausstellung Berlin, Berlin 1987, S. 167–184; Wolfgang Pehnt, Die Architektur des Expressionismus, Stuttgart 1973.

42 Bruno Taut, Nieder der Seriosismus!, a.a.O., S. 11.

43 Walter Gropius, Schreiben an Karl-Ernst Osthaus vom 2. 2. 1919: »Lieber Osthaus … ich habe mich sehr darüber gefreut, daß Du beginnst, Taut richtig zu erkennen. Ich halte ihn für ganz außerordentlich fähig und auch als Mensch so hoch über den leider so zahlreichen Architektenhochstaplern (Behrens, Paul, Muthesius usw.) stehend, daß ich Bedeutendes von ihm erwarte …«, zit. nach: Arbeitsrat für Kunst 1918–1921, a.a.O., S. 117.

44 Adolf Behne, Die Zukunft unserer Architektur, in: Sozialistische Monatshefte, 27. 1931, 31. Januar, S. 90–94, zit. nach Iain Boyd Whyte, Bruno Taut, Baumeister einer neuen Welt, a.a.O., 178. Siehe dort insbes. Kap. 23 ›Das Ende einer Avantgarde‹, dem diese Hinweise entnommen sind.

45 »Wenn die Welt von Einsicht und Güte wird geleitet werden, helfen wir ihr, zu bauen. Und bis dahin hüten wir die reine Flamme … Wir leisten Zukunftsarbeit. Die Gegenwart müssen wir preisgeben …« Adolf Behne, Ruf zum Bauen, a.a.O., S. 78.

46 Mies van der Rohe, Bürohaus, in: G Nr. 1, Juli 1923, S. 3.

47 Ebenda.

48 Vgl. Adolf Behne, Architekten, in: Frühlicht, Neue Folge, Heft 2, 1921, nach Bruno Taut. Frühlicht 1920–1922, a.a.O., S. 126 ff.

49 Mies van der Rohe, Baukunst und Zeitwille, in: Der Querschnitt, 4. 1924, H. 1, S. 31 f.

50 Carl Gottfried, Hochhäuser, in: Qualität. Internationale Propaganda für Qualitätserzeugnisse, 3. 1922, Heft 5, S. 63 ff.

51 Frühlicht, Neue Folge, Heft 4, 1922, S. 122–124 mit dem Beitrag von Mies – Zum Verhältnis von Mies zum Expressionismus siehe Wolfgang Pehnt, Wall and Crystal. Mies van der Rohe and German Expressionism, in: Inland Architect, March/April 1986, S. 20–27.

52 Theo van Doesburg, Cornelis van Eesteren, Auf dem Weg zu einer kollektiven Konstruktion, in: De Stijl, 1923–1925, Nr. 6/7, S. 89 f. – Siehe in diesem Kontext, Werner Gräff, Es kommt der neue Ingenieur, in: G Nr. 1, Juli 1923, S. 4.

53 Ludwig Hilberseimer, Konstruktion und Form, in: G Nr. 3, Juni 1924, S. 14, sowie Großstadtarchitektur, Stuttgart 1927, S. 101 f.

54 Le Corbusier, Kommende Baukunst, Stuttgart 1926, zit. nach der Neuausgabe unter dem Titel: Ausblick auf eine Architektur, Berlin 1963, S. 40.

55 Vgl. die bei Wasmuth verlegte, unter Architekten der zwanziger Jahre weitverbreitete Publikation Werner Lindner, Die Ingenieurbauten in ihrer guten Gestaltung, Berlin 1923.

56 Erich Mendelsohn, Amerika, Bilderbuch eines Architekten, Berlin 1926, S. 13.

57 Ebenda.

58 So benutzt Hilberseimer, Berliner Architektur der 20er Jahre, Berlin 1967, S. 61, diesen Nietzsche-Aphorismus zur Charakterisierung des berühmten Projekts zu einem Bürogebäude in Beton von Mies van der Rohe.

59 Mies van der Rohe, Industrielles Bauen, in: G Nr. 3, Juni 1924, S. 8.

60 Vorwort zur Buchpublikation ›Bau und Wohnung‹, hrsg. v. Deutschen Werkbund Stuttgart 1927. – Zum Wandel der Mies'schen Positionen in den zwanziger Jahren siehe meine Studie, Mies van der Rohe. Das kunstlose Wort. Gedanken zur Baukunst, Berlin 1986.

61 Bruno Taut, Der Sozialismus des Künstlers, in: Sozialistische Monatshefte, 25. 1919, Bd. 52, S. 259–262.

62 Martin Wagner, Amerikanische Bauwirtschaft, Berlin 1925.

63 Siedlungen der zwanziger Jahre – heute. Vier Berliner Großsiedlungen 1924–1984, Bauhaus-Archiv, Berlin 1985; Liselotte Ungers, Die Suche nach einer neuen Wohnform. Siedlungen der zwanziger Jahre damals und heute, Stuttgart 1983.

64 Bruno Taut, Die Auflösung der Städte oder Die Erde eine gute Wohnung, Hagen 1920.

65 Ludwig Hilberseimer, Das Formproblem eines Weltstadtplatzes, in: Das Neue Berlin. Monatshefte für Probleme der Großstadt, Heft 2, Februar 1929, S. 39; vgl. auch ders., Entwicklungstendenzen des Städtebaus, in: Die Form, 4. 1929, S. 209–211.

66 Walter Curt Behrendt, Der Sieg des neuen ›Baustils‹, Stuttgart 1027

Fig. 61   *Julius Klinger. "Erste Admirals-Redoute" poster,*
1913. SMPK Kunstbibliothek, Berlin.

Abb. 61   *Julius Klinger. »Erste Admirals-Redoute«, Plakat,*
1913. SMPK Kunstbibliothek, Berlin.

Angela Schönberger

It's a Joy to Live – Spirits Are Rising

Angela Schönberger

Es ist eine Lust zu leben, die Geister bewegen sich...

Berlin, capital of a united Germany since 1871, imperial residence and center of political and military power, had by the turn of the century become a world city. Its hurried pace, its impatient, blunt speech, and its humor were notorious. Rapid growth in every field of business and commerce had made the city a melting pot that attracted and absorbed people of the most diverse backgrounds from all over the German empire. An interconnected transportation system of subways and elevated trains, begun in 1896, linked the capital with surrounding towns like Charlottenburg, Schöneberg, and Wilmersdorf. By 1920 these independent communities had become incorporated in Greater Berlin.

The first electric streetcar had plied its way through Lichterfelde, one of Berlin's many residential suburbs, in 1881. In 1903, a railcar built by the Allgemeine Electricitätsgesellschaft (AEG) and driven by a three-phase electric motor set a world record of 210.2 kilometers an hour on the Marienfelde-to-Zossen line. The automobile, the zeppelin, and the airplane, film and photography, the typewriter and new technology in newspaper printing created a swiftly expanding transportation and communications network unprecedented in its complexity and size. The mechanization of life had begun.

Berlin's existence and its imperial power depended mainly on new industries. With Borsig and other large firms producing machine tools, and, even more important, with electrical companies like Siemens and AEG developing new products, Berlin became a leading industrial power in the world. At the same time, and in the wake of Paris and London, Berlin burgeoned into an important center for banking and trade, exploiting its ideal position between Eastern and Western Europe.

Berlin was an intellectual center as well. With Humboldt University, the State Museums, the German Archaeological Institute, and the Kaiser Wilhelm Society, to name only a few of the important research institutions, the city increasingly developed into a locus of intellectual inquiry unrivaled throughout Germany.

Yet the turn of the century also witnessed a growing malaise on the part of liberally minded citizens, architects, and artists over cultural life under the

Berlin, seit 1871 Hauptstadt des neugegründeten Deutschen Reiches, Residenz des Kaiserhauses, Zentrum der politischen und militärischen Macht, hatte sich bis zur Jahrhundertwende zu einer Weltstadt entwickelt. Ihre Geschäftigkeit, Hektik, Kaltschnäuzigkeit, ihr Witz waren berühmt und berüchtigt. Durch eine rapide Expansion auf allen Gebieten der Wirtschaft und des Handels wurde die Stadt zu einem Schmelztiegel, der Menschen unterschiedlichster Herkunft und Bildung aus allen Gebieten des Deutschen Reiches anzog und absorbierte. Ein dichtes Verkehrsnetz mit Hoch- und Untergrundbahnen, seit 1896 im Bau und ständig wachsend, verband die umliegenden Städte, z.B. Charlottenburg, Schöneberg oder Wilmersdorf, mit der Hauptstadt. Die erste elektrische Straßenbahn fuhr bereits 1881 durch Lichterfelde, einen der vielen Villenvororte Berlins. 1903 erreichte ein Drehstromwagen der AEG mit einer Geschwindigkeit von 210,2 km/h auf der Strecke Marienfelde–Zossen den damaligen Weltrekord. Das Automobil, Zeppelin und Flugzeug, Film und Fotografie, die Schreibmaschine und die Erfindung des Rotationsdrucks schufen eine bis dahin nicht gekannte Verkehrs- und Kommunikationsdichte, die sich mit immenser Geschwindigkeit ausbreitete. Die Mechanisierung des Lebens hatte begonnen.

Zur zentralen Lebensader und damit zum bedeutendsten Machtfaktor der Reichshauptstadt wurde die Großindustrie. Neben dem Maschinenbau durch Borsig und andere erlangte vor allem die Elektroindustrie mit den Firmen Siemens und AEG Führungsniveau auf dem Weltmarkt. Nach Paris und London entwickelte sich Berlin um die Jahrhundertwende zu einer bedeutenden Bank- und Handelsmetropole mit einer Schlüsselstellung zwischen Ost- und Westeuropa.

Um die Jahrhundertwende machte sich bei Teilen des liberalen Bürgertums, bei Architekten und Künstlern immer mehr ein Unbehagen an der Wilhelminischen Kultur und der offiziellen Kulturpolitik breit. Insbesondere riefen die herrschenden sozialen und hygienischen Mißstände im Wohnungswesen wie auch die gesamte gesellschaftspolitische Situation nach Reformen. Solche komplexen und vielschichtigen historischen Zusammenhänge können hier nur

Kaiser and the official arts policy of his government. Even more obviously in need of reform were widespread social injustices and poor housing conditions, indeed the entire socio-political situation in the capital. The "rental barracks" of working-class districts like Kreuzberg, Wedding, Prenzlauer Berg, or Neukölln, for example, earned Berlin the nickname of "the Petrified City." Such complex and multifarious historical circumstances were the source and impetus of turn-of-the-century reform movements that set out to cure the discontents of civilization as if they were an illness – by means of natural medicine, nudism, health food, garden cities, and, not least, the *Reformkleid,* a new fashion in dress that was adopted in Germany's artistic circles and which finally liberated women from disfiguring corsets.

The Jugendstil, a reform movement in the arts around 1900, represented a basic philosophical and aesthetic reaction not only to the historical revivals of the preceding century but to the increasing mechanization of modern life itself. Organizations and groups of artists formed to oppose the machine and to advocate artistic quality and craftsmanly execution in the manufacture of things for everyday use. The year 1897 saw the founding in Munich of the Vereinigte Werkstätten für Kunst im Handwerk (the Associated Workshops for Art in Craftsmanship), followed in 1898 by the Dresdner Werkstätten für Handwerkskunst (Workshops for the Crafts). Soon these and other groups were producing furniture of straightforward design with an emphasis on structural honesty. Among the leading personalities of this movement were Richard Riemerschmid, Bruno Paul, Bernhard Pankok, and Hermann Obrist. Along with Munich and Dresden, Darmstadt developed into a center for fine craftsmanship and architecture, noted for its artists' colony at Mathildenhöhe, headed by Josef Maria Olbrich. Peter Behrens in particular caused a sensation there with a house he built for himself in which every detail was of his own design – a true *Gesamtkunstwerk.*

In about 1906, as resistance to applied ornament grew, advocates of simple, functional objects for everyday use began to gain a hearing. The beauty of things, they argued, should inhere solely in the simple forms dictated by their use. A corollary of this general demand for functionality and sobriety in architecture and applied art was an acceptance of machine-made goods, providing that adequate designs were relied on. The first standardized, mass-produced furniture was displayed in 1906, at an arts and crafts exhibition in Dresden. In 1907 the Deutsche Werkbund was established for the purpose of creating an alliance of art, craftsmanship, and industry.

angedeutet werden. Trotzdem muß man sie erwähnen, weil sie der Ausgangspunkt und die Basis für die um die Jahrhundertwende einsetzenden Reformbewegungen sind, mit denen man das Unbehagen an der Kultur wie eine Krankheit heilen zu können glaubte: durch Naturheilkunde, Freikörperkultur, Reformwarenhäuser, Gartenstädte und Reformkleider, die die Frauen endlich von dem den Körper deformierenden Korsett befreiten.

Die Stilbewegung um 1900 war in ihrer philosophischen und ästhetischen Grundhaltung nicht nur eine Reaktion auf den Historismus, sondern auch auf die zunehmende Mechanisierung des Lebens; und sie war natürlich nicht auf Berlin beschränkt, sondern im ganzen Reich formierten sich um die Jahrhundertwende Organisationen und Gruppen einzelner Künstler, die gegen die Maschine opponierten und wieder ein vom Handwerk künstlerisch gestaltetes Gebrauchsgerät forderten. So wurden 1897 in München die »Vereinigten Werkstätten für Kunst im Handwerk« gegründet und 1898 die »Dresdner Werkstätten für Handwerkskunst«. Führende künstlerische Persönlichkeiten dieser Bewegung waren Richard Riemerschmid, Bruno Paul, Bernhard Pankok und Hermann Obrist. Neben München und Dresden entwickelte sich als weiteres Zentrum für Kunsthandwerk und Architektur die »Künstlerkolonie auf der Mathildenhöhe« unter dem Patronat des Großherzogs von Hessen und der Leitung von Joseph Maria Olbrich in Darmstadt. Dort erregte vor allem Peter Behrens mit seinem als Gesamtkunstwerk gestalteten Wohnhaus Aufsehen.

Mit der nun allgemein einsetzenden Ablehnung ornamentalen Dekors wurde seit etwa 1906 immer mehr ein puristisches, zweckbetontes Gebrauchsgerät gefordert. Die Schönheit der Gegenstände sollte allein in der sachlichen, dem Zweck des Gegenstandes entsprechenden Form zum Ausdruck kommen. Mit dem allgemeinen Ruf nach Zweckmäßigkeit und Sachlichkeit in Architektur und angewandter Kunst war die vorbehaltlose Anerkennung maschineller Verarbeitung verbunden, für die adäquate Formen gefunden werden mußten. Auf der Kunstgewerbeausstellung in Dresden 1906 wurden zum ersten Mal typisierte Serienmöbel gezeigt. 1907 erfolgte die Gründung des Deutschen Werkbundes, dessen Anliegen die Verbindung von Kunst, Handwerk und Industrie war. Sein Programm sah die Synthese zwischen künstlerischer und industrieller Produktion vor.

Kunsthandwerklich gearbeitete Möbel und Gebrauchsgegenstände konnten die Berliner um die Jahrhundertwende vor allem im Hohenzollern-Kunstgewerbehaus in der Leipziger Straße sehen und kaufen. Dieses war von Hermann Hirschwald 1879 mit

Fig. 62   *Henri van de Velde. Hohenzollern-Kunstgewerbe-haus, Berlin, 1904. Main entrance, Leipziger Strasse.*

Abb. 62   *Henri van de Velde. Hohenzollern-Kunstgewerbe-haus, Berlin, 1904. Haupteingang Leipziger Straße.*

Around the turn of the century, handcrafted products could be purchased in only a few exclusive stores in Berlin. One of the principal outlets was the Hohenzollern-Kunstgewerbehaus on Leipziger Strasse, a department store in which the public "would always find the most outstanding products of contemporary German and especially Berlin craftsmanship exhibited and for sale." The store was to provide "a central outlet for the entire range of Berlin arts and crafts, in which none of the quality workshops, large or small, would remain unrepresented."[2] The Kunsthaus had

einer Ladenetage in der Straße Unter den Linden eröffnet worden. Nach dem Umzug in die Leipziger Straße wurde 1899 Henri van de Velde mit der Leitung des Ateliers und der Werkstätten sowie mit dem Ausbau der Geschäftsräume (1901) beauftragt *(Abb. 62)*. Im Kunsthaus sollte das Publikum nicht nur »stets die erlesensten Erzeugnisse des deutschen und besonders des berlinischen zeitgenössischen Kunstgewerbes ausgestellt finden«, sondern es wurde auch durch Veranstaltungen über die internationalen Strömungen informiert.[2] So zeigte das Hohenzollern-Kunstgewer-

Fig. 63   *Curt Stoeving. Bronze desk-top objects for the "Moderne Wohnräume" exhibition, 1902.*

Abb. 63   *Curt Stoeving. Diverse Bronzegeräte für den Schreibtisch für »Moderne Wohnräume«, 1902.*

begun with a first-floor shop on Unter den Linden, opened in 1879 by Hermann Hirschwald. After its move to Leipziger Strasse, Henri van de Velde was commissioned in 1899 to head the studio and workshops *(fig. 62)*. Later, in 1901, he became responsible for the design of the business premises as well.

Exhibitions of international arts and crafts were also held in the Hohenzollern salesrooms. These included so-called reform clothing in 1902; the work of the Parisian jeweler René Lalique in 1903; and in 1904, handcrafted furniture by the Wiener Werkstätte. Among the crowds of avid buyers, Julius Lessing, director of the Berlin Kunstgewerbemuseum, could frequently be seen admiring the displays; as he explained, a stroll through the Hohenzollern Kunsthaus was among the most instructive experiences to be had in the field of applied art. Representatives of foreign museums likewise visited Hirschwald's institution to make acquisitions for their modern collections. The Wiener Werkstätte show, for which Josef Hoffmann and Koloman Moser provided a Viennese ambience,

behaus 1903 in seinen Räumen das Werk des Pariser Juweliers René Lalique und 1904 Kunsthandwerk der »Wiener Werkstätte«. Neben dem kauflustigen Berliner Publikum stattete ihm auch Julius Lessing, Direktor des Kunstgewerbemuseums, zahlreiche Besuche ab und erklärte, daß ein Gang durch die Räume des Hohenzollern-Kunstgewerbehauses zum Lehrreichsten gehöre, was auf dem Gebiet des Kunsthandwerks geboten werden könne. Aber auch Vertreter ausländischer Museen besuchten regelmäßig das Hirschwaldsche Institut, um dort Neuerwerbungen für ihre musealen Sammlungen aufzustöbern. Von großem Einfluß auf die Entwicklung des Berliner Möbeldesigns in Richtung einer geradlinigen und puristischen Formgebung war die bereits erwähnte Ausstellung »Wiener Werkstätte«, die von Josef Hoffmann und Koloman Moser ganz im Wiener Stil inszeniert wurde.

Den eigentlichen Auftakt für das neue Kunstgewerbe in Berlin bildete 1902 die Ausstellung »Moderne Wohnräume« im Warenhaus Wertheim. Dieser revolutionäre Bau einer neuen Architekturgattung war erst

exerted a strong influence on Berlin furniture designers to develop simple and functional forms.

The real impetus for a new approach to craftsmanship in Berlin came, however, from an exhibition entitled *Moderne Wohnräume (Modern Interiors),* held in 1902 at the Wertheim Department Store. Here, for the first time, Berlin audiences were introduced to work by the most significant artists of the period. The organization and design of the show were handled by the architect Curt Stoeving *(fig. 63).* Both he and Max Osborn, one of the day's most knowledgeable art critics, described the purpose of the exhibition in the magazine *Deutsche Kunst und Dekoration (German Art and Decoration).* Stoeving explained that "the rooms installed at Wertheim to create the overall impression of complete Berlin apartments were intended to give onlookers of every degree of taste and

wenige Jahre zuvor (1896/97) von Alfred Messel errichtet worden. Hier sah das Berliner Publikum zum ersten Mal Arbeiten der bedeutendsten Künstlerpersönlichkeiten jener Zeit. Die Gesamtleitung und Gestaltung der Ausstellung »Moderne Wohnräume« hatte der Architekt Curt Stoeving *(Abb. 63)* übernommen. Zusammen mit Max Osborn, einem der kenntnisreichsten Kunstkritiker der Zeitschrift »Deutsche Kunst und Dekoration«, beschrieb er das Vorhaben folgendermaßen: »Wohnräume, wie sie als eine Gesamt-Anlage nach Art vollständiger Berliner Wohnungen ... durch das Warenhaus A. Wertheim ... errichtet wurden, (sollten) Beschauern jeden Bildungs-Grades die Möglichkeit (geben), die einfache Geschlossenheit dieser modernen Räume zu empfinden, die praktische Nutzanwendung der Möbel zu sehen und solche zu mäßigen Preisen in bester Ausführung zu kaufen.«[3]

Fig. 64 *August Endell. Dining room for the "Moderne Wohnräume" exhibition, 1902.*

Abb. 64 *August Endell. Speisezimmer in »Moderne Wohnräume«, 1902.*

Fig. 65 *Peter Behrens. Dining room for the "Moderne Wohnräume" exhibition, 1902.*

Abb. 65 *Peter Behrens. Speisezimmer in »Moderne Wohnräume«, 1902.*

Fig. 66 *Peter Behrens. Soup bowl from dinner service for the "Moderne Wohnräume" exhibition, 1902. Produced by Porzellanfabrik Gebr. Bauscher, Weiden. Private collection.*

Abb. 66 *Peter Behrens. Terrine aus dem Speiseservice für »Moderne Wohnräume«, 1902. Hersteller: Porzellanfabrik Gebr. Bauscher, Weiden. Privatbesitz.*

education an opportunity to perceive the simple unity of these modern interiors, to recognize the practical utility of the furnishings, and to purchase the same at reasonable prices in the best quality."[3] Contributors to the exhibition included Richard Riemerschmid, Peter Behrens, the Danish designers Thorwald Jörgensen and Carl Petersen, Paul Ludwig Troost, Paul Schultze-Naumburg, M. H. Baillie Scott, Patriz Huber, and August Endell, whose dining room *(fig. 64)* in a rather startling color scheme prompted Osborn to report: "Endell has ventured forth into a very bold color composition: the walls were papered in violet, the ceiling was tinted pastel green, the floor carpeted in dark green frisé; blue slipcovers were chosen for the furniture, a light, waxed oak for the woodwork; and baseboards, window and door frames were painted red!"[4] The Wertheim exhibition was intended to be educational as well. "It is very important that the crowds who daily flow through the store," declared Osborn, "become acquainted with good taste, and realize that opulence is not the point."[5]

The point was to build, show, and sell furniture of good quality and exemplary design that was within the reach of a broad public. Of all of the exhibits, Peter Behrens's dining room excited the greatest interest. Max Osborn's description is worth quoting at length:

An der Ausstellung waren Richard Riemerschmid, Peter Behrens, die Dänen Thorwald Jörgensen und Carl Petersen, Paul Ludwig Troost, Paul Schultze-Naumburg, M. H. Baillie Scott und aus Berlin Patriz Huber beteiligt.

Über ein in provokanter Farbigkeit gehaltenes Speisezimmer von August Endell *(Abb. 64)* berichtet Osborn: »Endell wagte sich zu einer sehr kecken koloristischen Komposition vor: Die Wand erhielt eine violette Tapete, die Decke ward zartgrün getönt, der Fußboden mit dunkelgrünem Fries belegt, zu den Möbeln wurden blaue Stoffbezüge gewählt, als Holz hell gewachste Eiche genommen, die Fußleiste, Fenster- und Türumrahmungen rot gestrichen!«[4]

Der Wertheim-Ausstellung wurde eine große erzieherische Wirkung zugesprochen. »Es ist sehr wesentlich, daß die Menge, die täglich das Warenhaus durchströmt, einen so diskreten, soliden Geschmack kennenlernt, daß sie sieht: es kommt nicht auf den Prunk an.«[5]

Man wollte Möbel schaffen, Möbel zur Schau stellen, die von guter Qualität waren: hervorragend gestaltet und für ein breites Publikum geeignet. Das Speisezimmer von Peter Behrens *(Abb. 64–69)* erregte unter allen Arbeiten das größte Aufsehen. Es soll deshalb ausführlicher beschrieben werden, so wie Max Osborn

This is a logically composed, unified creation in which every detail has been subjected to an ordering purpose. Behrens began with a linear ornament whose basic form is a rectangle, which is generally subdivided by parallel or perpendicular lines into several smaller, rectangular or square sections. This "abstract" figure, composed of ruled lines, appears as flat ornament on the walls, where it is stenciled on the plaster over a wainscoting of white lacquered mats and tinted in several colors; it appears again, in blue, on the china tableware, and again in the carpet, slightly altered but in similar nuances of blue; and it is to be repeated in relief-work on the silver, which we are still awaiting. Nor is that the last of this ornamental motif. It takes on three-dimensional shape and burgeons into rectangular-section, absolutely original brackets,

es gesehen hat: »Es ist eine streng durchgeführte, einheitliche Schöpfung, in der sich jede Einzelheit einem ordnenden Willen unterwarf. Behrens ging dabei von einem geradlinigen Ornament aus, dessen Grund-Form ein Rechteck ist, und das durch parallele oder in rechten Winkeln zu einander stehende Linien meist in mehrere kleinere, rechteckige oder quadratische Teile weiter zerfällt. Diese aus Lineal-Strichen entstandene »abstrakte« Figur tritt als Flach-Ornament an den Wänden auf, wo sie über einem Paneel von weißlackierten Spahn-Matten auf den Putz schabloniert und in mehreren Farben getönt ist, sie erscheint ebenso, in Blau, auf dem Porzellangeschirr, sodann, gleichfalls in blauen Nuancen, wenig verändert auf dem geknüpften Teppich, sie soll in Relief-Arbeit auf dem Silberzeug auftreten, das wir noch zu erwarten haben. Damit ist jedoch der Herrschafts-Bezirk dieses

Fig. 67 *Peter Behrens. Flatware for the "Moderne Wohn-räume" exhibition, 1902. Produced by Sächsische Metallwarenfabrik August Wellner Söhne AG, Aue i. Sachsen, and J. J. Rückert, Mainz. Hessisches Landesmuseum, Darmstadt.*

Abb. 67 *Peter Behrens. Teile aus dem Eßbesteck für »Moderne Wohnräume«, 1902. Hersteller: Sächsische Metallwarenfabrik August Wellner Söhne AG, Aue i. Sachsen, und J. J. Rückert, Mainz. Hessisches Landesmuseum, Darmstadt.*

Fig. 68   *Peter Behrens. Gold-rimmed drinking glasses for
the "Moderne Wohnräume" exhibition, 1902. Produced by
Benedikt von Poschinger Glass Factory, Oberzwieselau.
Hessisches Landesmuseum, Darmstadt; private collection.*

Abb. 68   *Peter Behrens. Gläser mit Goldrand für »Moderne
Wohnräume«, 1902. Hersteller: Kristallglasfabrik Benedikt von
Poschinger, Oberzwieselau. Hessisches Landesmuseum,
Darmstadt; Privatbesitz.*

which in turn have influenced the design of the
rectilinear gas-jet composition; it has affected the
structure of the furniture, buffet, and sideboard,
here too stipulating the straight line as principle; it
has determined the form of the aluminum fittings,
which stand out very pleasingly against the dark
elmwood; and finally, it has played its part in the
construction of the chairs, in the design of their
backs.[6]

The significance of this exhibition at the Wertheim
Department Store cannot be sufficiently emphasized.
As Max Osborn noted in his review, it marked the
inception of a democratic art in Imperial Germany of
the Wilhelminian era:

     … the great principle underlying all contemporary

ornamentalen Gedankens nicht erschöpft; er nimmt
drei-dimensionale Gestalt an und wächst sich zu
viereckigen, völlig originellen Wand-Armen aus, die
ihrerseits wiederum in der Bildung der geradlinigen
Gas-Kronen-Komposition mitgewirkt haben; er hat
sich auf den Bau der Möbel, des Büffets und der
Kredenz eingewirkt und auch diesen die gerade Linie
als Gesetz vorgeschrieben, hat die Form der Alumi-
nium-Beschläge bestimmt, die sich von dem dunkeln
Rüstern-Holz sehr gut abheben, und hat schließlich
beim Bau der Stühle, bei der Gestaltung der Lehnen
seine Hand mit im Spiele gehabt.«[6]

Die Bedeutung dieser Ausstellung im Warenhaus
Wertheim im Jahre 1902 kann nicht genügend hervor-
gehoben werden. Wie sehr sie auch als Auftakt einer
demokratischen Kunst in der Zeit des Wilhelminischen

Fig. 69   *Peter Behrens. Dining-room chair for the "Moderne Wohnräume" exhibition, 1902. Cooper-Hewitt Museum, The Smithsonian Institution's National Museum of Design, New York.*

Abb. 69   *Peter Behrens. Speisezimmerstuhl für »Moderne Wohnräume«, 1902. Cooper-Hewitt Museum, The Smithsonian Institution's National Museum of Design, New York.*

effort in the arts and crafts, which characteristically enough came over to us from England, America, and Belgium, is a fundamentally democratic one. All of the typically democratic qualities it embodies sharply distinguish this movement from the artistic tendencies of earlier epochs, and it was only natural that on the path to its prime goal, the crafts movement should sooner or later have converged with that other very significant factor in democratic society represented by the department store.[7]

This association of modern crafts with the department store, as well as Osborn's characterization of the department store as a democratic institution, is extremely illuminating. It was not the official society of court and aristocracy that furthered these efforts to improve design, but the retail trade. The initiative was taken by manufacturers and individual businessmen.

Kaiserreiches angesehen wurde, soll ein weiteres Zitat von Max Osborn belegen: »Das große Prinzip des ganzen kunstgewerblichen Sehnens unserer Zeit, das bezeichnenderweise von England, Amerika und Belgien zu uns herüberkam, ist im Kern ein demokratisches, in dieser Eigenschaft beruhen eben die charakteristischen Merkmale, die es von den künstlerischen Tendenzen aller früheren Epochen scharf unterscheiden, und es ist nur natürlich, daß das Kunst-Handwerk auf dem Wege zu jenem nächsten freien Ziel früher oder später mit einem so bedeutsamen anderen Faktor der demokratischen Kultur, wie ihn das moderne Warenhaus darstellt, zusammentreffen mußte.«[7]

Die Verbindung von neuer kunsthandwerklicher Gestaltung und dem Warenhaus sowie die Charakterisierung des Warenhauses als Institution einer demokratischen Kultur ist äußerst aufschlußreich und damit auch bezeichnend für die Berliner Situation. Nicht die offizielle Gesellschaft, d. h. der Hof und die Aristokratie, setzten sich für die Förderung des Design ein, sondern die Warenhäuser. Industrielle und einzelne Händler übernahmen hier die Initiative.

Fig. 70   *Peter Behrens. AEG electric heater, c. 1908. Private collection.*

Abb. 70   *Peter Behrens. AEG Elektrischer Heizofen, um 1908. Privatbesitz.*

Fig. 71 *Alfred Grenander. View of music room interior, exhibited at A. S. Ball furniture showroom, 1905.*

Abb. 71 *Alfred Grenander. Hauptansicht des Musikzimmers, ausgestellt im Möbelgeschäft A. S. Ball, 1905.*

When in 1905 a second exhibition, this one entitled *Neue Wohnräume (New Interiors),* was mounted at Wertheim, again arranged by Curt Stoeving and with the same architects and artists as in 1902, the press drew attention to this development: "Many regret ... that it should have to be department stores that take it upon themselves to nurse our infant crafts industry .... Not every federal state can boast its Darmstadt throne. Berlin, for one, certainly cannot."[8] With this allusion to the Grand Duke of Hesse and his patronage of the exhibition *Ein Dokument deutscher Kunst (A Document of German Art)* in Darmstadt in 1901, the indifference of the Prussian government to the new crafts movement stood publicly accused.

In the same year, a great stir was created by the exhibition organized by Alfred Grenander at the A. S. Ball furniture factory on Potsdamer Strasse, in which interiors were presented that had been shown at the St. Louis Exposition in 1904. These included home fur-

Dieses Manko wurde anläßlich der Ausstellung »Neue Wohnräume«, die 1905 im Kaufhaus Wertheim, ebenfalls unter der Leitung von Curt Stoeving und mit denselben Architekten und Künstlern wie bereits 1902, stattfand, von der Presse deutlich angeprangert: »Viele bedauern..., daß gerade die Warenhäuser es sein müssen, welche bei unserem eigenen Kunsthandwerk die Ammenpflicht übernehmen... Nicht in jedem Bundesstaat steht ein Darmstädter Thron. In Berlin z. B. auch nicht.«[8] Mit dieser Anspielung auf das Mäzenatentum des Großherzogs von Hessen und seine vorbildliche Förderung der Ausstellung »Ein Dokument deutscher Kunst« in Darmstadt 1901 wurde das Desinteresse der Wilhelminischen Kultur an der neuen Kunstgewerbebewegung öffentlich mißbilligt.

Eine weitere Ausstellung erregte großes Aufsehen in Berlin. Alfred Grenander präsentierte ebenfalls 1905 Interieurs in den Räumen der Möbelfabrik A. S. Ball in der Potsdamer Straße, die auf der Weltausstellung in

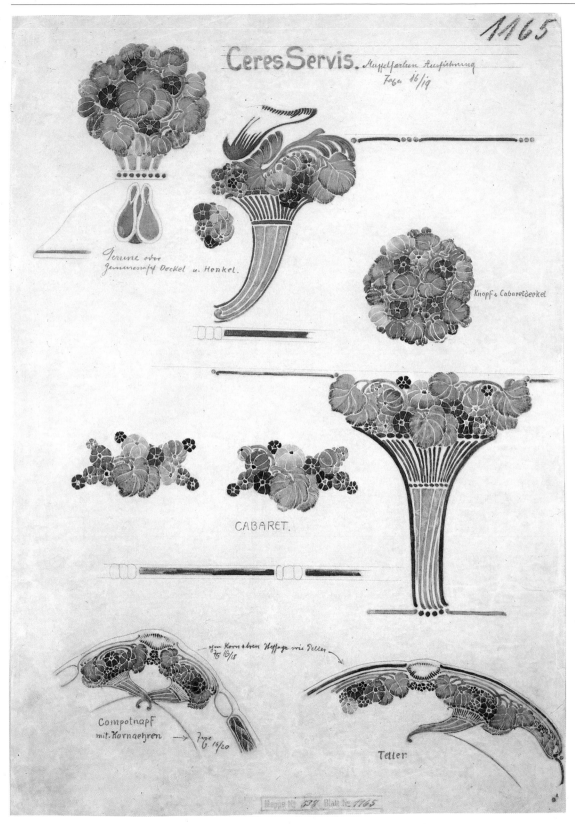

Fig. 72 / Abb. 72

Fig. 73   *Theo Schmuz-Baudiss. Soup bowl, from the "Ceres" dinner service, 1913. Produced by KPM (Königliche Porzellan Manufaktur), Berlin. Berlin-Porzellansammlung Belvedere, Berlin.*

Abb. 73   *Theo Schmuz-Baudiss. Terrine aus dem Tafelservice ›Ceres‹, 1913. Hersteller: KPM (Königliche Porzellan-Manufaktur), Berlin. Berlin-Porzellansammlung Belvedere, Berlin.*

Fig. 72   *Theo Schmuz-Baudiss. Design for the "Ceres" dinner service, 1912. Graphite, watercolor, and gilt. KPM-Archiv, Schloss Charlottenburg, Berlin.*
The "Ceres" dinner service was designed for the 150th anniversary of the KPM (Königliche Porzellan-Manufaktur). In 1914 it was shown in the Deutsche Werkbund Exhibition in Cologne.

Abb. 72   *Theo Schmuz-Baudiss. Dekorentwürfe für das Tafelservice ›Ceres‹, 1912. Graphit, Aquarell, und Gold. KPM-Archiv, Schloß Charlottenburg, Berlin.*
Das Tafelservice ›Ceres‹ wurde für das 150. Jubiläum der KPM (Königliche Porzellan-Manufaktur) entworfen. 1914 wurde es auf der Werkbund Ausstellung in Köln gezeigt.

Fig. 74   *Lab porcelain, 1920s. Produced by KPM*
(Staatliche Porzellan-Manufaktur), Berlin.
Abb. 74   *Laborporzellan, 20er Jahre. Hersteller:*
KPM (Staatliche Porzellan-Manufaktur), Berlin.

nishings by Marie Philipp, E. Schneckenberg, and Rudolf and Fia Wille of Berlin, along with Grenander's own designs *(fig. 71)*, and work by Charles Rennie Mackintosh. "It has been a long time since craftsmanship in Berlin has been able to register such a great success," *Deutsche Kunst und Dekoration* commented in its review of the opening.

> The ladies and maidens of the Westend in particular were seen to glide with bright, caressing glances through the tasteful and brilliant rooms, and now all obstinate Berlin is in raptures over the new decorative ideal and the young German style. Everyone here is still very much impressed by the great victory won by German handcrafts in St. Louis; indeed only now has the import of this astonishing circumstance become apparent, now that duplicates of the prizewinning pieces are on show and Berlin positively swarms with Grands Prix .... Another thing Berliners are learning from this exhibition is that the modern style is by no means an effusion of novelty, caprice, or faddish-

St. Louis gezeigt worden waren: u. a. Zimmereinrichtungen von Marie Philipp, E. Schneckenberg und Rudolf und Fia Wille aus Berlin, seine eigenen Arbeiten *(Abb. 71)* und Arbeiten von Ch. R. Mackintosh. »Einen solchen offenkundigen Erfolg hat das Kunstgewerbe in Berlin lange nicht zu verzeichnen gehabt«, schreibt die »Deutsche Kunst und Dekoration« anläßlich der Ausstellungseröffnung.

»Namentlich die Frauen und die Jungfrauen des Westens wandelten mit strahlenden und liebkosenden Augen durch die geschmackvollen und glänzenden Räume, und jetzt schwärmt das obstinate Berlin für das neue, dekorative Ideal und für den jungdeutschen Stil. Man steht hier immer noch unter dem Eindruck des großen Sieges, den das deutsche Kunstgewerbe in St. Louis erfochten hat, ja jetzt wird erst eigentlich die Bedeutung der überraschenden Tatsache ruchbar, da manches über das große Wasser heimgekehrt ist, die Doubletten der preisgekrönten Arbeiten gezeigt werden und Berlin von Grand Prix nur so wimmelt ... In dieser Ausstellung wird den Berlinern des ferneren noch klar gemacht, daß der moderne Stil keineswegs ein Ausfluß von Neuerungswut, von Laune oder sonst eine Willkürlichkeit ist, er erwächst vielmehr folgerichtig aus umgeänderten Lebensbedingungen, aus neuen Anforderungen an die *Hygiene*. An Stelle von Kerzen oder Lampenbeleuchtung ist das bewegliche *elektrische Licht* getreten, Kachelöfen und Kamine haben den *Gittern* der *Zentralheizungen* Platz gemacht, und wer es irgendwie ermöglichen kann, nimmt auch zu den Segnungen der *Ventilation* seine Zuflucht. Es ist klar, daß alle diese *neuen Voraussetzungen* auch zu *neuen* Formen und Abmessungen führen mußten.«[9]

1907 überraschte Bruno Paul auf der »Großen Berliner Kunstausstellung« das Publikum mit seinen eleganten, kostbaren Luxus-Interieurs. Es lohnt sich, bei ihm etwas ausführlicher zu verweilen. Er war neben Hermann Muthesius und Peter Behrens für das Berliner Kulturgeschehen der Vorkriegszeit eine außerordentlich wichtige Persönlichkeit. 1907 wurde Bruno Paul auf Empfehlung Wilhelm von Bodes, dem Generaldirektor der Staatlichen Museen, von Wilhelm II. als Leiter der »Unterrichtsanstalt des Berliner Kunstgewerbemuseums« und später Direktor der »Vereinigten Staatsschulen für freie und angewandte Kunst« in den preußischen Staatsdienst berufen.

Bruno Paul studierte und arbeitete zunächst in München als Illustrator für die satirische Zeitschrift »Simplicissimus«. Möbel nach seinen Entwürfen wurden bei großen Veranstaltungen von internationaler Bedeutung präsentiert, z. B. auf der »Internationalen Ausstellung für moderne, dekorative Kunst« in Turin 1902, der Weltausstellung in St. Louis 1904 und der

Fig. 75 *Marguerite Friedlaender-Wildenhain. "Hallesche Form" mocha service, 1930. Produced by KPM (Staatliche Porzellan-Manufaktur), Berlin.*
Abb. 75 *Marguerite Friedlaender-Wildenhain. Mokkaservice »Hallesche Form«, 1930. Hersteller: KPM (Staatliche Porzellan-Manufaktur), Berlin.*

ness of any sort, but that it has emerged logically from altered living conditions, from new demands made on hygiene. Candles and lamps have been replaced by portable electric lighting, tile stoves and fireplaces have made way for the grilles of central heating, and anyone who can afford to will certainly avail himself of the blessings of ventilation. It is obvious that these new circumstances could not but lead to new forms and proportions.[9]

In 1907, Bruno Paul surprised Berlin with the elegant, superbly made, luxurious, and quite severely rectilinear interiors he entered at the *Grosse Berliner Kunstausstellung*. Paul is a man worth discussing at length. His importance to the development of the arts in Berlin prior to the First World War is matched only by that of Hermann Muthesius and Peter Behrens. In 1907, on the recommendation of Wilhelm Bode, director general of the State Museums, Wilhelm II took Bruno Paul into the Prussian civil service, to head Berlin's

»Deutschen Kunstgewerbeausstellung« in Dresden 1906. Für seine Formensprache charakteristisch ist eine konstruktive und geradlinige Klassizität.

Ein Zeitgenosse beschrieb ihn als einen, der »die klaren Augen des Ingenieurs und die Arbeitshände des Pioniers«[10] hatte, und ein anderer als Deutschen, »der sich als Erzieher zur Eleganz« hervortue.[11] Bruno Pauls Formensprache war der der Wiener Werkstätte verwandt, besonders in der Verwendung rechteckiger, kubischer und quadratischer Elemente. Als Ergebnis seines spektakulären Erfolgs auf der »Großen Berliner Kunstausstellung« 1907 wurde er mit der Innenraumgestaltung des Zentralhotels in der Friedrichstraße (1909) und der Ausstattung des Cafés Kerkau (1910) beauftragt. Außer seinen großbürgerlichen Villeneinrichtungen entwickelte er bereits 1906 Typenmöbelprogramme, d. h. billige, maschinell gefertigte Möbel, die von den »Vereinigten Werkstätten für Kunst im Handwerk« in München seriell hergestellt wurden.

Ab 1907 entwarf Bruno Paul Schiffsinterieurs für die Überseedampfer des Norddeutschen Lloyds und 1925/26 dann den Straßenbahnwagen T 24 für eine Berliner Straßenbahngesellschaft. Er gehörte zu den Gründungsmitgliedern des Deutschen Werkbundes. Neben seiner Tätigkeit als Möbeldesigner und Lehrer an der Unterrichtsanstalt des Kunstgewerbemuseums in Berlin war er auch ein vielbeschäftigter Architekt. Durch seine so umfassende Arbeit übte er einen großen Einfluß auf die Entwicklung des Industriedesign in Deutschland aus.

Den entscheidenden Anteil auf dem Weg zum Industrial Design in Deutschland hatte unbestritten der Deutsche Werkbund. Mehrere Faktoren waren für seine Gründung bestimmend. Mit der Ausstellung »Ein Dokument Deutscher Kunst« auf der Mathildenhöhe in Darmstadt 1901 setzte die neue Bewegung im Kunstgewerbe und die Abkehr vom ornamentalen Jugendstil ein. Ein weiterer Schritt war die »Deutsche Kunstgewerbeausstellung« in Dresden 1906, wo die Vertreter des neuen Kunstgewerbes zusammenkamen und intensiv über das Verhältnis von Kunsthandwerk und Kunstindustrie diskutierten. Durch ausgewählte Exponate, die für eine zweckgerechte, modernen Bedürfnissen angemessene Gestaltung, etwa von Büro- und Schulräumen, Bahnhofshallen, Eisenbahnwagen sowie unprätentiös eingerichteten Wohnungen vorgesehen waren, kritisierte man das auf ästhetische Effekte zielende Jugendstil-Kunstgewerbe. Die Ausstellung war ein vielbeachtetes Ereignis. Der Hamburger Architekt Fritz Schumacher schrieb im Katalog-Vorwort: »Die große Zahl der gezeigten Erzeugnisse weist darauf hin, daß bei deren Herstellung nicht die Hand sondern die Maschine für die Ausführung eines künst-

Kunstgewerbemuseum School, later the Associated State Schools of Fine and Applied Arts. Paul, architect, furniture designer, and gifted teacher, lastingly influenced furniture design in Berlin, indeed product design altogether.

After studying in Munich, Paul worked as an illustrator for the satirical magazine *Simplicissimus,* before turning to furniture design. Soon his work was being shown at such important events as the 1902 International Exposition of Modern Decorative Arts in Turin, the St. Louis Exposition of 1904, and the German Arts and Crafts Exhibition in Dresden in 1906. His style is characterized by an emphasis on structure and a rectilinear classicism. One of Paul's contemporaries described him as a man with the "clear eye of an engi-

lerischen Entwurfes ausschlaggebend ist ... Eine der wichtigsten neuzeitlichen Kulturaufgaben«, führt er fort, »besteht darin, das Schaffen solcher Gebrauchsgegenstände in gesunde Bahnen zu lenken, die in ihrer Massenherstellung den Bedarf und dadurch den Geschmack unserer Zeit beherrschen.«

Gut gestaltete Produkte würden auch den wirtschaftlichen Erfolg bringen. In dieser abgekürzten Formel wurden bereits die Ziele des Werkbundes angesprochen. Einer der wichtigsten Verfechter des Werkbund-Gedankens war Hermann Muthesius, der bei dessen Gründung eine Schlüsselstellung einnehmen sollte. Muthesius hatte von 1896 bis 1903 als Kulturattaché in London die englische Kunstgewerbebewegung eingehend kennengelernt und war seit

Fig. 76 *Marguerite Friedlaender-Wildenhain (form) and Trude Petri (decoration). Tea and coffee cups with saucers and sugar bowl, from the "Hallesche Form" service, 1930. Produced by KPM (Staatliche Porzellan-Manufaktur, Berlin. Private collection.*

Abb. 76 *Marguerite Friedlaender-Wildenhain (Form) und Trude Petri (Dekor). Tee- und Mokkatasse mit Untertassen und Zuckerschale, aus dem Service »Hallesche Form«, 1930. Hersteller: KPM (Staatliche Porzellan-Manufaktur) Berlin. Privatbesitz.*

neer and the capable hands of a pioneer."[10] Josef August Lux said that he "excelled as an instructor in elegance."[11] The formal syntax of his designs was related to that of the Wiener Werkstätte, particularly in its use of rectangular, square, and cubic elements.

As a result of his spectacular success at the *Grosse Berliner Kunstausstellung* in 1907, Paul was commissioned to design the interiors of the Central Hotel on Friedrichstrasse in 1909, and furnishings for the Café

1903 als Referent des preußischen Handelsministeriums für die Kunstgewerbeschulen wieder in Berlin ansässig. Bei einem in dieser Eigenschaft im Jahr 1906 gehaltenen Vortrag über »Die Bedeutung des Kunstgewerbes« prangerte er vehement die Kunstindustrie an, die nur mit Imitationen historischer Stile und Surrogaten arbeitete.

Er verlangte von Kunsthandwerkern und Industrie: »keine Imitation irgendwelcher Art, jeder Gegenstand

Fig. 77 *Marguerite Friedlaender-Wildenhain. "Hallesche Form" coffee pots, 1930. Produced by KPM (Staatliche Porzellan-Manufaktur), Berlin. Private collection.*

Abb. 77 *Marguerite Friedlaender-Wildenhain. Kaffeekannen »Hallesche Form«, 1930. Hersteller: KPM (Staatliche Porzellan-Manufaktur), Berlin.*

Kerkau in 1910. Besides doing interior decoration for a prosperous clientele, as early as 1906 he developed a line of *Typenmöbel,* inexpensive machine-made furniture that was mass produced by the Vereinigte Werkstätten für Kunst im Handwerk in Munich. In 1907, Paul also designed the first of a number of interiors for North German Lloyd liners, and from 1925 to 1926, the T 24 streetcar for a Berlin transport company.

Bruno Paul was a founding member of the Deutsche Werkbund. In addition to designing furniture and teaching at the Kunstgewerbemuseum School in Berlin, he ran a prospering architectural office. In all these diverse activities he exerted a great influence on the development of industrial design in Germany.

The greatest contribution of all to German industrial design was undoubtedly made by the Deutsche Werkbund. Various factors contributed to the estab-

wirke als das, was er ist, jedes Material trete in seinem eigenem Charakter in Erscheinung.«[12]

Seine Kritik wurde vom Fachverband für die wirtschaftlichen Interessen des Kunstgewerbes als Beleidigung aufgefaßt und führte zu einer Eingabe an das Ministerium für Handel und Gewerbe, die beinahe die Entlassung Muthesius' aus dem preußischen Staatsdienst zur Folge gehabt hätte.

Trotz dieser Widerstände wurde 1907 der Deutsche Werkbund von Künstlern, Architekten, Kunsthandwerkern und Fabrikanten mit dem Ziel der Veredelung der gewerblichen Arbeit im Zusammenwirken von Kunst, Industrie und Handwerk in München gegründet.

Zu den Gründungsmitgliedern gehörten neben Hermann Muthesius auch Peter Behrens und Bruno Paul. Bald kamen weitere Berliner Künstler hinzu wie Alfred Grenander, Walter Gropius, Bruno Möhring,

Fig. 78 *Gerhard Marcks and Wilhelm Wagenfeld. "Sintrax" coffee maker, manufactured from 1925 to the present. Produced by Jenaer Glaswerke Schott & Gen., Jena. Private collection. Wagenfeld introduced this handle design in 1930.*
Abb. 78 *Gerhard Marcks und Wilhelm Wagenfeld. Kaffeemaschine »Sintrax«, um 1925 bis heute. Hersteller: Jenaer Glaswerke Schott & Gen., Jena. Privatbesitz. Seit 1930 existiert das Modell mit dem von Wagenfeld gestalteten Griff.*

Fig. 79 *Wilhelm Wagenfeld. Tea service, after 1934. Produced by Jenaer Glasswerke Schott & Gen., Jena. Private collection.*
Abb. 79 *Wilhelm Wagenfeld. Tee-Service nach 1934. Hersteller: Jenaer Glaswerke Schott & Gen., Jena. Privatbesitz.*

Fig. 80   *Wilhelm Wagenfeld. Wire holder with three cups for boiling eggs, c. 1932. Produced by Jenaer Glaswerke Schott & Gen., Jena. Private collection.*
Wilhelm Wagenfeld was one of the leading proponents of "Gute Form" in mass-produced commodities. During the thirties he worked for Jenaer Glaswerke and as the artistic director of Lausitzer Glaswerke. Wagenfeld's design won the Grand Prix at the World Exhibition in Paris in 1937.

Abb. 80   *Wilhelm Wagenfeld. Drahtgestell mit drei Eierkochern, um 1932. Hersteller: Jenaer Glaswerke Schott & Gen., Jena. Privatbesitz.*
Wilhelm Wagenfeld gehört zu den führenden Künstlern, die die »Gute Form« des serienmäßig hergestellten Gebrauchsgegenstandes populär machten. In den 30er Jahren war er sowohl für die Jenaer Glaswerke als auch als künstlerischer Leiter der Lausitzer Glaswerke tätig. Seine Entwürfe wurden auf der Weltausstellung in Paris 1937 mit dem Grand Prix ausgezeichnet.

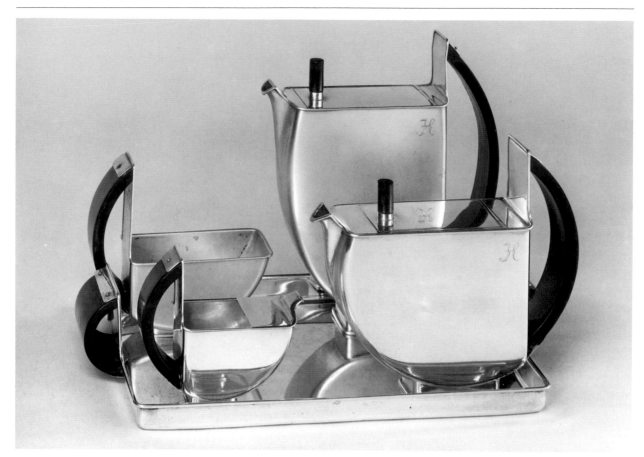

Fig. 81 *Karl Heubler. Tea and coffee service, c. 1925. Pro-duced by the Reimann School, Berlin. Bröhan-Museum, Berlin.*

Abb. 81 *Karl Heubler. Tee- und Kaffeeservice, um 1925. Her-steller: Schule Reimann, Berlin. Bröhan-Museum, Berlin.*

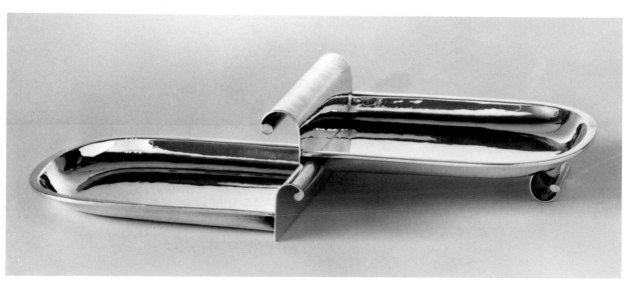

Fig. 82 *Emmy Roth. Candy dish, 1926. Produced by Emmy Roth. Private collection.*

Abb. 82 *Emmy Roth. Konfektschale, 1926. Hersteller: Emmy Roth. Privatbesitz.*

Fig. 83 *Andreas Moritz. Flatware, c. 1925. Produced by Andreas Moritz. SMPK Kunstgewerbemuseum, Berlin.*
Abb. 83 *Andreas Moritz. Besteck, um 1925. Hersteller: Andreas Moritz. SMPK Kunstgewerbemuseum, Berlin.*

lishment of this association. In 1901, the *Ein Dokument deutscher Kunst* exhibition in Darmstadt had marked the inception of a new movement in the arts and crafts and a departure from the ornamental excesses of Jugendstil. Subsequently, at the third German Arts and Crafts Exhibition in Dresden, in 1906, advocates of the new approach hotly debated the relationship between hand-craftsmanship and industrial manufacture. On view at Dresden were designs adapted to modern needs, from furnishings for offices and schools, railway stations and railway cars, to unpretentious home interiors.

A concrete challenge to Jugendstil design and its emphasis on aesthetic effect, the exhibition attracted wide attention. In the preface to the catalogue, the Hamburg architect Fritz Schumacher wrote: "The great number of products on exhibit indicates that it is the machine, not the hand, that is crucial for the execution of an artistic design . . . . One of the most significant tasks of modern civilization will be to guide the creation of such useful objects along healthy lines, for by their

Emil Lettré, Hans Poelzig, Curt Stoeving, Bruno Taut und Heinrich Tessenow.

Unter den Berliner Firmen traten neben der AEG die Königliche Porzellan-Manufaktur (KPM), die Glas- und Mosaikwerke Gottfried Heinersdorff & Co, die Deutsche Glasmosaik-Gesellschaft Puhl & Wagner, die Bronzegießerei S. A. Loevy, das Hohenzollern-Kunstgewerbehaus, weiterhin der S. Fischer Verlag, die Druckerei Hollerbaum & Schmidt, die die Plakate und Prospekte von Lucian Bernhard, Julius Klinger *(Abb. 61)* und Julius Gipkens (alle drei ebenfalls Werkbund-Mitglieder) druckte, schließlich der Verband der Deutschen Waren- und Kaufhäuser dem Werkbund bei. Sehr schnell gewann der Werkbund, der seinen Geschäftssitz in Berlin am Schöneberger Ufer 36a hatte, im ganzen Reich an Bedeutung, was sich in seiner steigenden Mitgliederzahl, der Auflagenhöhe seiner Jahrbücher und vor allem in seinen Ausstellungsaktivitäten, besonders der großen Ausstellung 1914 in Köln, zeigte.

In Berlin war seit 1882 die Trennung der künstlerischen Ausbildung in die »freien« und die »angewandten« Künste erfolgt. Mit dieser Aufteilung ging auch die Trennung der Zuständigkeit der staatlichen Behörden einher. Für die freien Künstler war weiterhin das Kultusministerium zuständig, für die angewandten Künste das Ministerium für Handel und Gewerbe. Damit verbunden waren künftig auch unterschiedliche Interessen und Intentionen durch die beaufsichtigenden Behörden, die für die Designgeschichte und das Verständnis von Design bis heute äußerst aufschlußreich sind. Design war nicht mehr Sache der Kultur, sondern stand von nun an im Dienste der Wirtschaft. Die Trennung beinhaltete von vornherein Konflikte, die heute noch wirken, die oftmals unsichere Beurteilung von Designkriterien womöglich erklären und mit der Wertschätzung von Design in Deutschland überhaupt zu tun haben mögen.

Ausbildungsmöglichkeiten für Designer in Berlin gab es zunächst an der staatlichen Unterrichtsanstalt des Kunstgewerbemuseums. Als Bruno Paul 1907 zu ihrem Direktor ernannt wurde, zählte diese etwa 100 Studenten. Sie war in eine Tagesschule mit Fach- und Ergänzungsunterricht und eine Abendschule vor allem für im Beruf stehende Handwerker eingeteilt. Die Aufnahmebedingungen waren streng. Neben künstlerischer Begabung wurde eine abgeschlossene Lehrzeit in einem gewerblichen Betrieb verlangt. Acht Tage dauerte die Aufnahmeprüfung. Emil Orlik unterrichtete die Klasse für graphische Gestaltung und Buchkunst. Ludwig Sütterlin, der Reformator der deutschen Schreibschrift, lehrte Schriftzeichen. Emil Rudolf Weiss, der sich durch seine Mitarbeit an den Insel-

Fig. 84   *Lucian Bernhard. "Osram AZO," poster, before 1914.*
SMPK Kunstbibliothek, Berlin.

Abb. 84   *Lucian Bernhard. »Osram AZO«, Plakat, vor 1914.*
SMPK Kunstbibliothek, Berlin.

mass production they will determine the needs and hence the taste of our epoch." And, Schumacher concluded, well-designed products would also mean good business for manufacturers and the country. In essence these were the aims of the Werkbund.

One of the most outspoken advocates of these aims was Hermann Muthesius, who was to play a key role in the founding of the Werkbund. While serving as German cultural attaché in London from 1896 to 1903, Muthesius had closely followed the English Arts and Crafts movement, and upon his return to Berlin, he became an adviser on applied art education to the Prussian Ministry of Commerce. In this capacity, he gave a lecture, "The Significance of Applied Art," in 1906, roundly attacking manufacturers who were satisfied to produce imitations of past styles. He demanded of artisans and industry that they make "no imitations of any kind; every object should be effective for what it is; every material should display its intrinsic

Büchern und anderen buchkünstlerischen Unternehmen einen Namen gemacht hatte, unterrichtete die Fachklasse für dekorative Malerei und Musterzeichnen. Josef Wackerle war für die dekorative Plastik zuständig, und Bruno Paul selbst leitete die Klasse für Architektur und Raumgestaltung. Außerdem gab es da Lehrwerkstätten für Steindruck, Tapetendruck, Buchdruck und Glasmalerei.

Die Trennung in der Ausbildung zwischen freier und angewandter Kunst war nicht konfliktlos, und deshalb gab es zunehmend Bestrebungen, diese wieder unter der Hoheit des Kultusministeriums zu vereinigen. Wilhelm Waetzoldt, der Nachfolger Wilhelm von Bodes, setzte sich energisch für eine Vereinigung der Schulen ein.

»Es ist ein Irrtum an eine ideale Vereinigung der Interessen von Kunst und Industrie zu glauben, sie widerstreiten einander: Das Interesse der Industrie ist gerichtet auf Massenherstellung und Massenabsatz

qualities."[12] Since this criticism was considered injurious to the economic interests of German craftsmanship, the trade association lodged an official protest with the Ministry that nearly resulted in Muthesius's dismissal from the civil service.

Despite resistance of this sort, however, artists, architects, craftsmen, and manufacturers gathered in Munich in 1907 to found the Deutsche Werkbund, with the aim of improving product design and manufacture through an alliance of art, industry, and crafts. The founding members of this group, besides Muthesius, included Peter Behrens and Bruno Paul. They were soon joined by such Berlin artists as Alfred Grenander, Walter Gropius, Bruno Möhring, Emil Lettré, Hans Poelzig, Lilly Reich, Theo Schmuz-Baudiss, Curt Stoeving, Bruno Taut, and Heinrich Tessenow.

Among the member firms of the Werkbund were the AEG, KPM (Königliche Porzellan-Manufaktur), Gottfried Heinersdorff & Co. Glass and Mosaic Works, Puhl & Wagner German Glass Mosaic Corporation, the S. A. Loevy Bronze Foundry, the Hohenzollern Kunstgewerbehaus, S. Fischer Publishers, the printers Hollerbaum & Schmidt (who printed posters and brochures by the three Werkbund members Lucian Bernhard,

bei möglichst geringen Selbstkosten und Fehlgriffen. Das bedingt ein Entgegenkommen dem Massengeschmack und den Massenbedürfnissen.« Waetzoldt vertrat hier als Kunsthistoriker und vortragender Rat im Kultusministerium 1917 einen programmatischen und illusionslosen Standpunkt, der sich von den Intentionen des Werkbundes unterschied.[13]

Bruno Paul folgte ebenfalls immer mehr dieser Meinung und bemühte sich deshalb zielstrebig um eine ganzheitliche Künstlerausbildung. Dies gelang allerdings erst nach dem Ersten Weltkrieg. 1924 wurde die Vereinigung der Unterrichtsanstalt des Kunstgewerbemuseums mit der Akademischen Hochschule für Bildende Künste vollzogen. Die Unterrichtsanstalt zählte zu diesem Zeitpunkt 1000 Studenten. Die neue Institution erhielt den Namen »Vereinigte Staatsschulen für freie und angewandte Kunst« mit drei Abteilungen: Architektur, freie Kunst und angewandte Kunst. Zu den Lehrern zählten unter anderen Emil Orlik, Bruno Paul, Emil Rudolf Weiss, Alfred Grenander, César Klein und Karl Hofer.

Die Kunstgewerbe-Bewegung um 1900 löste vielfältige Aktivitäten in Berlin aus. Es war eine kleine private Anstalt, die als erste das Werkstättenprinzip,

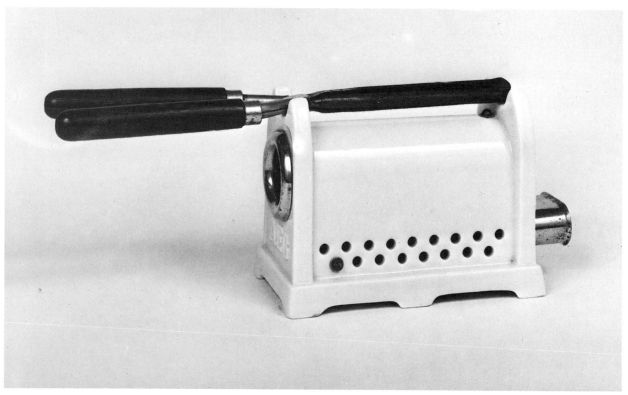

Fig. 85 AFG electric curling iron, c. 1920. Designed and produced by AEG. Private collection.

Abb. 85 AEG Elektrischer Brennscherenwärmer, um 1920. Entwurf und Hersteller: AEG. Privatbesitz.

Julius Klinger *(fig. 61),* and Julius Gipkens), and finally, the Association of German Retail Trade and Department Stores.

Soon the Werkbund's ideal spread throughout Germany. Its membership list grew, its yearbooks were printed in large editions, and above all its exhibitions were well attended – especially the landmark exhibition of 1914 in Cologne.

Training in the fine and applied arts had been conducted separately at Berlin schools since 1882. This separation was reflected on the administrative level, with the Ministry of Education remaining responsible for the fine arts while the applied arts came under the jurisdiction of the Ministry of Commerce. The resulting divergence of departmental interests and purposes has affected the history of German design and public attitudes toward design to this day. Instead of being

wie es dann auch vom Bauhaus praktiziert wurde, eingeführt hat. Die 1902 von Albert und Klara Reimann gegründete Reimann-Schule war eine außerordentlich erfolgreiche private Unterrichtsanstalt für angewandte Kunst. Albert Reimann stellte kunstgewerbliche Arbeiten her, die als Modelle für die Fabrikate der Bronze- und Silberwarenfabriken, Goldschmiedewerkstätten und keramischen Fabriken dienten. Die Schule expandierte in kürzester Zeit, und der Unterricht wurde ausgeweitet. Zu den Metallwerkstätten kamen Fachschulklassen für Mode- und Plakatkunst hinzu; letztere wurde von Julius Klinger, dem führenden Plakatmaler, geleitet. 1912 wurde der Reimann-Schule die Höhere Fachschule für Dekorationskunst angegliedert. Diese Einrichtung zur Ausbildung von Schaufensterdekorateuren war einer Initiative des Deutschen Werkbundes zusammen mit dem Deutschen Verband

Fig. 86   *Gudrun Germann. Advertisement for an electric hair dryer, after 1930. Private collection.*

Abb. 86   *Gudrun Germann. Plakatentwurf für einen elektrischen Haartrockner, nach 1930. Privatbesitz.*

Fig. 87   Telephone, 1924–27. Designed and produced by Siemens & Halske AG., Berlin. Siemens-Museum, Munich. Since 1900 the development of Siemens telephones has illustrated the emergence of functionalist design. Size was reduced and shapes were simplified over the years, while materials were changed from precious woods to lacquered metal, and finally to a molded plastic compound.

Abb. 87   Telefon, 1924–27. Entwurf und Hersteller: Siemens & Halske AG., Berlin. Siemens-Museum, München. Die hervorstechenden Merkmale der gebrauchsfunktionalen und gestalterischen Entwicklung der Siemens-Telefongeräte ab 1900 sind neben der Größenreduzierung der Formwandel und neue Materialien. Die Entwicklungslinie läuft von edel verarbeitetem zu lackiertem Holz, lackiertem Stahlblech und schließlich Preßstoff mit den Eigenschaften eines zu seiner Zeit faszinierenden Materials, das zu neuer Gestaltung herausforderte.

considered a branch of art or an adjunct of the nation's cultural life, design became a handmaiden of commerce. This distinction involved conflicts that still persist, and that perhaps explain the widespread insecurity to be found in Germany even now in evaluating design achievements.

In Berlin, the first courses in design were given at the Kunstgewerbemuseum School. When Bruno Paul became its director in 1907, the institution numbered about a hundred students. Instruction was divided into daytime courses in specialized fields and a night school that was attended primarily by working artisans and craftsmen. The admission requirements were extremely stringent; besides artistic talent, an apprenticeship with a commercial firm was required of all applicants. The admission test lasted a full week. The Museum School class in printmaking and book design was headed by Emil Orlik; Ludwig Sütterlin, the reformer of German penmanship, taught lettering. Emil Rudolf Weiss, known for his book designs for Insel Verlag and other fine printing enterprises, taught an

für das kaufmännische Unterrichtswesen und dem Verband Berliner Spezialgeschäfte zu verdanken. Ein Kuratorium, dem unter anderen Hermann Muthesius, Peter Behrens, Theo Schmuz-Baudiss und der jeweilige Geschäftsführer des Deutschen Werkbundes angehörten, überwachte den Unterricht. Die Reimann-Schule war sowohl eng mit dem Gedankengut des Deutschen Werkbundes als auch mit dessen Organisation verbunden. Arbeiten aus der Reimann-Schule wurden in den Werkbund-Jahrbüchern veröffentlicht, in seinen Rechenschaftsberichten diskutierte man die Entwicklung der Schule.

Im gesellschaftlichen Leben Berlins waren vor allem die Kostümbälle der Schule berühmt, für die Julius Klinger die Plakate entwarf. In den 20er Jahren wurden jeweils bis zu 1000 Schüler, von denen viele aus dem Ausland kamen, ausgebildet. Das Unterrichtsprogramm umfaßte etwa 30 Fächer, darunter Mode, Werbung, Foto und Film, Metallarbeiten (Abb. 81) und Schaufensterdekoration. Der Akzent lag auf dem Praktischen und Angewandten. Nach 1933 fanden ver-

advanced class in decorative painting and pattern design. Josef Wackerle was responsible for applied sculpture, and Bruno Paul himself headed the courses in architecture and interior design. The school also had workshops in lithography, wallpaper design, printing, book production, and glass painting.

The separation of fine and applied arts training was not without its absurdities, and repeated efforts were made to reunite the two streams under the administration of the Ministry of Education. Wilhelm Waetzoldt, Wilhelm Bode's successor, devoted a great deal of energy to this enterprise, declaring in 1917, "It is a mistake to believe in an ideal unity of artistic and commercial interests; they conflict with one another. The interests of industry focus on mass production and mass distribution, while keeping investment costs and miscalculations at a minimum. This entails adaptation to mass tastes and mass needs."[13] This was a pragmatic and hard-headed point of view opposed to Werkbund ideals, and Paul, like Waetzoldt, was soon to come around to it, leading him to invest a great deal of time and effort in advancing the cause of unified art education. His tenacity was not rewarded until after the First World War, when the Kunstgewerbemuseum School was combined with the Academy of Fine Arts in 1924. The School had about a thousand students at the time of the merger. The new institution, christened the Associated State Schools of Fine and Applied Arts, had three departments: architecture, fine art, and applied art. Its faculty included Emil Orlik, Bruno Paul, Emil Rudolf Weiss, Alfred Grenander, César Klein, and Karl Hofer.

Around 1900 the Arts and Crafts movement stimulated a host of activities in Berlin, including the founding of a small, private institution at which the workshop idea that was to become so central to such later schools as the Bauhaus was first introduced. The Reimann School, opened by Albert and Klara Reimann in 1902, became an extraordinarily successful private school of applied art. Albert Reimann was a gifted craftsman whose candlesticks, coffee services, and desk sets served as prototypes for manufacturers of bronze and silver products, goldsmiths' workshops, and pottery factories. The school he founded expanded rapidly, and its curriculum was extended. In addition to offering courses on metalworking, the school added courses in fashion and in poster design, the latter department being headed by the renowned poster artist Julius Klinger. In 1912 the Reimann School was incorporated into the Advanced College of Decorative Art, an institution for the training of window-display decorators that had been founded through the combined initiative of the Werkbund, the German Associa-

diente Bauhauskünstler an der Schule noch Arbeitsmöglichkeiten. Reimann selbst mußte emigrieren und verkaufte die Schule 1935 an den Architekten Hugo Häring. Bei einem Luftangriff 1943 wurden sämtliche Gebäude zerstört. Damit war das Ende der Unterrichtsanstalt besiegelt.

Die Geschichte der deutschen Industrie ist eng mit den politischen und wirtschaftlichen Entwicklungen verknüpft, die Geschichte des Design und der guten Form wiederum ist mit der Entwicklung der Industrie verbunden. Sie ist aber auch abhängig von einzelnen Unternehmerpersönlichkeiten.

Das größte Verdienst kommt hier unbestritten der Firma AEG zu. Mit der Entscheidung, Peter Behrens als künstlerischen Beirat in das Unternehmen zu holen, leistete sie Pionierarbeit.

Andere Firmen wie z. B. die Siemens & Halske A. G., die in Berlin ebenfalls eine führende Position in der Elektrotechnik innehatte, folgten nicht dem Beispiel der AEG.

Die Gestaltung ihrer Haushaltsgeräte war zweckmäßig, sachlich und funktionsgerecht. In den 20er Jahren wurden unter dem Namen »Protos« Elektroherde, Staubsauger (Abb. 89), Toaster, elektrische Wasserkessel, Turbowascher und seit 1928 elektrische »Heizbügler«, d. h. Bügeleisen, produziert. In die Architekturgeschichte ging die Firma Siemens vor allem mit dem Bau von Produktionsstätten und Werksiedlungen ein, die bis 1915 von dem Architekten Karl Janisch und ab 1915 von Hans Hertlein errichtet wurden.

Die kulturelle Leistung der Firma Siemens lag vor allem in ihren vorbildhaften sozialen Einrichtungen, die von der Altersversorgung über Betriebskrankenkasse und Erholungsheime bis zu den großen Wohnsiedlungen für die Mitarbeiter reichte.

Die Staatliche Porzellan-Manufaktur (KPM), die seit ihrer Gründung 1763 zunächst als Eigentum des Königs, dann als Eigenbetrieb des Staates Preußen und schließlich des Landes Berlin ununterbrochen besteht, zählt mit ihrer über 200 Jahre alten Geschichte zu den ältesten Manufakturen der Stadt. Neben der Herstellung von künstlerischen, figürlichen Porzellanen und Servicen bildet die Produktion von technischem Porzellan (Abb. 74), das seit etwa 1820 hergestellt wird, einen wichtigen Wirtschaftsfaktor der Manufaktur. Gerade dieses technische Weiß-Porzellan hat in den 20er Jahren die Gestaltung von Gebrauchsgeschirr beeinflußt. Von 1908–1925 war Theo Schmuz-Baudiss künstlerischer Direktor der KPM. Seine Bedeutung für das Unternehmen lag vor allem in seiner eigenen Arbeit (Abb. 72–73). Besonders auf dem Gebiet der Überlaufglasuren und der Un-

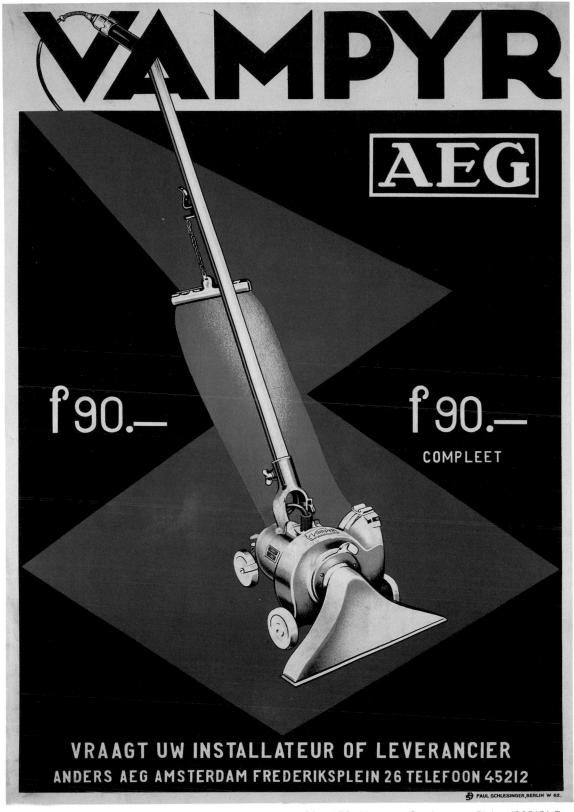

Fig. 88 *AEG "Vampyr" vacuum cleaner, poster, c. 1930–31. Unidentified designer. Private collection.*

Abb. 88 *AEG »Vampyr«-Staubsauger, Plakat, 1930/31. Entwurf unbekannt. Privatbesitz.*

tion for Commercial Education, and the Association of Berlin Specialty Shops. Instruction was supervised by a committee whose members included Hermann Muthesius, Peter Behrens, Theo Schmuz-Baudiss, and the current business manager of the Werkbund.

The Reimann School was closely allied with the Werkbund and its philosophy; its designs were published in the Werkbund yearbooks and its developments discussed in their annual reports. The school's costume balls, for which Julius Klinger designed the posters, soon became a high point in the Berlin social season. During the 1920s, the student body was comprised of up to one thousand students, many of whom came from abroad. The curriculum encompassed about thirty fields, including fashion, advertising, photography and film, metalworking *(fig. 81),* and window display design. The accent lay on practical, useful design. After 1933, many accomplished Bauhaus artists were able to continue their work at the Reimann School. Reimann himself was forced to emigrate, and in 1933 sold the school to the architect Hugo Häring. During an air raid in 1943, all of the school buildings were destroyed, sealing its demise.

The history of German industry has always been closely linked with political and economic developments, just as the history of design has been influenced by industrial developments. Yet much of the best in past German design can be traced back to the initiative of individual businessmen and entrepreneurs.

The greatest corporate contribution to German design was unquestionably that of the AEG, whose decision to hire Peter Behrens as the company's architect and designer was a pioneering one. His teakettles, clocks, toasters, fans, and electric heaters were so well designed that they furthered AEG's image in the domestic market. During the 1920s Siemens & Halske AG, another large Berlin electrical corporation, manufactured a line called "Protos" that included electric ranges, vacuum cleaners *(fig. 89),* toasters, electric water heaters, "turbo" washing machines, and from 1928 on, electric irons. The company neglected to follow AEG's example in hiring an art director to oversee production, however, and the design of its household appliances remained merely straightforward, practical, and functional. Siemens's contribution lay, instead, primarily in the field of workers' benefits, with an unprecedented range of amenities that extended from a company health service and pension plan to recreation facilities and well-designed housing for employees. Siemens made architectural history by employing the architects Karl Janisch (until 1915) and Hans Hertlein (after 1915) to design its production facilities and employees' housing.

terglasurmalerei machte er sich durch neue Methoden und perfekte Techniken einen Namen.

Nach dem Ersten Weltkrieg mußte die Produktion von Kunstporzellan eingeschränkt werden, da die zur Verfügung stehenden Rohstoffe in erster Linie für das technische Porzellan gebraucht wurden. Die Entwicklung der Manufaktur zu einem Staatsbetrieb mit modernen Gestaltungsideen gelang erst unter der Leitung von Günther von Pechmann (1929–1938), der sich 1924 mit seinem Buch »Die Qualitätsarbeit, ein Handbuch für Industrielle, Kaufleute, Gewerbepolitiker« Ansehen verschafft hatte. 1925 gründete er in München die dem Bayerischen Nationalmuseum angeschlossene »Neue Sammlung«, das erste deutsche Design-Museum. Von Pechmann war Gründungsmitglied des Deutschen Werkbundes, und somit war seine Berufung nach Berlin als künstlerischer Leiter der KPM für ihn gleichzeitig auch Werkbundaufgabe. Er sah hier die Möglichkeit, endlich »auch das Porzellan in die neue Formgebung einzubeziehen ... und modernes Gebrauchsporzellan zu schaffen.«[14]

Seiner Initiative ist die Arbeitsgemeinschaft zwischen der KPM und der Kunstgewerbeschule Burg Giebichenstein bei Halle zu verdanken, an der Marguerite Friedlaender-Wildenhain und der Bildhauer Gerhard Marcks arbeiteten. Diese beiden Künstler kamen nach der Schließung des Bauhauses in Weimar, dessen Schüler sie gewesen waren, im Jahre 1925 an die Burg Giebichenstein. 1930 brachte die KPM das erste Porzellan von Marguerite Friedlaender-Wildenhain, das Kaffee-, Mokka-und Teeservice »Hallesche Form« *(Abb. 75–77)* heraus. Im gleichen Jahr folgte das Tafelservice »Burg Giebichenstein« in Weiß- und Seladonporzellan mit Rillendekor.

Ebenfalls 1930 entwarf Marguerite Friedlaender-Wildenhain das erste ausschließliche Gebrauchsservice der KPM für die Flughafengesellschaft Halle/Berlin. Gerhard Marcks entwickelte rechteckige und quadratische Rohkost- und Konfektschalen von damals sensationeller Sachlichkeit, in denen die technische Form von chemischen Abdampfschalen für das Gebrauchsgeschirr übernommen wurde. Trude Petri entwickelte 1931 das berühmte Service »Urbino«. Es ist neben dem von Hermann Gretsch für Arzberg entworfenen Service »1382« das wohl bekannteste Tafelporzellan der 20er Jahre und wird heute noch hergestellt.

Die Jahre nach dem Ersten Weltkrieg waren in Deutschland von einer ungeheuren Aufruhr- und Umbruchstimmung erfüllt, die Architekten, Maler, Bildhauer, Schriftsteller und Musiker gleichermaßen ergriff. In Berlin bildeten sich 1918 die »Novembergruppe« und der »Arbeitsrat für Kunst«. Zu den

KPM, the Staatliche Porzellan-Manufaktur, had, since its establishment in 1763, passed through phases of royal, Prussian state, and Berlin municipal ownership. In addition to high-quality traditional china and figurines, the manufactory had produced technical porcelain for laboratory use *(fig. 74)* since about 1820. During the 1920s this laboratory porcelain had a considerable influence on the design of household tableware. The artistic director of KPM from 1908 to 1925 was Theo Schmuz-Baudiss, whose importance to the company lay particularly in his own superb design talent *(figs. 72–73)*. He made a name for himself by introducing many new production methods and by perfecting techniques, especially in the fields of glazes and in underglaze painting.

After the First World War, the production of fine porcelain had to be reduced since the available raw materials were required for laboratory porcelain. The development of the factory into a public-owned enterprise with modern design ideas did not come about

führenden Köpfen zählten Walter Gropius, Bruno Taut und der Kunstkritiker Adolf Behne. »Die Kunst soll nicht mehr der Genuß weniger, sondern Glück und Leben der Masse sein. Zusammenschluß der Künste unter den Flügeln einer großen Baukunst ist das Ziel.«[15] 1919 übernahm Walter Gropius die Leitung des Staatlichen Bauhauses in Weimar, das entscheidenden Einfluß auf Architektur und Gestaltung im Stil der neuen Sachlichkeit hatte; und in seiner kurzen, wechselvollen Geschichte spiegelte es die Widersprüche der Weimarer Republik zwischen Revolution und Reaktion.

In den Kriegsjahren war der Wohnungsbau fast vollständig zum Erliegen gekommen, allein in Berlin fehlten mehr als eine Million Wohnungen. Um der größten Not entgegenzutreten, wurde zunächst billigen Volkswohnungen Priorität eingeräumt. Die kleinen Wohnungen erforderten auch einen neuen Einrichtungsstil. Da der Wohnraum jetzt mehrere Funktionen vereinigte, kam es zur Konstruktion von Mehrzweckmöbeln und Anbausystemen.

Fig. 89 *"Protos" vacuum cleaner, 1927. Designed and produced by Siemens-Schuckertwerke, Berlin.*

Abb. 89 *»Protos«-Staubsauger, 1927. Entwurf und Hersteller: Siemens-Schuckertwerke, Berlin.*

Fig. 90 *Lilly Reich. Kitchen in a cupboard, 1931*
Fig. 90 *Lilly Reich. Kochschrank, 1931.*

until Günther von Pechman became its director (1929–38). Von Pechman had attracted wide attention in 1924 with a book entitled *Die Qualitätsarbeit: Ein Handbuch für Industrielle, Kaufleute, und Gewerbepolitiker (Quality Work: A Handbook for Industrialists, Businessmen, and Commercial Policymakers)*, and in 1925 he founded the Neue Sammlung, the first design museum in Germany, affiliated with the Bavarian National Museum. Von Pechman was also a founding member of the Werkbund, and as such he considered his new position as artistic director of KPM a superb chance to put Werkbund principles into practice. Here at last was an opportunity "to bring porcelain into the sphere of modern design . . . and to create modern chinaware for daily use."[14]

Thanks to von Pechman's initiative, a collaboration was arranged between KPM and the School of Arts and Crafts at Burg Giebichenstein, near Halle, where Marguerite Friedlaender-Wildenhain and sculptor Gerhard Marcks were on the faculty. Both artists had attended the Bauhaus, and when that school was forced to move from Weimar to Dessau in 1925, they went to Burg Giebichenstein. Friedlaender-Wilden-

Im Oktober 1925 erschien das erste Heft der Zeitschrift »Die Form« als neues Publikationsorgan des Werkbundes. Der Herausgeber Walter Curt Behrendt umriß in seinem Geleitwort die aktuellen Probleme einer zeitgemäßen Gestaltung: »Die Zeitschrift wird die Aufgaben der Formgestaltung für alle Gebiete des gewerblichen und künstlerischen Schaffens behandeln. Alle gestaltende Arbeit findet ihr Ende und ihren sichtbaren Ausdruck in der Form. Form ist Ordnung. Die neue Welt der Arbeit aber, die um uns entstanden ist, hat für sich bisher noch keine Ordnung gefunden. Die Grundlagen der gestaltenden Arbeit haben eine vollständige Umwandlung erfahren, neue Arbeitsverfahren, neue Werkzeuge, neue Werkstoffe sind eingeführt, und diese tiefgreifenden Umwälzungen haben umgestaltend zurückgewirkt auf unsere Wirtschafts-, Lebens- und Gesellschaftsformen. Sie haben die alte Arbeitsordnung mit ihren festgefügten Bindungen zerstört, die überlieferten Formen zerbrochen und altgewohnte, durch Jahrhunderte gültige Begriffe ihres Sinnes beraubt.«[16]

In diesem Zitat kommt die Hoffnung, aber auch die politische Unsicherheit zum Ausdruck, die mit der Frage verbunden war, in welche Richtung sich das Design in Deutschland entwickeln würde. Zu den Werkstoffen, die durch neue Arbeitsverfahren auch zu einer neuen Form führten, zählt das Stahlrohr im Möbelbau.

Seine Materialeigenschaften kamen den Vorstellungen einer neuen, sachlichen Wohnkultur in den 20er Jahren in ganz besonderer Weise entgegen. Die Stahlrohrmöbel versinnbildlichten die Vorstellungen von Hygiene, Leichtigkeit, Transparenz, Funktionalität, Anonymität und Sachlichkeit *(Abb. 1, 94–97)*. Marcel Breuer entwarf während seiner Bauhaus-Lehre das erste Modell eines aus gebogenem Stahlrohr gestalteten Sessels, den »Wassily-Sessel« *(Abb. 96)*, der ursprünglich für das Meisterhaus Wassily Kandinskys in Dessau bestimmt gewesen sein soll. Erst die dritte, überarbeitete Fassung dieses Sessels ging 1928 in die Produktion und wird bis heute in leicht veränderter Form noch hergestellt. Stahlrohrmöbel galten als avantgardistisch und wurden zunehmend modern.

So wurden sie in Ausstellungen wie z.B. »Die Wohnung« in der Weißenhof-Siedlung in Stuttgart 1927, der Werkbund-Ausstellung in Paris 1930 und der Deutschen Bauausstellung in Berlin 1931 gezeigt.

Die deutsche Stahlrohrmöbelproduktion lag zunächst weitgehend bei Berliner Betrieben. Die »Berliner Metallgewerbe Joseph Müller« in Lichtenrade stellten die ersten Stahlrohrmöbel von Mies van der Rohe her *(Abb. 1)*. Die »Standard-Möbel Lengyel & Co.« in der Burggrafenstraße 5 fertigten seit 1926 Marcel

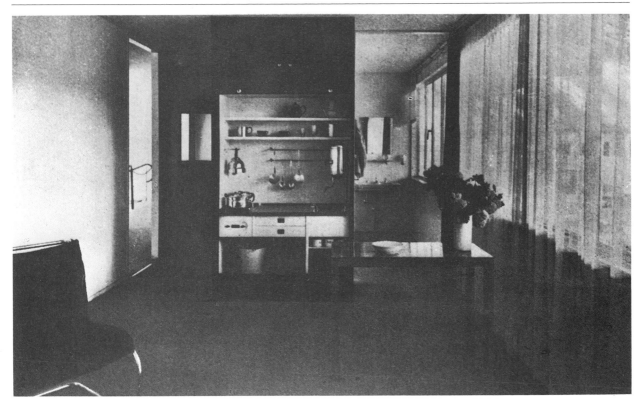

Fig. 91 *Lilly Reich. Apartment in a boarding-house, 1931.*   Abb 91 *Lilly Reich. Apartment in einer Pension, 1931.*

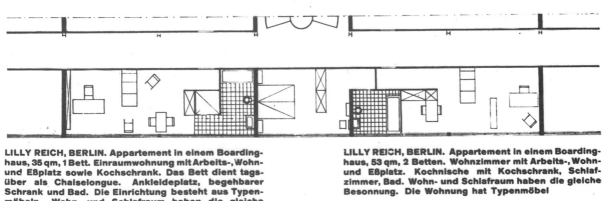

LILLY REICH, BERLIN. Appartement in einem Boarding-haus, 35 qm, 1 Bett. Einraumwohnung mit Arbeits-, Wohn-und Eßplatz sowie Kochschrank. Das Bett dient tags-über als Chaiselongue. Ankleideplatz, begehbarer Schrank und Bad. Die Einrichtung besteht aus Typen-möbeln. Wohn- und Schlafraum haben die gleiche Besonnung

LILLY REICH, BERLIN. Appartement in einem Boarding-haus, 53 qm, 2 Betten. Wohnzimmer mit Arbeits-, Wohn-und Eßplatz. Kochnische mit Kochschrank, Schlaf-zimmer, Bad. Wohn- und Schlafraum haben die gleiche Besonnung. Die Wohnung hat Typenmöbel

Fig. 92 *Lilly Reich. Apartment in "Die Wohnung unserer Zcit", 1931.*

Abb. 92 *Lilly Reich. Apartment in »Die Wohnung unserer Zeit«, 1931*

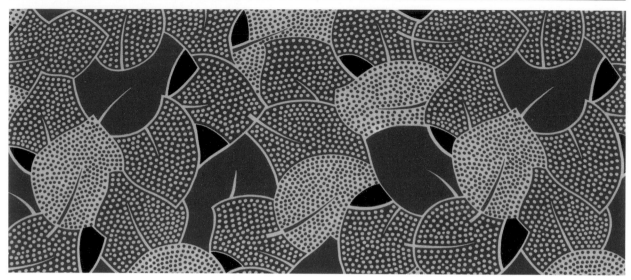

Fig. 93 *Dress fabric, 1920–30. Printed silk. Unidentified designer and manufacturer. Deutsches Textilmuseum, Krefeld.*

Abb. 93 *Seidendruck-Kleiderstoff, 1920–30. Entwurf und Hersteller unbekannt. Deutsches Textilmuseum, Krefeld.*

hain's first design to be produced by KPM was a coffee and tea service in 1930, called "Hallesche Form" *(figs. 75–77)*, followed the same year by a table service, "Burg Giebichenstein," in white and celadon glaze with ripple decor. The new departure in these designs was the translation into porcelain of forms traditionally produced by hand on the potter's wheel and the successful adaptation of craft methods for mass production. In 1930, Friedlaender-Wildenhain also designed the first exclusively commercial tableware ever manufactured by KPM, a service for the Halle-Berlin Airport Association.

Gerhard Marcks designed rectangular and square salad and candy dishes for KPM whose startlingly functional look derived from the shapes of chemical reduction dishes. In 1931, Trude Petri, another talented KPM designer, developed a service called "Urbino" that was to become famous – indeed, with Hermann Gretsch's "Arzberg 1382," probably the most famous tableware design of the period. (Both, incidentally, are still being manufactured today.) Petri's "Urbino" united the aesthetic of age-old Chinese design with the functionalism of technology, building on tradition to develop new forms. She was inspired to realize this merger by an exhibition of Chinese art held in 1929 at the Prussian Academy of Arts. In 1934 Trude Petri was forced to emigrate, and she left for the United States.

The years after the First World War were a time of turmoil and upheaval in Berlin that left none of the arts unaffected. The Novembergruppe and the Arbeitsrat

Breuers Stühle an. Diese Firma wurde 1929 von der Gebrüder Thonet AG in Frankenberg (Hessen) übernommen. Für Desta (Deutsche Stahlmöbel GmbH) *(Abb. 94)*, in der Teltower Straße 47/48 ansässig, entwarfen seit 1929 die Gebrüder Luckhardt *(Abb. 95)*, Erich Mendelsohn und Mart Stam. Aber auch diese Firma konnte sich gegen den übermächtigen Konkurrenten, die Thonet AG, nicht behaupten und wurde schließlich 1932 ebenfalls von Thonet übernommen.[17]

1931 wurde »Die Wohnung unserer Zeit« auf der Deutschen Bauausstellung Berlin auf dem Messegelände unter dem Funkturm zum ersten Mal einem breiten Publikum vorgestellt *(Abb. 98)*. Die Gestaltung dieser Ausstellungssektion innerhalb der großen Bauausstellung war Mies van der Rohe zusammen mit Lilly Reich übertragen worden. Die aktuellen Themen dieser Jahre wie die Wohnung für das Existenzminimum, der Raum für einen Sportsmann (Marcel Breuer) und der Gemeinschaftsraum (Walter Gropius) wurden zur Diskussion gestellt. Man verstand die Wohnung als Teil des »Industrialisierungsprozesses, der alle unsere Gebrauchsgegenstände erfaßt hat... auch die Wohnung ist ein Gebrauchsgegenstand.«[18]

Mies van der Rohe hatte also für die Ausstellung folgendes Programm entwickelt: »Die Wohnung unserer Zeit gibt es noch nicht. Die veränderten Lebensverhältnisse aber fordern ihre Realisierung. Die Voraussetzung dieser Realisierung ist das klare Herausarbeiten der wirklichen Wohnbedürfnisse. Das wird die Hauptaufgabe der Ausstellung sein. Eine

für Kunst (Working Council for Art) were both formed in 1918, led by such men as Walter Gropius, Bruno Taut, and the art critic Adolf Behne. "Art must cease being the pleasure of a few and must become happiness and life for the people. An alliance of arts beneath the pinions of a great architecture is our goal."[15] In 1919, Walter Gropius became president of the Bauhaus in Weimar. The Bauhaus was to exert a decisive influence on architecture and design in the new *Sachlichkeit*, or functional style, and its short, checkered history was to reflect the dilemma of a republic caught between revolution and reaction.

During the war years, the construction of housing had come almost to a standstill; in Berlin alone, the shortage amounted to over a million apartments. To meet this emergency, priority was given to inexpensive housing developments. The small apartments in these new developments required a new style of furnishing. Since their living rooms had to serve several functions, designers developed multipurpose furniture and modular systems that could be added to at will.

weitere Aufgabe wird es sein, die geeigneten Mittel für die Befriedigung dieser neuen Wohnbedürfnisse aufzuzeigen. Nur so wird die heute bestehende Diskrepanz zwischen wirklichem Wohnbedürfnis und falschem Wohnanspruch, zwischen notwendigem Bedarf und unzulänglichem Angebot, überwunden.

Sie zu überwinden ist eine brennende wirtschaftliche Forderung und eine Voraussetzung für den kulturellen Aufbau«.[19] In den Flachbauten von Mies van der Rohe und Lilly Reich waren die Idealvorstellungen einer Wohnung der Zukunft verwirklicht, während die Kleinstwohnungen mit ihrem Minimum an Raum und Ausstattung die realen wirtschaftlichen Verhältnisse jener Tage ausdrückten.

Lilly Reich arbeitete seit 1926 mit Mies van der Rohe in einem gemeinsamen Büro. Für die Bauausstellung 1931 in Berlin hatte sie ein Erdgeschoßhaus und Apartments für ein Boardinghaus entworfen und diese mit Typenmöbeln eingerichtet *(Abb. 91–92)*. Vor allem ihr Küchenschrank *(Abb. 90),* für eine Kleinstwohnung gedacht, war eine geniale gestalterische Leistung. In

Fig. 94   *DESTA-Stahlmöbel. Front cover of catalogue, 1931–1932. Bauhaus-Archiv, Berlin.*

Abb. 94   *DESTA-Stahlmöbel. Vordere Umschlagseite eines Kataloges, 1931/32. Bauhaus-Archiv, Berlin.*

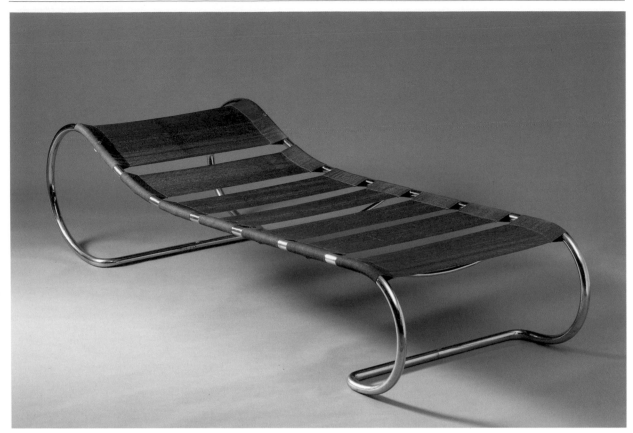

Fig. 95   *Hans und Wassili Luckhardt. Chaise longue, after 1931. Produced by DESTA, Berlin. Private collection.*

Abb. 95   *Hans und Wassili Luckhardt. Liege, seit 1931. Hersteller: DESTA, Berlin. Privatbesitz.*

In October 1925, the first issue of *Die Form* came out, the new official organ of the Werkbund. Its publisher, Walter Curt Behrendt, outlined the current problems facing contemporary design in his editorial:

> This magazine intends to discuss the tasks of design in every field of commercial and artistic creation. All creative work finds its end and visual expression in form. Form is order. The new world of work that has risen up around us, however, has yet to find an order for itself. The principles of creative work have experienced a complete transformation; new methods, new tools, new materials have been introduced, and these profound changes have in turn affected the way we conduct our lives, manage the economy, run society. They have destroyed the old labor system with its solid bonds, smashed traditional conventions, and rendered meaningless familiar concepts that had been held valid for centuries.[16]

diesem 2 m hohen und 1,30 m breiten Möbel waren ein elektrischer Herd, ein Spülbecken, Regale und Hängesysteme eingebaut. Mit einem Rolladen wurde der Schrank geschlossen. Die Küche mit ihren Geräten verschwand hinter einer neutralen Fassade.

Auf der Ausstellung waren weitere Typen von Kleinwohnungen zu sehen, die u. a. von Ludwig Hilberseimer, Hugo Häring, Erwin Gutkind, Marcel Breuer und Josef Albers entworfen worden waren. Typisch war die Ost-West-Ausrichtung der Grundrisse für sonnendurchflutete und gut belüftbare Wohnungen. Sie waren fast ausschließlich mit Stahlrohrmöbeln, vor allem von der Thonet AG, eingerichtet. Bauhaustapeten schmückten die Wände. Aufbaumöbel mit wenigen Grundelementen waren für alle Wohnbereiche gleichermaßen geeignet. Die Ausstellung wollte die Weichen für ein kollektives, in freier Verbundenheit geführtes Leben stellen: Wohnräume für eine klassenlose Gesellschaft sollten gestaltet werden.

Fig. 96   *Marcel Breuer. Club armchair, 1925–26. Produced by Standard-Möbel, Berlin. Cooper-Hewitt Museum, The Smithsonian Institution's National Museum of Design.*
Abb. 96   *Marcel Breuer. Armlehnstuhl, 1925–26. Hersteller: Standard-Möbel, Berlin. Cooper-Hewitt Museum, The Smithsonian Institution's National Museum of Design.*

Fig. 97   *Marcel Breuer. Tubular-steel stool, 1931. Model B 8, Eisengarn fabric. Produced by Thonet, Frankenberg/Eder. Private collection.*
Abb. 97   *Marcel Breuer. Stahlrohrhocker Modell B 8, mit blauem Eisengarnbezug, 1931. Hersteller: Thonet, Frankenberg/Eder. Privatbesitz.*

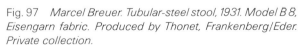

These words are expressive of both the hope and the political insecurity that were associated with the future of German design and the direction it would take.

Steel tubing was one of the new furniture materials whose handling required new methods, which led in turn to new forms *(figs. 1, 94–97)*. Its qualities were particularly well suited to the modern, hygienic, and functional homes envisioned by 1920s designers. Marcel Breuer, while still a Bauhaus student, designed the first prototype of a chair in bent steel-tube, later dubbed the Wassily Chair *(fig. 96)* and said to have been originally intended for Wassily Kandinsky's faculty house in Dessau. It did not go into production until 1928, in a third, improved version, and it is still being manufactured today in a slightly altered form.

The propagation of steel-tube furniture made rapid progress. Examples were shown at many exhibitions, including *Die Wohnung (The Home)* at the Weissenhof Development in Stuttgart in 1927, the 1930 Werkbund exhibition in Paris, and the German Building Exhibition of 1931 in Berlin.

The steel-tube furniture produced in Germany came mainly from four companies in Berlin. Mies van der Rohe's first designs *(fig. 1)* in this material were executed by Josef Müller's Metalworking Shop at 32 Lichtenrader Strasse. Lengyel & Co. Standard Furniture, 5 Burggrafenstrasse, began manufacturing Marcel Breuer's chairs in 1926 (and sold their premises and designs to the Thonet brothers in 1929). Erich Mendelsohn, Mart Stam, and the Luckhardt brothers designed for DESTA-Stahlmöbel, 47–48 Teltower Strasse, from 1929 *(figs. 94–95);* but this company, too, was unable to compete with the all-powerful Thonet Corporation, which swallowed them up in 1932.[17]

At the 1931 German Building Exhibition at the Berlin Fairgrounds, the issue of contemporary apartment design was introduced to a wide public for the first time *(fig. 98)* in the exhibition *Die Wohnung unserer Zeit (Apartments for the Present Day)*. Marcel Breuer designed a "room for the sportsman," and Walter Gropius contributed a "community room." In the section of the exhibition designed by Mies van der Rohe and Lilly Reich, such topical issues as apartments for people living at subsistence level were tackled and debated. The apartment was understood to be an industrial product in the creation of which "every one of our commodities has been involved ... even the apartment is a commodity."[18] In an article on the exhibition that Mies van der Rohe wrote for *Die Form*, he pointed out the exhibition's goals:

> The apartment for our age does not yet exist. But changed living conditions demand that it be re-

1931, am Vorabend der Machtergreifung durch die Nazis und auf dem Höhepunkt der Weltwirtschaftskrise mit 6 Millionen Arbeitslosen, konnte dies aber nur eine Illusion bleiben.

Anmerkungen

1 Der Titel dieses Essays ist das Motto des Artikels von Curt Stoeving: »Eine Gesamtanlage Moderner Wohnräume im Warenhaus A. Wertheim Berlin unter künstlerischer Leitung von Curt Stoeving« in: Deutsche Kunst und Dekoration, Band 11, Sonderheft März 1903, S. 257 f.

2 Ludwig Pietsch: »Das Hohenzollern-Kunstgewerbehaus. Aus Anlaß seines 25-jährigen Bestehens.« in: Deutsche Kunst und Dekoration Band 15, 1904/05, S. 171

3 Curt Stoeving, a. a. O., S. 257

4 Max Osborn: »Die modernen Wohn-Räume im Waren-Haus von A. Wertheim zu Berlin.« in: Deutsche Kunst und Dekoration, Band 11, Sonderheft März 1903, S. 267

5 Max Osborn, a. a. O., S. 266

6 Max Osborn, a. a. O., S. 263

7 Max Osborn, a. a. O., S. 259

8 E. Högg: »Neue Wohnräume, neues Kunstgewerbe – dem Hause eigen. Nach Entwürfen von Künstlern unter Leitung von Prof. Curt Stoeving« in: Deutsche Kunst und Dekoration, Band 16, 1905, S. 643 ff.

9 M. Rapsilber und A. S. Ball: Ausstellung unter Leitung von Prof. A. Grenander. in: Deutsche Kunst und Dekoration, Band 16, 1905, S. 395 ff.

10 H. Michel in: Deutsche Kunst und Dekoration, Band 19, 1906/07, S. 112

11 Joseph August Lux: »Das neue Kunstgewerbe in Deutschland«, 1908, S. 141

12 Hermann Muthesius: »Die Bedeutung des Kunstgewerbes« in: Hohe Warte, 3, 1906/07, S. 235

13 Wilhelm Waetzoldt: Die Entwicklung des kunstgewerblichen Unterrichtswesens in Preußen. Nach Bode, A.: Bruno Paul als Direktor der Unterrichtsanstalt des Kunstgewerbemuseums und ihrer Nachfolgeorganisation. in: Stadt, 10, 1982, S. 12

14 Günther von Pechmann: »Zur Situation der Staatlichen Porzellanmanufaktur Berlin« in: Werk und Zeit, 1961, S. 4

15 Die Freiheit 12. 12. 1918. Architekturprogramm des Arbeitsrates für Kunst.

16 Walter Curt Behrendt: Geleitwort. in: Die Form, 1, 1925

17 Jan van Geest und Otokar Máčel: »Stühle aus Stahl. Metallmöbel 1925–1940«, 1980

18 Ludwig Hilberseimer: Die Wohnung unserer Zeit. in: Die Form, 6, 1931

19 Wilhelm Lotz: Die Halle II auf der Bauausstellung. in: Die Form, 6, 1931, S. 241 ff.

alized. The prerequisite for this will have to be a clear definition of the requirements now placed on living space. This will be one main task of the exhibition. Another task will be to point out the means best adapted to satisfying these new requirements. Only in this way can the present discrepancy between true housing needs and false housing demands, between essential requirements and insufficient supply, be overcome. To overcome these is a burning economic necessity and a precondition of cultural advancement.[19]

The flat-roofed buildings by Mies van der Rohe and Lilly Reich represented just such a realization of these ideals, while the "minimum-space apartments," with their radically reduced floor space and spare furnishings, expressed the true economic conditions of the time.

Lilly Reich had shared an office with Mies since 1926. The 1931 Berlin Building Exhibition included her designs for a single-story house and for apartments for a boardinghouse furnished with standardized furniture *(figs. 91–92)*. Her kitchen cabinet *(fig. 90)* for a utility apartment was a particular stroke of design genius. Just 2 meters high by 1.3 meters wide, this cabinet contained a built-in electric range, a sink, shelves, and a series of hooks and brackets, all concealed behind a sliding shutter. The kitchen nook with its appliances disappeared behind a neutral facade.

Further types of small apartments were also on view at the exhibition, designed by Ludwig Hilberseimer, Hugo Häring, Erwin Gutkind, Marcel Breuer, and Josef Albers, among others. Most of the floor plans were characteristically east-west oriented to ensure plenty of sunlight and good ventilation. The furniture was of the steel-tube variety, almost without exception, most of it supplied by the Thonet brothers. Bauhaus wallpaper decorated the walls; the furniture, consisting of a few basic units, was equally suited to all the living areas. This exhibition foresaw collective life in a society of free individuals, and attempted to design living spaces for a classless society. In 1931, however, on the eve of the Nazi takeover and at the height of the Depression, with six million Germans unemployed, such aims were fated to remain an illusion.

Fig. 97a   *Marcel Breuer. Tubular-steel étagère, after 1928. Produced by Thonet, Vienna. Private collection.*
Abb 97a   *Marcel Breuer. Stahlrohr-Étagère, nach 1928. Hersteller: Thonet, Wien. Privatbesitz*

Footnotes

1   The title of this article was a motto by Curt Stoeving for his article "Eine Gesamtanlage Moderner Wohnräume im Warenhaus A. Wertheim Berlin unter Künstlerischer Leitung von Curt Stoeving," in *Deutsche Kunst und Dekoration,* special issue, March 1903, vol. 11, pp. 256–257.

2 L. Pietsch, "Das Hohenzollern-Kunstgewerbehaus. Aus Anlass seines 25-jährigen Bestehens," *Deutsche Kunst und Dekoration,* vol. 15, 1904–05, pp. 171ff.

3 *Deutsche Kunst und Dekoration,* vol. 11, 1902–03, p. 257.

4 *Ibid.,* p. 267.

5 *Ibid.,* p. 266.

6 *Ibid.,* p. 263.

7 *Ibid.,* p. 259.

8 E. Högg, *Deutsche Kunst und Dekoration,* vol. 16, 905, p. 643 ff.

9 M. Rapsilber and A. S. Ball, "Berlin, Ausstellung unter Leitung von Professor A. Grenander," *Deutsche Kunst und Dekoration,* vol. 16, 1905, pp. 395 ff.

10 *Deutsche Kunst und Dekoration,* vol. 19, 1906–07, p. 112.

11 Joseph August Lux, *Das neue Kunstgewerbe in Deutschland,* (1908), p. 141.

12 Hermann Muthesius, "Die Bedeutung des Kunstgewerbes," in *Hohe Warte,* vol. 3, 1906–07, p. 235.

13 Andreas Bode, "Bruno Paul als Direktor der Unterrichtsanstalt des Kunstgewerbemuseums und ihrer Nachfolgeinstitutionen," *Stadt,* vol. 10, 1982, p. 12.

14 Günther von Pechman, "Zur Situation der Staatlichen Porzellanmanufaktur Berlin," in *Werk und Zeit,* 1961, p. 4. and Margarete Jarchow, *Die Staatliche Porzellan-Manufaktur Berlin (KPM) 1918–1938: Institution und Produktion,* doctoral dissertation, University of Hamburg, 1984.

15 Architectural program of the Arbeitsrat für Kunst. Published in *Die Freiheit,* Dec. 12, 1918.

16 Walter Curt Behrendt, foreword to the new *Die Form,* vol. 1, 1925.

17 Jan van Geest and Otokar Macel, *Stühle aus Stahl, Metallmöbel, 1925–1940* (Cologne, 1980).

18 Ludwig Hilberseimer, "Die Wohnung unserer Zeit," *Die Form,* 6, 1931.

19 Quoted in Wilhelm Lotz, "Die Halle II auf der Bauausstellung," *Die Form,* 6, 1931, pp. 241 ff.

Fig. 98   *View of the exhibition "Die Wohnung unserer Zeit,"*
Berlin 1931.

Abb. 98   *Blick in die Ausstellungshalle »Die Wohnung*
unserer Zeit«, Berlin 1931.

Fig. 99   *Alfred Messel. Wertheim Department Store, 1896.*
Berlin-Mitte, Leipziger Strasse (destroyed).

Abb. 99   *Alfred Messel. Warenhaus Wertheim, 1896.*
Berlin-Mitte, Leipziger Straße (zerstört).

Tilmann Buddensieg
From Academy to Avant-garde

In the Beginning Was Alfred Messel

Wherever architectural renewal heralded the developments of the twentieth century, academically trained and historically aware architects were to be found at the source. Just as Amsterdam had its H. P. Berlage (1856–1934), Vienna its Otto Wagner (1841–1918), Boston its H. H. Richardson (1838–1886), and Chicago its Louis Sullivan (1856–1924), Berlin had Alfred Messel (1853–1909). Yet how different was Messel's influence on the following generation, despite accomplishments that were equal to those of the giants just named. Berlage and Wagner were father figures, inspiring teachers, conscious pioneers in both their building and their writings. Messel owed his major work, the Wertheim Department Store *(fig. 99),* not to a logical development or theoretical reflection but solely to careful and conscientious preparation for a specific architectural task. He avoided drawing conclusions from the result, chose to develop it no further, and formed no school.

The enthusiasm and praise of a younger generation, which included Henri van de Velde, Peter Behrens, August Endell, and Bruno Taut, not to mention the accolades of the critics, seem only to have put Messel on the defensive. Apparently none of these young innovators received moral support from this shy, ailing man who tended, on the contrary, to belittle them. Although the young Bruno Taut declared that he would build on Messel's achievement, Messel found a successor more to his taste in his friend Ludwig Hoffmann (1852–1932), Berlin City Architect, designer of numerous schools, humanely conceived hospitals, including the particularly attractive Virchow-Hospital, museums, public baths, and countless other community projects, few of which were of lasting interest. Everything Messel experimented with in the way of the historical-revival repertoire, all of his new solutions for unprecedented building tasks, Hoffmann reestablished in a kind of academic retrogression, bolstering historical accuracy with the paternalistic authority of his city office.[1]

Tilmann Buddensieg
Von der Akademie zur Avantgarde

Am Anfang war Alfred Messel

In allen Zentren der architektonischen Erneuerung zum zwanzigsten Jahrhundert hin ist die Geburtshilfe der akademisch geschulten und geschichts-bewußten Baumeister von größter Wichtigkeit gewesen. Wie Amsterdam H. P. Berlage (geb. 1856), Wien Otto Wagner (geb. 1841), Boston H. H. Richardson (geb. 1838), Chicago Louis Sullivan (geb. 1856), so hatte Berlin Alfred Messel (1853–1909). Doch wie anders als die der genannten ist Messels Wirkung auf die folgende Generation, bei gleicher geschichtlicher Leistung! Berlage und Wagner sind große Vaterfiguren, ausstrahlende Lehrer, im Schreiben und Bauen sich des Anfangs und des Neuen bewußt gewesen. Messel hat sein Hauptwerk, das Kaufhaus Wertheim *(Abb. 99),* nicht einer konsequenten Entwicklung, keiner theoretischen Reflexion zu verdanken, sondern der aufmerksamen Zweckerforschung einer neuen Bauaufgabe. Er hat jede Schlußfolgerung und Weiterentwicklung vermieden, keinerlei Schulbildung betrieben. Er war sicher eher defensiv gegen den Enthusiasmus und die Verehrung einer jüngeren Generation, der keine Geringeren als Henri van de Velde, Peter Behrens, August Endell, Bruno Taut angehörten, von den Hymnen der Kritik ganz zu schweigen. Keiner dieser jungen Neuerer dürfte je wohlwollende Förderung, manchmal eher blanke Ablehnung erfahren haben von dem scheuen kränklichen Mann, den fortzusetzen das eigentliche Ziel des jungen Bruno Taut war und der sich stattdessen legitim fortgesetzt sah in Ludwig Hoffmann (1852–1932), seinem Freunde, dem Berliner Stadtbaumeister von allerhand Schulen, Krankenhäusern, wie dem sehr schönen Virchow-Krankenhaus, Museen, Badeanstalten, zahllosen kommunalen Bauaufgaben, viele ohne bleibendes Interesse. Alles, was Messel am historischen Formenrepertoire in Frage stellte, zur Veränderung freigab, alle seine Neuformulierungen neuer Bauaufgaben, das wird von Ludwig Hoffmann wieder in seinem akademischen Rückbezug befestigt, in seiner historischen Richtigkeit mit obrigkeitlicher Autorität ausgestattet.[1]

Fig. 100   *Alfred Messel. Wertheim Department Store, 1904–1905. Berlin-Mitte, Voss-Strasse (destroyed).*

Abb. 100   *Alfred Messel. Warenhaus Wertheim, 1904/05. Berlin-Mitte, Voßstraße (zerstört).*

After Messel, all architectural progress was bound up with private and commercial commissions, while Hoffmann's municipal and federal architecture stagnated. Court architecture became the target of withering criticism, indeed ridicule. With the Siegesallee (Avenue of Victories), the Dom (Cathedral), the Kaiser Friedrich Museum, and countless construction projects in which the Kaiser intervened to insure that Berlin would be hailed as "the most beautiful city in the world," Wilhelm II dissipated a three-hundred-year history of Hohenzollern cultural leadership. The Royal Court Opera, intended to crown the Kaiser's only city-planning undertaking in Berlin, on Königsplatz, opposite the Reichstag, turned out to be a colossal fiasco. Paul Westheim, a leading art critic of the twenties, called its planning history the "most grotesque architectural farce of all time."[2] Reconstructed castles and manor houses, memorial churches, the Imperial Palace at Posen – all affirmed the failure of Wilhelm II as patron. Only Strasbourg received an imperial residence that still serves the different purposes of a different age astonishingly well.

Although influential advisers such as Wilhelm Bode and Ludwig Hoffmann managed to convince Wilhelm to commission important architects of the period, as in

Seit Messel ist aller Fortschritt mit der Privat- und Unternehmerarchitektur verbunden, die städtische und staatliche Architektur Hoffmanns bleibt stehen. Die Baukunst des Hofes geht rückwärts, verfällt der vernichtenden Kritik, ja dem Hohngelächter. Mit Siegesallee, Dom, Kaiser-Friedrich-Museum, mit zahllosen Bauten, in deren Planung der Kaiser eingriff, um Berlin zur »schönsten Stadt der Welt« zu machen, hat Wilhelm II. die dreihundertjährige Führungsrolle der Hohenzollern verspielt. Das Scheitern der königlichen Hofoper als Vollendung des einzigen städtebaulichen Unternehmens des Kaisers in Berlin am Königsplatz gegenüber dem Reichstag – Paul Westheim nannte dessen Planungsgeschichte die »groteskeste Architekturkomödie aller Zeiten«[2] – bedeutete den Bankrott des Kaisers als Bauherr. Rekonstruierte Burgen und Pfalzen, Gedächtniskirchen, das Kaiserschloß in Posen können diese Bilanz nicht ändern. Nur Straßburg erhielt eine Kaiserresidenz, die für andere Zwecke in anderen Zeiten erstaunlich gut funktioniert.

Gelang es einflußreichen Ratgebern wie Bode und Hoffmann, den widerstrebenden Kaiser zu Aufträgen an die bedeutenden Architekten der Zeit, wie Messel für das Pergamon-Museum ab 1907, zu bewegen, so lastete sein Geschmack wie ein Fluch der Maßlosigkeit

the case of Messel for the Pergamon Museum in 1907, even here the Kaiser's grandiose tastes seemed to cast a pall over the results. Messel the court architect produced the Pergamon Museum and the Imperial German Embassy in Rome. But Messel the private architect designed the Wertheim store, the AEG Administration Building, an apartment house complex for the Berlin Building and Savings Association, and the Oppenheim Residence.[3] It was through these private projects, rather than the royal commissions, that he had his greatest influence.

The Wertheim cathedral at Leipziger Strasse served as a model for department stores in provincial towns across the land, conferring on these towns some of the prestige of the capital city. Messel's Wertheim, particularly the Voss-Strasse facade *(fig. 100)*, also inspired the little-known Berlin houses of August Endell and the exteriors of the AEG Turbine Factory and the Small Machinery Factory. This same free composition of independent and asymmetrical elements appears in his Oppenheim Residence *(fig. 101)* of 1908, a transmission of the classicism of the estates of the Prussian nobility to the suburban mansions of the new ruling class in commerce and industry.[4] And Bruno Taut, even in his modernist houses like those in the Berlin-Eichkamp settlement *(fig. 102)*, displays, perhaps unconsciously, his admiration for Messel's love of asymmetry.

Fig. 101 *Alfred Messel. Oppenheim Residence, 1908. Berlin-Wannsee, Am Grossen Wannsee 43, 45 (formerly Grosse Seestrasse 16), (1970 photo). Detail of back wing.*
Abb. 101 *Alfred Messel. Villa Oppenheim, 1908. Berlin-Wannsee, Am Großen Wannsee 43, 45 (früher Große Seestraße 16) (Zustand 1970). Detail des hinteren Flügels.*

Fig. 102 *Bruno Taut. Berlin-Eichkamp development, 1925–1927. Duplexes on Zikadenweg (early photo).*

Abb. 102 *Bruno Taut. Siedlung Berlin-Eichkamp, 1925–27. Doppelhäuser am Zikadenweg (ursprünglicher Zustand).*

Fig. 103   *Bernhard Sehring. Tietz Department Store,*
1899–1900. Berlin-Mitte, Leipziger Strasse (destroyed).

Abb. 103   *Bernhard Sehring. Warenhaus Tietz, um*
1899–1900. Berlin-Mitte, Leipziger Straße (zerstört).

Fig. 104   *Paul Wallot. Reichstag, Berlin 1884–94 (early photo).*

Abb. 104   *Paul Wallot. Das Reichstagsgebäude, Berlin 1884–94 (ursprünglicher Zustand).*

Wertheim – A New Department Store on Leipziger Platz, Farewell to the Shop and the Shopkeeper

Adolf Behne introduced his important book *Der moderne Zweckbau (Modern Functional Architecture)* in 1926 with a lengthy analysis of the Wertheim store of 1896–1904; Julius Posener discussed Messel almost as exhaustively as he did Muthesius; Nikolaus Pevsner and Henry-Russell Hitchcock both paid him homage. And yet Messel, whose oeuvre was decimated in the last war, has still to receive international recognition.

Messel the academic, after mastering composition, proportion, the whole interlocking network of historical styles, proceeded to disassemble them into their component parts. He then, with equal sovereignty and a grand disregard for the strictures of unity, reassembled them – "freely," as he himself put it in one of his rare statements. Thus he resolved the Renaissance palace scheme, liberating himself from ties of proportion in the shape of columns, applied orders, and pilasters, and from the rhythmic strictures of capitals and bases. He was free to determine the height of the whole and its parts, spacing and relations, as he saw fit.

auch auf diesen Bauten. Messel, der Hofarchitekt, baute das Pergamon-Museum und die Kaiserlich Deutsche Botschaft in Rom. Messel, der Privatarchitekt, schuf das Kaufhaus Wertheim, das Verwaltungsgebäude der AEG, das Doppelwohnhaus für den Berliner Bau- und Sparverein und die Villa Oppenheim – alles Bauten von folgenreicher Bedeutung für die Zukunft.[3]

Die Wertheim-Kathedrale an der Leipziger Straße lieferte zahllosen Kaufhäusern bis in die entfernteste Provinz den Standard ihrer Fassaden und den Bezug zur Metropole.

Messels Wertheim inspirierte aber auch die zu wenig beachteten Berliner Wohnhäuser von August Endell, die Fabrikwände der Turbinenhalle an der Berlichingen- und der Kleinmotorenfabrik an der Volta-Straße. Die lockere, gesimslose Gruppierung der Bauteile von Wertheim an der Voßstraße *(Abb. 100)* enthält schon die Gruppenbildung aus Treppen- und Lastentürmen mit Geschoßbauten, wie sie das AEG-Ensemble am Humboldthain beherrschen.

Die Villa Oppenheim *(Abb. 101)* von 1908 zeigt die gleiche souveräne Komposition selbständiger, unverbundener und asymmetrischer Bauglieder, die den Stil frühklassizistischer Landgüter des preußischen Adels,

Fig. 105 *Alfred Messel. Tenement house for the "Bauge-nossenschaft des Berliner Spar- und Bauvereins von 1892," 1893. Berlin-Moabit, Sickingenstrasse 7–8 (1986 photo).*

Abb. 105 *Alfred Messel. Mietshaus für die »Baugenossen-schaft des Berliner Spar- und Bauvereins von 1892«, 1893. Berlin-Moabit, Sickingenstraße 7–8 (Zustand 1986).*

In the Wertheim store, Messel extended the almost uninterrupted surface of glass over five stories, leaving almost no solid wall. And he stretched Gothic-derived pillars without bases from sidewalk to nonchalantly plumped-on hip roof. His design introduced the paradigm of the department store as a merger of separate shops, summarizing his new whole through a multiplication of display windows in a vertically articulated glass facade.

Bernhard Sehring, in his Tietz Department Store of 1900 *(fig. 103)*, simultaneously went one step further, by minimizing the floor divisions with a seemingly unsupported glass surface – his prototype of the curtain wall. Sehring took a step backward, however, when he inserted heavily sculpted portals in an overblown baroque style.[5] But it was Messel's reformulation of the support system in a glazed multistory building that strengthened Behrens, Gropius, and Bruno Taut, not to mention Mendelsohn and Mies, in their own design convictions. Said spokesman Behne, "He gave us courage to depart from the conventional scheme."[6] This had even greater consequences than Otto Wag-

den Vorstadtvillen der neuen Oberschicht in Handel und Industrie übergibt.[4]

Bruno Tauts Bewunderung für Messel läßt, vermutlich unbewußt, noch in die völlig voraussetzungslos erscheinenden Häuserwände der Siedlung Eichkamp *(Abb. 102)* die Messelsche Asymmetrie eingehen.

Wertheim – das neue Warenhaus am Leipziger Platz, der Abschied von Laden und Geschäft

Adolf Behne leitet sein wichtiges Buch von 1926 »Der moderne Zweckbau« mit einer langen Analyse des Kaufhauses Wertheim von 1896–1904 ein, Julius Posener erörtert Messel fast so ausführlich wie Hermann Muthesius, Nikolaus Pevsner und Henry-Russell Hitchcock erwiesen ihm ihre Reverenz, aber eine internationale Anerkennung ist Messel, dessen Werk im letzten Kriege grausam zerstört wurde, noch nicht zuteil geworden.

Messel, der Akademiker, vermochte das makellos beherrschte Wertgefüge der historischen Stile, der

Fig. 106   *Tenement house, late 19th century. Berlin-Moabit, Sickingenstrasse 76–77 (1986 photo). This building is located opposite the tenement house by Messel.*

Abb. 106   *Mietshaus, Ende des 19. Jhs. Berlin-Moabit, Sickingenstraße 76–77 (Zustand 1986). Dieses Haus steht gegenüber dem Mietshaus von Messel.*

ner's contemporaneous but merely verbal "Gird your-selves! Onward!"[7] And, though evidence for this is hard to come by, Wagner's "creative modern architects" were also stimulated by such edifices of turn-of-the-century Berlin, mistakenly labeled Wilhelminian, as Paul Wallot's Reichstag *(fig. 104)* of 1894. The power of the building expressed the opposing forces of a new German parliamentarism, not the Kaiser's court architecture. (Wilhelm II, speaking in Rome in April 1893, termed it "the apex of tastelessness.")

A model of the building earned both American public approval in Chicago in 1893 and praise from the twenty-two-year-old Bruno Taut. Hermann Muthesius, in 1901, called the Reichstag a "generative structure" that marked "the beginning of a new epoch in German architecture" and heralded "a liberation from the fetters of stylistic imitation."[8] Fritz Schumacher confessed, "We are all indebted to [Wallot] for a touch of liberating inspiration." Similar tribute was paid to Wallot by Max Berg, designer of the Century Hall in Breslau, as well as by two of his other collaborators on the Reichstag, Heinrich Straumer and Wilhelm Kreis.[9]

Komposition und der Proportionen in seine Bestandteile aufzulösen. Er fügt sie souverän und unter Verzicht auf die Fessel der Einheit zusammen, – nunmehr »frei«, wie er das selbst in einem seiner seltenen Zeugnisse nannte. So löst er das Schema des Renaissancepalastes auf, befreit sich von der Proportionsfessel der Säulen, Säulchen und Pilaster, von dem Ordnungszwang der Kapitelle und Basen. Er kann die Höhe des Ganzen und der Teile, Abstände und Relationen frei bestimmen. Er wiederholt die kaum unterteilten Glasflächen der Läden und Schaufenster im Erdgeschoß mauerlos über fünf Stockwerke, zieht ununterbrochene, durchlaufende gotisierende Pfeiler vom Straßenpflaster ohne Sockel und Bogen bis zum wie zufällig übergestülpten Dach. Messel führt damit das Paradigma des Warenhauses als eine Verschmelzung der Einzelläden ein und bildet dieses in der vertikal strukturierten Glas-Fassade als einer Summe von Schaufenstern zu einem neuen Ganzen ab.

Bernhard Sehring geht im Warenhaus Tietz *(Abb. 103)* von 1900 zugleich einen Schritt weiter – sein Prototyp der Curtain Wall verschmilzt die Geschosse zu

The New Apartment House – Farewell to the Bourgeois Facade, Enter the Common Man

Finally, Alfred Messel tackled a third field of modern architecture, the urban apartment building for the upper levels of the working population (a contemporary spoke of "low-echelon civil servants, the petty bourgeoisie"),[10] and reformulated it so radically that he deserves to be called a pioneer of modern mass housing.

In his extensive work for the Building Cooperative of the Berlin Building and Savings Association (founded in 1892 and still active today), Messel overcame the fundamental contradiction of nineteenth-century lower-class housing. According to Rudolf Eberstadt, "The plan [and the elevation] of the typical apartment block is cut to fit the 'grand' front apartment; it is entirely unsuited to the small flat, and simply cannot be corrected."[11] Messel served from 1893 on the board of the Building Cooperative, which made him one of the few academic architects of the period to take an active interest in reforming housing conditions.[12]

The Cooperative, as its bylaws stated, intended to "make healthy apartments available to the less-well-off at reasonable prices," but at the same time "to encourage Cooperative members to become aware of social problems." The practical goal for the almost eighty percent of the Cooperative's low-income members who lived outside the working-class areas proper in 1899 was to achieve their integration into middle-class districts, and hence to prevent their isolation in huge enclaves and to avoid "class segregation" like that prevailing in England.

The first Cooperative project, on Sickingenstrasse 7–8 (fig. 105) in Berlin-Moabit, got under way in 1893 – a five-story building with a spacious courtyard, flanked by lateral wings and closed by a transverse wing set unusually far back for Berlin standards. A garden with a playground, a library, laundry room, bathrooms, and shops provided social amenities generally lacking in low-income housing.[13] It is not easy to explain just what was pioneering about this otherwise conventional-looking building; yet without doubt, it stood at the beginning of the superb contribution that Berlin made to housing for the less-privileged sectors of the population. The five-story house has six entrances on stairwells serving a total of six commercial shops on the ground floor, twenty-six one-room apartments, fifty-

einer von Stützen befreiten Glasfläche – und einen Schritt zurück, in der barocken und skulpturalen Überladung der Portalwände.[5] Es ist aber Messels Neuformulierung des Stützensystems in einem verglasten Stockwerkbau, die Behrens, Gropius und Bruno Taut, aber auch Mendelsohn und Mies in ihren eigenen Entwürfen bestärkte. »Er macht Mut, vom konventionellen Schema abzugehen.«[6] Das war noch folgenreicher als Otto Wagners gleichzeitiges, aber 1895 nur geschriebenes »kräftiges, ermunterndes ›Vorwärts‹!«[7]

Solche Ermunterung zogen die »modern schaffenden Architekten« (Otto Wagner) im Berlin der Jahrhundertwende auch aus einem als ›Wilhelminisch‹ mißverstandenen Bau wie Paul Wallots Reichstag (Abb. 104) von 1894. Die Macht des Gebäudes verbildlicht die opponierenden Kräfte eines neuen deutschen Parlamentarismus, keineswegs Kaiserlichen Hofstil. (Wilhelm II. nannte ihn [im April 1893 in Rom] »den Gipfel der Geschmacklosigkeit«.)

Ein Modell des Baues erregte die Anerkennung des amerikanischen Publikums in Chicago 1893, wie die Bewunderung des 22jährigen Bruno Taut. Hermann Muthesius bezeichnet den Reichstag 1901 als einen »Schöpfungsbau«, mit dem »ein neuer Zeitabschnitt in der deutschen Baukunst« beginne und der »die Befreiung von den Fesseln der Stilnachahmung« eingeleitet habe[8], und Fritz Schumacher bezeugt: »Wir alle verdanken ihm ein Stück erlösender Anregung.« Diesen Tribut zollte Wallot auch Max Berg, der Erbauer der Breslauer Jahrhunderthalle, wie Heinrich Straumer und Wilhelm Kreis Mitarbeiter am Reichstag.[9]

Das Neue Mietshaus – der Abschied von der bürgerlichen Fassade, der Wohnungsbau der kleinen Leute

Alfred Messel hat endlich einen dritten Bereich des Modernen Bauens, das Städtische Mietshaus der Oberschicht des Arbeiterstandes, – ein Zeitgenosse spricht vom »Unterbeamtenstand, dem kleinen Mittelstand«[10] –, in einer so radikalen Weise umformuliert, daß er am Anfang des modernen Massenwohnungsbaues steht.

In seiner umfangreichen Arbeit für die noch heute bestehende Baugenossenschaft des Berliner Spar- und Bauvereins von 1892 überwindet er den Grundwiderspruch der Wohnarchitektur für die unteren Bevöl-

---

Fig. 107 *Bruno Taut. Tenement building, 1910. Berlin-Neukölln, Kottbusser Damm (photo 1984).*

Abb. 107 *Bruno Taut. Miets- und Geschäftshaus, 1910. Berlin-Neukölln, Kottbusser Damm (Zustand 1984).*

Fig. 107 / Abb. 107

Fig. 108   *Bruno Taut and Martin Wagner. Horseshoe Development, 1925–30. Berlin-Britz, interior of the horseshoe (early photo).*

Abb. 108   *Bruno Taut und Martin Wagner. Hufeisensiedlung, 1925–31. Berlin-Britz, das Innere des »Hufeisens« (ursprünglicher Zustand)*

two one-and-a-half to two-room apartments, and two three-room apartments. Floor space averaged between 31 and 93 square meters. Twenty-four apartments are visible in the formal articulation of the facade, in striking contrast to the inexpressive monotony of most tenement fronts. Just opposite the Messel building this is vividly confirmed by a contemporary tenement house *(fig. 106)*.

Messel's apartment block was the first building of its type to derive its composition from the small elements of the one or two small rooms that comprised the plain dwellings of plain people. A momentous advance in architectural syntax, formulated for the new urban class produced by the Industrial Revolution, it marked the end of upper-class conventions cheapened for mass consumption. The "socially nonexistent" (the term is Ernst Bloch's) had achieved aesthetic presence in a new architecture, one that severed itself completely from the desiccated Schinkel school. Messel's "powerfully immediate intuition," which enabled him to "tear down . . . a rigid and ordered conceptual

kerungsschichten im 19. Jahrhundert, wie ihn Rudolf Eberstadt formulierte: »Der Grundriß (und die Fassade!) der Mietskaserne ist auf die ›herrschaftliche‹ Vorderwohnung zugeschnitten; für die Kleinwohnung dagegen ist er untauglich und schlechthin unverbesserlich.«[11] Alfred Messel gehörte der Baugenossenschaft seit 1893 als Vorstandsmitglied an und ist somit einer der wenigen akademischen Architekten der Zeit, die sich für die Reform der Arbeiterwohnungen interessierten.[12] Die Genossenschaft wollte gemäß ihrer Satzung »Minderbemittelten gesunde Wohnungen zu billigen Preisen verschaffen«, zugleich aber sollte der Genosse »zur Anpassung an den sozialen Gedanken« erzogen werden. Es lag hier das punktuelle Bemühen vor, für die 1899 fast 80% einkommensschwachen Mitglieder der Genossenschaft außerhalb der eigentlichen Arbeiterviertel auf der untersten Ebene die Integration an bürgerliche Wohnviertel zu erreichen und somit die Isolation der Arbeiterbevölkerung in riesigen Vierteln, die »Segregation der Klassen«, wie in England, zu vermeiden.

Das erste Bauprojekt in der Sickingenstraße 7–8 *(Abb. 105)* in Berlin-Moabit ist ein 1893 begonnenes 5-geschossiges Doppelhaus mit großem Hofraum, den die Seitenflügel und ein abgerücktes Quergebäude rahmen. Eine Gartenanlage mit Kinderspielplatz, Bibliothek, Waschküche, Baderäume und Geschäfte schaffen sonst fehlende soziale Einrichtungen.[13] Es ist nicht ganz leicht, sich das Bahnbrechende in dem konventionell erscheinenden Bau zu verdeutlichen. Doch steht er am Anfang des glanzvollen Berliner Wohnungsbaus für die Minderbemittelten. Das 5-geschossige Doppelhaus hat an 6 Aufgängen insgesamt 6 Ladenwohnungen, 26 1-Zimmer-Wohnungen, 52 1½–2-Zimmer-Wohnungen, 2 3-Zimmer-Wohnungen zwischen 31 und 93 m². 24 Wohnungen erscheinen deutlich sichtbar im formalen Aufbau der Fassade, sehr im Gegensatz zu der inhaltslosen Einförmigkeit gleichzeitiger Mietshausfassaden *(Abb. 106)*, wie sie in der gleichen Straße gegenüber stehen. Messels Doppelhaus ist der erste Bau, dessen »Komposition« aus den kleinen Elementen der ein bis zwei Stuben der kleinen Wohnungen der kleinen Leute gewonnen wird. Das ist der folgenreichste Schritt architektonischer Sprachgebung für eine seit der industriellen Revolution entstandene Klasse der städtischen Bevölkerung und das Ende einer bloß niedersten Ausformung der Architektur der Oberschichten. Das »soziale Nichts« (Ernst Bloch) erhält ästhetische Präsenz als eine neue Architektur. Sie löst sich völlig von der ausgetrockneten Schinkelschule ab. Messels »Zertrümmern« eines »starren und regelmäßigen Begriffsgespinstes« durch eine »mächtige gegenwärtige Intuition« bedeutet den

Fig. 109 *Bruno Taut and Martin Wagner. Horseshoe Development, 1925–31. Berlin-Britz, housing blocks by Martin Wagner, Stavenhagener Strasse (early photograph).*

Abb. 109 *Bruno Taut und Martin Wagner. Hufeisensiedlung, 1925–31. Berlin-Britz, Wohnzeile von Martin Wagner, Stavenhagener Straße (ursprünglicher Zustand).*

web,"[14] signified a liberation from conventions that had become oppressive.

Messel was nevertheless a total stranger to revolutionary impulses and utopian claims of the sort that would so move his admirers, Bruno Taut and Adolf Behne, twenty years later. His was a more liberal approach to problem solving: to do what just passed as feasible, on a small scale, as a stimulus for the next step ... leading to many more next steps, which, only after 1919, through the limited efforts of cooperative building societies, garden cities, and industrial housing, would emerge in public housing as the true pacemaker of the entire Neues Bauen movement. This process characterized Amsterdam and Rotterdam as much as it did Frankfurt and Berlin. It was a long road from Berlage's and Messel's beginnings to the mass housing of 1930.

The Berlin Directory for 1911 lists eighty-two tenants at Sickingenstrasse 7–8; with their wives, children, and relatives, the building's inhabitants probably totaled about two hundred. Thirty-seven occupations are detailed. Exactly half the tenants were metal and factory workers, most of them probably

Abschied von oppressiv gewordenen Konventionen.[14]

Messel ist jeder revolutionäre Impuls fremd, jeder utopische Anspruch, wie der seiner Bewunderer Bruno Taut und Adolph Behne, 20 Jahre später. Es war ein eher liberaler Lösungsversuch, das gerade noch Mögliche in kleinem Maßstab zu tun, als Anreiz für den nächsten Schritt, viele nächste Schritte, die erst nach 1919, über begrenzte Genossenschaftsbemühungen, Gartenstädte und die Siedlungen der Industrie hinaus, zu einem Wohnungsbau als eigentlichem Schrittmacher der gesamten Bewegung des Neuen Bauens werden sollte. Das gilt für Amsterdam und Rotterdam wie in gleichem Maße für Frankfurt und Berlin. Ein weiter Weg von Berlages und Messels Anfängen zum Massenwohnungsbau um 1930!

Im Jahre 1911 verzeichnet das »Adreßbuch für Berlin und seine Vororte« 82 Bewohner; mit Ehefrauen, Kindern, Verwandten wird man in der Sickingenstraße 7–8 sicher über 200 Personen annehmen dürfen. 37 verschiedene Berufe werden genau benannt. Exakt die Hälfte sind Metall- und Fabrikarbeiter, sicher zumeist in der nahen Turbinenfabrik der AEG tätig oder in der Maschinenfabrik von Ludwig Loewe. Ein Viertel

Fig. 110   *Adolf Behne, "Max Taut: Bauten und Pläne," Berlin 1927. Cover design and typography, Johannes Molzahn. Private collection.*
Abb. 110   *Adolf Behne, »Max Taut. Bauten und Pläne«, Berlin 1927. Entwurf des Einbandes und Typographie Johannes Molzahn. Privatbesitz.*

employed in the nearby AEG turbine plant or at Ludwig Loewe's machine-building factory. One quarter of them were employed in trades; the last quarter were clerical workers and widows. Skilled workers and office employees who were without the benefits of such cooperative self-help or industrial patronage lived invisibly in apartments facing the back courtyards of middle-class Berlin apartment houses.

It was only fifty years earlier that Berlin's rising middle class had found a distinct form of architectural expression in the work of Karl Friedrich Schinkel. In 1828 this great Prussian neoclassicist, with impressions of England still fresh in his mind, had built a residence for Tobias Christoph Feilner, on Ritterstrasse. This house – with its terra-cotta ornamentation made in Feilner's own stove-manufacturing plant and its air of an aesthetically refined English factory building – departed radically from the aristocratic and courtly style of ornamentation and facade design then considered *de rigueur* for the middle classes. In Schinkel's

der Bewohner sind Handwerker, ein Viertel kleine Angestellte und Witwen. Außerhalb solcher genossenschaftlichen Selbsthilfe oder industriellem Patronat wohnten diese Facharbeiter unsichtbar in den Hinterhöfen der Mietshäuser eines Bürgertums, das erst seit Schinkel seinen eigenen architektonischen Ausdruck gefunden hatte.

Schinkel hatte 1828 dem Fabrikanten Feilner, mit den noch frischen Eindrücken seiner Englandreise von 1826, ein Wohnhaus in der Ritterstraße erbaut. Radikal unterscheidet sich sein Fabrikantenhaus, im selbst produzierten Terrakottaschmuck aus seiner Ofenfabrik und im Charakter eines ästhetisch verfeinerten englischen Fabrikbaus, von einer sozial vorgeschriebenen Teilhabe am Dekorations- und Fassadenstil des Hofes und der Aristokratie.

Diese Emanzipation eines bürgerlichen Ausdrucksvermögens im Medium der Architektur bestand im Sinne Schinkels auf dem Recht jedes Individuums, »zu bauen wie man wolle«. Aus dieser Freiheit der Hausbesitzer folgert Schinkel das Recht des Individuums, vom gleichförmigen Formenkanon des Barock abzuweichen und die Pflicht, infolge der »sehr verschiedenen Vermögens- und Berufsverhältnisse« und infolge »verschiedener individueller Ansicht des Lebens« von der »gleichartigen Form der Wohnungen« abzuweichen.[15] Feilner wünschte ausdrücklich, daß man sein Haus als das eines Terrakottafabrikanten erkennen könne. Die bürgerliche Freiheit der Individualität des Geschmackes wählt sich ihren Stil aus der besser und besser erforschten Architektur der Menschheitsgeschichte und nicht mehr aus der Residenz des Souveräns.

Verschwindet diese Wählbarkeit und Käuflichkeit der Gestalt des Hauses durch die eine Person des Besitzers und Bewohners, dann wird die bürgerliche Wohnung zur Ware, die nur noch auf ihren Gebrauchswert, nicht mehr auf den Geschmack des Bauherrn bezogen werden kann. Der Stil der Mietshäuser wird jetzt zur Spekulation im Hinblick auf die vermuteten Geschmacks-Clichés und die sozialen Hoffnungen potentieller Mieter gewählt. Das hat Schinkel mit bemerkenswerter Klarsicht in London am 10. Juni 1826 gesehen und beschrieben: »10.000 Häuser werden jährlich gebaut, lauter Spekulation, die durch die sonderbarsten Gestaltungen reizbar gemacht werden sollen. Oft sieht man lange Reihen von Palästen, die nichts anderes als viele drei und vier Fensterbreiten aneinandergeschobene Privatwohnungen sind, denen man gemeinschaftliche Architektur gegeben hat.«[16]

Diese immer »sonderbarer« werdende Gestaltung, die »Losgelassenheit der Künste«, auch der Architektur, seit Hegel, erreicht nach 1870 auch Berlin. Das

eyes, this emancipation of bourgeois expression in architecture consisted in the right of every individual "to build as he wishes," and Feilner deliberately sought to have his house immediately recognizable as that of a terra-cotta manufacturer. From the house owner's freedom of choice Schinkel then derived the architect's right to depart from the homogeneous baroque cliché. In view of his clients' "extremely varied financial and professional situations" and "differing individual conceptions of life," Schinkel felt it his duty to depart from "boring types of dwellings."[15] The individual's right to express his own taste implied selecting a style from a history of architecture that was becoming better researched by the day, as well as ceasing to take pointers from a sovereign.

In the opposite case, where the style of a bourgeois dwelling is not decided according to the whims and pocketbook of its owner and inhabitant but by the developer, the house remains a mere commodity whose value is determined primarily by its use. This was the case with tenement houses, the style of which was usually chosen according to stereotypes of the supposed tastes and social ambitions of potential

»chaotische Durcheinander aller Stile«, den »Tumult aller Stile«, den Nietzsche schon 1873 in der Kleidung, in den Zimmern, in den Häusern und beim »Gang durch die Straßen« der Städte beklagte,[17] breitete sich in den Neubauvierteln der Gründerzeit, von der Naunynstraße in Kreuzberg bis zum Kurfürstendamm aus. Hier brach die Schinkelsche Einheit der Besitzer, Erbauer oder Bewohner mit dem selbstgewählten Stil des Einzelhauses auseinander. So entstanden tausende von Mietshäusern, wie die des Maurermeisters Götze von 1885 in der Courbièrestraße in Schöneberg. Hier wird die Fassade, unabhängig von der Größe der Wohnungen, der Einheit einer symmetrischen und dekorativen Komposition unterworfen, als sei es eines der Tiergarten-Palais von Hitzig, Adler oder M. Gropius. Die Obergeschosse werden halbiert, die Etagen und die Fensterabstände verkürzt.[18]

Messel verzichtet auf diese symmetrische Stufung der Einzelelemente zur Hierarchie einer bürgerlichen Fassade. Über dem rustizierten Untergeschoß mit Läden, Portalen und den zugehörigen 24 Wohnungen erheben sich die drei Geschosse und die Dachwohnungen erstmals in der Berliner Architektur ohne ach-

Fig. 111 *Bruno Taut. Onkel-Tom Development, 1926–31. Berlin-Zehlendorf, Waldhüterpfad (1926–27) (early photograph).*

Abb. 111 *Bruno Taut. Waldsiedlung »Onkel Toms Hütte«, 1926–31. Berlin-Zehlendorf, Waldhüterpfad (1926–27) (ursprünglicher Zustand).*

occupants. Schinkel realized and described this with remarkable clairvoyance in 1826: "Ten thousand houses are built annually in London, all on speculation, to which they attempt to lend interest by the strangest designs. Often one sees long rows of palaces that are nothing but a lot of three- and four-window-broad private apartments jammed together and given an icing of public architecture."[16] The "icing" got ever stranger, and the arts and architecture ever more "frenzied," as Hegel noted, until by 1870 the wave had reached Berlin. The "chaotic jumble of styles," the "tumult of every style" that Nietzsche had already decried in 1873 in clothing, interiors, houses, and just "walking down the street,"[17] now inundated the new *Gründerzeit*, or boomtown, districts from Naunynstrasse in the east to Kurfürstendamm in the west. Schinkel's romantic notion of an owner who is also contractor and inhabitant was shattered. Instead thousands of apartment blocks such as that of 1885 by the mason Götze rose up around Berlin. In these, the elevation, regardless of apartment size, was subjected to the unity of a symmetrical and decorative composition as though it were a fashionable Tiergarten town house by Friedrich Hitzig, Friedrich Adler, or Martin Gropius. The upper stories were halved and the window spacings reduced.[18]

In his Sickingenstrasse house, Messel rejected the symmetrical arrangement of separate elements that had been common in the hierarchy of the bourgeois facade. Above the rusticated ground floor with its shop-fronts, portals, and its twenty-four apartments, rise three stories, with a fourth under the roof, which – for the first time in Berlin architecture – lack any axial relationship to the ground floor, any strict definition of floor levels, and are completely without such decorative elements as pilasters, pediments, capitals, or stucco figures. The "Bavarian" style of the building was a vernacular one to tenants who, since they were not classically educated, did not run their lives according to the terms of a classical education. Only the balcony bands – a functional, not an ornamental motif – subtly underscore the horizontal lines of the different stories, which are undistinguished by cornices or moldings. The balconies run the length of the facade and pull the many small apartments together into a diversified whole, even beyond the vertical dividing wall in the center. In place of the widespread and extreme attempts to create an original style of ornamentation in *Gründerzeit* facades, Sickingenstrasse expresses community spirit in its balcony structure, which, moreover, extends out beyond the plane of the wall, and opens the apartments to the street. The balcony is no longer the focus of the isolated middle-class apart-

sialen Zusammenhang mit dem Sockelgeschoß, ohne strenge Geschoßteilung und völlig ohne dekorative Elemente wie Pilaster, Giebel, Kapitelle, Stuckfiguren. Der »bayrische« Stilcharakter des Hauses ist »volkstümlich« für Bewohner, die außerhalb der klassischen Bildung und darum nicht innerhalb klassischer Ordnungen leben. Einzig die Balkonbänder, – also ein Funktionsmotiv, kein Dekorationselement –, betonen die Horizontallinien der Geschosse, die durch keine Gebälke oder Gesimse unterschieden sind. Die kontinuierlichen Balkons fassen die vielen kleinen Wohnungen zu einer vielgliedrigen Einheit zusammen, auch über die vertikale Trennwand der Mitte hinweg. Statt der extremen Lust am bloß dekorativen Anderssein der Hausfassaden der Gründerzeit finden wir in der Sickingenstraße die genossenschaftliche Gemeinschaft in der Einheit des Balkongerüstes, das zudem eine eigene Raumzone vor der Wand definiert und die Wohnungen zur Straße öffnet.

Der Balkon ist nicht Mitte der einen abgesonderten bürgerlichen Wohnung, sondern beherrschendes Verbindungsglied aller. Das noch heute erlebbare Anderssein des Messelschen Hauses ist kein Stil-, Stukkateuroder Künstlerunterschied, sondern der sichtbare Ausdruck einer gesellschaftlich unterschiedenen und um ihre eigene Präsenz ringenden Klasse.

Wieder gelingt Messel in strenger Rücksicht auf eine neue Aufgabe die Ablösung von einer Konvention. Er ermöglicht das Ende der bürgerlichen Fassade als Maske von Arbeiterwohnungen. Er gewinnt ein neues Gesicht für das Mietshaus aus der Summe kleiner Elemente, die sich kraft ihrer Funktion zusammenfügen, nicht aus der verwässerten und manipulierten Rhetorik der Renaissance-Fassade.

Das setzt den Anfang zur »fortschreitenden Vereinfachung« der Wohnarchitektur bis hin zum »Serienbau« der zwanziger Jahre, mit seiner »Aneinanderreihung weniger Elemente«. So beschreibt Bruno Taut dreißig Jahre nach Messels Mietshaus seine Vorstellungen der gleichen »Genossenschaftsarchitektur«.[19]

Wieder überläßt es Messel seinen Nachfolgern, die »Nürnberger« Dächer und Giebel abzunehmen, auf kleinbürgerliche Konzessionen, wie das barocke Portal und das würdige Treppenhaus, zu verzichten, die dem Genossenschaftsprogramm der »sozialen Anpassung« entsprachen. In Walter Curt Behrendts, den Zeitstil von 1910 treffendem Begriff von der »einheitlichen Blockfront« werden diese Tendenzen zu einem modernen Großstadtstil. Der junge Bruno Taut betrachtete 1913 »eine Weiterführung Messels im Prinzip als sein Schaffen überhaupt«. Die starke Rhythmik des zum Glück rekonstruierten Mietshauses am Kottbusser Damm *(Abb. 107)* ist dafür ein eindrucksvolles Zeugnis.[20]

Fig. 112 *Bruno Taut. Onkel-Tom Development, 1926–31. Berlin-Zehlendorf, Waldhüterpfad (1984 photo).*

Abb. 112 *Bruno Taut Waldsiedlung »Onkel Toms Hütte«, 1926–31. Berlin-Zehlendorf, Waldhüterpfad (Photo 1984).*

ment, but a symbolic link among all the inhabitants. The uniqueness of Messel's design, still evident today, cannot be defined solely by its style, stuccowork, or aesthetic approach, but must also be understood as Messel's attempt to express visually the emergence of a distinct social class struggling for recognition.

Once again, solely by concentrating his powers on a new task, Messel managed to overcome architectural convention. He showed how to strip the mask of the middle-class facade from workingmen's housing, and how to give it new character by the addition of small elements that work together by dint of their function rather than through a watered-down and manipulated neo-Renaissance rhetoric.

This building marked the inception of an "increasing simplification" of apartment architecture toward the Serienbau of the 1920s, with its "sequences of a limited number of elements." The quotation is Bruno Taut's, used to describe the same kind of cooperative architecture thirty years after Messel's achievement.[19]

Messel left it to succeeding architects like Bruno Taut to remove the remaining concessions to middle-class taste: "Nuremberg" roofs and gables, baroque portals, and grand staircases – which, according to the

Unter den veränderten Bedingungen der Weimarer Republik mußte nicht mehr die »Anpassung« an bürgerliche Wohnformen gesucht werden. Bruno Taut und Martin Wagner betreiben in der Siedlung Britz *(Abb. 11, 44, 108–109)* »das große Befreiungswerk vom bürgerlichen Kunst- und Kulturgeschmack. Wiederholung ist ... das wichtigste Kunstmittel.« Das Ziel der »Kollektivität als stilbildender Faktor« ist von den beiden sozialistischen Humanisten Taut und Wagner klar und eindeutig gegen das Mißverständnis der »Kasernierung einer namenlosen Masse« abgegrenzt. So lauteten konservative Vorwürfe. Das Bezirksparlament von Berlin-Britz verlor nach Baubeginn der Hufeisensiedlung von Bruno Taut und Martin Wagner seine sozialdemokratische Mehrheit, der Taut versprochene Bauabschnitt gegenüber dem Hufeisen ging an die Deutsche Gesellschaft zur Förderung des Wohnungshaus (DEGEWO), die konventionelle Häuser im bayrischen Heimatstil errichtete. Nirgendwo anders als im Weimarer Berlin steht sich Baukunst als Ausdruck politischer und sozialer Gegensätze buchstäblich in der Straße gegenüber.

Aber auch von kommunistischer Seite wurden die Weimarer Siedlungen heftig kritisiert. Der sowjetische

Fig. 113 *Bruno Taut. Onkel-Tom Development, 1926–31. Berlin-Zehlendorf, Riemeisterstrasse garden front (1984 photo). The smooth, brightly-colored plaster of the garden facade reflects Taut's original scheme for the building.*

Abb. 113 *Bruno Taut. Waldsiedlung »Onkel Toms Hütte«, 1926–31. Berlin-Zehlendorf, Riemeisterstraße, Gartenfassade (Zustand 1984). Der glatte, stark farbige Stuck entspricht der ursprünglichen Fassadengestaltung Tauts.*

Cooperative's program had been metaphors of "social adjustment." In Walter Curt Behrendt's influential conception of the unified block front *(Einheitliche Blockfront)* of around 1910, these tendencies became the ferment of a modern metropolitan architectural style. In 1913 the young Bruno Taut stated that "principally the basis of my work will be the continuation of Messel." The forceful rhythm of his reconstructed apartment house on Kottbusser Damm *(fig. 107)* is impressive testimony to that ambition.[20]

In the changed conditions of the Weimar Republic, an "adjustment" to middle-class styles of living was no longer apposite. Bruno Taut and Martin Wagner, in their Horseshoe Development *(figs. 11, 44, 108–109)*, instituted "a great work of liberation from bourgeois taste in art and culture. Repetition is … the most impor-

Architekt Gretschucho polemisierte 1933 gegen den Zeilenbau der deutschen Architekten in Rußland. Ihnen fehlten die Points de vue, die klassische Achse, die Symmetrie; die politisch-propagandistische Bedeutung von Plätzen sei nicht erkannt.[21]

In der internen Diskussion der Avantgarde selbst wurde die Schwierigkeit, »großbürgerliche und proletarische, hochkapitalistische und sozialistische Architektur« formal überhaupt noch unterscheiden zu können, optimistisch als die Zukunftsutopie einer klassenlosen Gesellschaft interpretiert, aber auch als das formalistische Ende des »Internationalen Stiles«.[22]

Bruno Tauts Onkel-Tom-Siedlung *(Abb. 111–114)* in Zehlendorf, Erwin Gutkinds Wohnhausblock in Berlin-Lichtenberg *(Abb. 115)* und Ludwig Hilberseimers Entwurf für Reihenhäuser in Berlin-Ruhleben *(Abb. 116)*,

tant means of art." The two socialist humanists clearly distinguished their encouragement of "collectivity as a style-generating factor" from the production of more "barracks for the nameless masses," although their conservative critics did not. The Horseshoe Development was not even finished when the district council of Berlin-Britz lost its Social Democratic majority, and the site across the street, promised to Taut, went to a civil service building society, the German Society for Housing Development, which put up houses in a conventional Bavarian vernacular. Nowhere else but in Weimar Berlin did architecture express so forcefully conflicting social and political opinions – literally on the streets.

The Weimar housing developments also drew sharp criticism from the Communist camp. In 1933, the Soviet architect Gretschucho mounted a polemic against German row building in Russia, saying that the style lacked *points de vue,* classical axes, or symmetry, and showed no recognition of the political and propagandistic significance of city squares.

Equally important, within the vanguard itself the difficulty of formally distinguishing between "upper middle-class, proletarian, high capitalist, and socialist architecture" was interpreted not only optimistically, as the utopia of a classless society, but as the demise of the International Style in formalism.[22] Bruno Taut's Onkel-Tom Development *(figs. 111–114)* in Zehlendorf, Erwin Gutkind's houses in Berlin-Lichtenberg *(fig. 115),* Ludwig Hilberseimer's design for row houses in Berlin-Ruhleben *(fig. 116),* and the designs by Forbat and Gropius are hardly distinguishable in what concerns their system of rhythmical repetition. The elegant houses that the Luckhardt brothers and Alfons Anker built in Berlin for the film elite that formed around Fritz Lang *(figs. 18, 117)* follow the same formulae, but allow for the bourgeois luxury of intervening space, giving neighbors a certain amount of distance from one another.

Bruno Taut's own analysis of the Britz Development precisely defines its delicate balance between the ideal of the middle-class residence and apartment on the one hand, and architecture in the service of Communist state propaganda on the other. Even more significant, Taut's description renders this precarious middle position of "Weimar" visible, by explaining the derivation of the formal elements of his architectural design. The formal relationships, the rhythmic links and interactions – Taut says – are to express "the meaning of relations among men." He continues with a biological metaphor:

We conceive ... the collective mass of similar members as a living creature that does not simply

wie auch die Entwürfe von Forbat oder Gropius sind kaum noch individuell nach ihrem System rhythmischer Wiederholung zu unterscheiden. Die feinen Wohnungen der Berliner Film-Elite um Fritz Lang, von den Brüdern Luckhardt und Alfons Anker in Berlin-Dahlem *(Abb. 18, 117)* folgen dem gleichen Gesetz einer reihenden Wiederholung, nur mit dem bürgerlichen Luxus eines Zwischenraumes, des Abstandes zum Nachbarn.

Bruno Tauts eigene Analyse der Britzer Siedlung vermag ungemein genau ihre delikate Position zwischen der bürgerlichen Eigenheim- und Mietshaus-Ideologie auf der einen Seite, und einer Architektur im Dienste kommunistischer Staatspropaganda auf der anderen zu definieren. Wichtiger noch, er vermag diese »Weimarer« Mittellage in den formalen Elementen seiner architektonischen Konzeption sichtbar zu machen: Formale Beziehungen, rhythmische Verknüpfungen und Bewegungen zueinander, sie stellen mit den Mitteln der Architektur »die Bedeutung der Beziehungen von Mensch zu Mensch« dar: »Wir fassen dagegen die kollektive Masse gleichartiger Glieder wie

Fig. 114   *Bruno Taut. Onkel-Tom Development, 1926–31. Berlin-Zehlendorf, Argentinische Allee (1984 photo).*
Abb. 114   *Bruno Taut. Waldsiedlung »Onkel Toms Hütte«, 1926–31. Berlin-Zehlendorf, Argentinische Allee (Zustand 1984).*

Fig. 115 *Erwin Gutkind. Sonnenhof tenement house, 1926–1927. Berlin-Lichtenberg, Marie-Curie-Allee (formerly Caprivi-Allee), corner of Delbrückstrasse.*

Abb. 115 *Erwin Gutkind. Wohnhausblock Sonnenhof, 1926–27. Berlin-Lichtenberg, Marie-Curie-Allee (früher Caprivi-Allee), Ecke Delbrückstraße.*

and automatically obey commands but every member of which is infused with collective consciousness and is for that reason alive. Its general quality depends on the quality of its individual constituents. A key factor in this quality is the relation of each member to the next, which is why the vital current must suffuse the whole in its groups and sequences. What speaks to the emotions in

ein atmendes Wesen auf, das nicht starr einem Macht-wort folgt, sondern das in jedem einzelnen Gliede das kollektive Bewußtsein trägt und infolgedessen in sich lebendig ist. Seine Gesamtqualität hängt von der Qualität der einzelnen Glieder ab. Ein wichtiger Teil der Qualität ist die Beziehung von einem Glied zum anderen, und deswegen muß der Lebensstrom das Ganze in seinen Gruppen und Reihungen durchziehen. Was bei

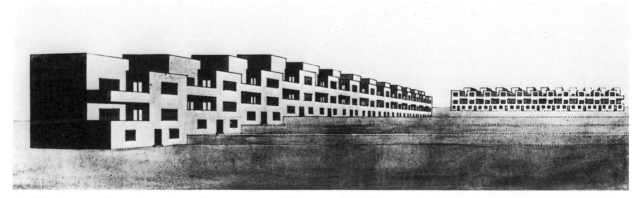

Fig. 116 *Ludwig Hilberseimer. Project for row houses, 1925. Berlin-Ruhleben.*

Abb. 116 *Ludwig Hilberseimer. Entwurf für Reihenhäuser, 1925. Berlin-Ruhleben.*

Fig. 117   *Hans and Wassili Luckhardt, Alfons Anker. Row houses, c. 1930. Berlin-Dahlem, Schorlemer Allee.*

Abb. 117   *Hans und Wassili Luckhardt, Alfons Anker. Reihenhauser, um 1900. Berlin-Dahlem, Schorlemer Allee.*

designs of this order is not the configuration of city squares or frontages, their lines in baroque or any other style, but rather (if the design is successful) an evocation of motion, of transitions between and among the groupings and rows.[23]

Anyone who sees the great sweeping horseshoe in Britz can still sense the "collective enjoyment," the "feeling of future, city, and brotherhood," so central to Expressionist architecture (Ernst Bloch). But the architects of the Neues Bauen were able to achieve this feeling only in the monads of the New Suburb, the New Business and Administrative Center, or in some utopian City of the Future – literally on the ruins of the old city, which Mies van der Rohe reduced to a dark backdrop to set off his crystalline visions. Wilhelm Büning marked the frontier between his "Weisse Stadt" *(fig. 118)* in Berlin-Reinickendorf and the neighboring prewar houses with a towerlike structure that served as a blunt negation of the community's continuity.

Ernst Bloch realized who the enemies of the egalitarian dream would be as early as 1923: "back-to-the-soilers" and "incapable developers who jerry-build tasteful fakes of the past out of the debris" of the present.[24]

solchen Anlagen jetzt zum Gefühl spricht, ist nicht die Bildung von Plätzen und Platzwänden, die barocke oder sonstige formale Linie, es liegt vielmehr, wenn eine solche Anlage glückt, in dem Ausdruck der Bewegung, von Überleitung der Reihen und Gruppen zueinander.«[23]

In Britz spürt jeder Besucher des Hufeisenrundes noch jenes expressionistische Gestaltungsverlangen aus einem und für einen »gleichheitlichen Genuß«, das »Zukunfts-, Stadt- und Kollektivgefühl« (Ernst Bloch). Aber die Architekten des Neuen Bauens vermochten dieses nur in der Monade der Neuen Vorstadtsiedlung, wie in Britz, Zehlendorf oder Siemensstadt, in der Neuen Geschäfts- und Verwaltungsstadt oder in einer utopischen Zukunftsstadt zu fühlen, – buchstäblich auf den Trümmern der alten Stadt. Diese durfte nur noch als schwarze Kulisse oder Collage die gläsernen Bauvisionen Mies van der Rohes rahmen. Wilhelm Büning grenzte seine »Weiße Stadt« *(Abb. 118)* in Berlin-Reinickendorf durch einen hohen Wohnturm von den Vorkriegsbauten ab, als brüske Negation der städtischen Kontinuität.

Ernst Bloch nennt schon 1923 die Feinde dieses egalitären Wunschbildes: die »Schollenphrase« und die

Fig. 118   *Wilhelm Büning. "Weisse Stadt" housing project, c. 1930. Berlin-Reinickendorf, Emmentaler Strasse 54, 56 (1984 photo).*

Abb. 118   *Wilhelm Büning. »Weiße Stadt«, um 1930. Berlin-Reinickendorf, Emmentaler Straße 54, 56 (Zustand 1984).*

Bruno Taut, Weimar architect incarnate, had to leave Germany immediately after Hitler's accession, torn away from numerous unfinished projects. He was a prime target of National Socialist hate. "You can burn obscenity and trash in word and image on the pyre," wrote a certain Professor Hoegg in February 1934. "But you cannot simply ask the Labor Service to demolish the trashy architecture of the postwar period. When humanity has long been transformed, for good or evil, its buildings will still stand as eloquent testimony to the philosophy it once held."[25] Two months after the Nazis came to power, in March 1933, Taut was forced to flee, to Stuttgart and then to Switzerland, where he received an invitation from the Japanese architectural association, which he followed via Marseilles, Naples, Athens, Istanbul, and Vladivostok.

Taut's successors in the Onkel-Tom Development in Zehlendorf propped pitched roofs on his row apartments and balconies in a grotesque and labored attempt at indigenous style, and drowned his bright colors in a rough, grayish plaster *(fig. 119)*. Architectural

»siedlerischen Nichtskönner, die aus den Trümmern geschmackvolle Vergangenheitsfälschungen flicken«.[24]

Bruno Taut, die Inkarnation »Weimarer« Architektur, mußte unmittelbar nach der Machtergreifung durch die Nationalsozialisten Deutschland verlassen, mitten aus einer rastlosen Tätigkeit. Der Haß der Nationalsozialisten verfolgte vor allem ihn: »Man kann Schmutz und Schund in Wort und Bild auf dem Scheiterhaufen verbrennen. Aber den Schundbau der Nachkriegszeit kann man nicht so ohne weiteres durch den Arbeitsdienst abtragen lassen. Wenn die Menschen längst Andere geworden sind – im Guten und Bösen – stehen noch ihre Bauwerke als beredte Zeugen ihrer früheren Gesinnung«, so ein Professor E. Högg im Februar 1934.[25]

Keine zwei Monate nach der Machtergreifung, im März 1933, muß Taut fliehen, über Stuttgart in die Schweiz. Hier erreicht ihn die Einladung des japanischen Architektenbundes, der er über Marseille, Neapel, Athen, Istanbul, Wladiwostok Folge leistet.

Bruno Tauts Nachfolger in der Onkel-Tom-Siedlung

ideals shifted from an urban, cooperative present to the village community of the past, complete with preindustrial half-timbering and fieldstone. Behind the Onkel-Tom Development, one pitched-roof detached house after another began to rise in 1936, wonderfully interspersed with greenery. The bitter but open controversy over row versus detached construction, flat or pitched roofs, international or vernacular style, was silenced. Argentinische Allee, Fischtalgrund, and Ithweg were not competing neighborhoods in the 1930s but expressions of abysmally deep political, ideological, and aesthetic differences. Today they are inhabited by Berliners who are quite peaceable and indistinguishable. The artistic differences remain irreconcilable.

The New AEG Administration Building – Farewell to the Palace

As with his Wertheim store, Messel took a historic if less dramatic step toward reorganizing architecture for administrative purposes. Messel achieved a subtle transformation of the Renaissance palace for modern purposes in the headquarters he designed in 1905 for AEG, on Friedrich-Karl-Ufer *(fig. 121)*, not a single stone of which still stands after the devastation of war and the building of the Wall. In this project Messel held, by the skin of his teeth, to the early Northern Italian palatial motifs of colossal orders, window balconies, base rustication, and lateral wings. To the extent that it was possible, he tried to turn a Renaissance palace into a modern administration building. Only a careful observer will note that the corner projections are visible as a slight broadening of the span. The central projection with its timid triangular pediment disappears in an almost undifferentiated sameness of pilasters and window-framing, underscored by the absence of any grand entrances. It is as if Messel left the relics of tradition as an invitation to a younger generation to discard them altogether.

The power of Messel's achievement lay in the subtlety of his transformation. Numerous bank buildings, clubs, and administrative offices all over Europe and Manhattan have been copied from Renaissance palaces, but rarely can they be considered to be intelligent adaptations suitable for new and different purposes. Messel himself defined his attitude toward tradition by saying: "In architecture everything rests on transformation. The originality of independent thinkers is not hampered by studying history. It is followers who do not have the benefit of appropriate reference points who produce monstrosities."[26]

in Zehlendorf setzen seinen Bau-Zeilen und den Balkonkreuzen grotesk wirkende steile Dächer auf *(Abb. 119)*, – mühsam herbeigeholter Heimatstil. Seine leuchtenden Farben werden in erloschenem Rauhputz ertränkt. Man will von der gegenwartsbewußten Genossenschaftsidee zur dörflichen Gemeinschaft mit vorindustriellem Fachwerk und Naturstein zurück. Hinter der Onkel-Tom-Siedlung in Zehlendorf reiht sich seit 1936 ein Einzelhaus mit steilem Dach, wunderbar durchgrünt, an das andere. Die bittere, aber offene Weimarer Polemik zwischen Zeilenbau und Einzelhaus, flachem und steilem Dach, internationalem oder Heimatstil ist am Ende. An der Argentinischen Allee, im Fischtalgrund und am Ithweg, – in den dreißiger Jahren nicht Nachbarschaft, sondern Ausdruck abgrundtiefer, politischer, ideologischer und ästhetischer Gegensätze –, wohnen heute die gleichen Berliner. Die künstlerischen Unterschiede bleiben unversöhnlich.

Der neue Verwaltungsbau der AEG – der Abschied vom Palast

Neben dem Schöpfungsbau des modernen Warenhauses gelingt Messel, weniger dramatisch, aber geschichtlich unverzichtbar, die Ahnung einer Neuorganisation des modernen Verwaltungsbaues in Berlin: Die AEG-Hauptverwaltung von 1905 am Friedrich-Karl-Ufer *(Abb. 121)*, von der kein Stein mehr nach der Kriegszerstörung und dem Mauerbau erhalten ist. Er hält sozusagen mit letzter Kraft an den alten oberitalienischen Palastmotiven der Kolossalordnung, der Fensterbalkone, der Sockelrustizierung und der Risalite fest. Er versucht, so viel als möglich vom italienischen Renaissance-Palast in einen modernen Begriff vom Verwaltungsbau einzubringen. Doch ist der Betrachter Zeuge, wie die Eckrisalite nur noch als winzige Jochverbreiterung erkennbar sind und der Mittelrisalit in der kaum noch unterschiedenen Gleichheit der Pilaster und Fenster und schließlich im Verzicht auf Portale sich verabschiedet. Der Dreiecks-Giebel der Risalite ist der dominierenden Summe des Gleichen untergeordnet, ein der Tradition verpflichtetes Relikt, auf das zu verzichten Messel eine jüngere Architektengeneration geradezu auffordert.

Die Veränderung ist der entscheidende Punkt. Es gibt eine endlose Zahl von schlichten und korrekten Kopien von Renaissance-Palästen, in Europa und Manhattan; aber sie können nur in den seltensten Fällen als intelligente Umformung ihrer sichtbaren Erscheinung, als Konsequenz neuer Funktionen angesehen werden: »In der Architektur beruht alles auf Weiterentwick-

The first AEG administration building, erected in 1892 by Cremer and Wolffenstein on Schiffbauer-damm *(fig. 120),* was totally different from Messel's structure in terms of function and style.[27] Emil Rathenau (1838–1915), the founder of the AEG, was an engineer from an old Jewish family. He chose to adapt a traditional palais form to serve both as his private residence and as his company quarters. On the main floor were Rathenau's living quarters, with those of his associates, Felix Deutsch and Paul Mamroth, located on the top floor. The executive offices were on the mezzanine, above the shops. Storage and administration were located in the invisible rear of the building. The functions of administration, storage, and distribution of large quantities of goods were almost completely concealed from view, though we can sense the pressure with which these new functions would soon invade the factory owner's private residence.

In Messel's AEG Administration Building, the Northern Italian city palace was translated into an expression of the concurrent functions and the collective enterprise of a large corporation. On the interior and exterior and from bottom to top, the building reminds one of Max Weber's notion of the increasing rationalization and anonymity of the modern world. This is the point at which Peter Behrens began, as he himself sensed[28] and as the influential art critic Karl Scheffler expressly stated: "The AEG," he said, enabled Behrens to "take Messel's empty chair."[29]

Industry – the New Gesamtkunstwerk – "Cathedral of Labor"

It was a misfortune of architectural history that neither Schinkel, with his English experiences of 1826, nor Messel, with his pioneering Wertheim store, was able to apply what he had learned to a large factory building. But it was equally fortunate that AEG should have hired Peter Behrens, a designer who had learned all Schinkel and Messel had to teach, and who to his dying day referred to himself as merely a "self-taught builder."

It was Emil Rathenau who must have brought in Peter Behrens. In 1881, Rathenau visited the Exposition internationale d'électricité in Paris. There he saw "the invention of the famous hermit of Menlo Park … Thomas Alva Edison's lighting system." This invention was "so brilliantly conceived and worked out down to the last detail that it might have been practically tested for decades … everything was finished with astonishing

lung. Die Originalität selbständiger Köpfe wird durch Studium des Überlieferten nicht behindert, die große Masse der Unselbständigen aber produciert ohne Anlehnung und Studium nur Scheußlichkeiten«, so definiert Messel selbst sein Verhältnis zur Überlieferung.[26]

Die Vielgliedrigkeit der organisatorischen Arbeitsabläufe, die Summe gleichzeitiger Funktionen, damit das sichtbare Verschwinden einer hierarchischen Zuordnung von Außen nach Innen und von Unten nach Oben erinnern an Max Webers Vorstellungen von der Rationalisierung und Anonymisierung der modernen Welt.

Das erste, 1892 am Schiffbauerdamm errichtete Verwaltungsgebäude der AEG *(Abb. 120)* von Cremer und Wolffenstein ist der Glücksfall eines anschaulichen Beleges für diese Entwicklung innerhalb der AEG selbst, vom Stadtpalais des industriellen Entrepreneurs zum Verwaltungssitz eines modernen Großbetriebes[27]. Die neue Machtelite der Industrie geht zunächst den Weg der Anpassung an überlieferte und heimische Palastformen des 18. Jahrhunderts. In dieser sind die neuen Funktionen der Verwaltung, des Lagerns und Ausstellens großer Warenmassen noch nahezu unsichtbar geblieben. Sie beginnen das Gebäude, das in der Belletage noch die Stadtwohnung des Fabrikbesitzers enthielt, zu sprengen.

Messels Verwaltungsgebäude überführt die pathetische Sprache oberitalienischer Stadtpaläste aus ihrem immer individuellen Bezug zum Hausherrn in das Kollektivbild eines großen Unternehmens. Hier schließt das Werk von Peter Behrens unmittelbar an, das hat er selber so empfunden[28] und ist von Karl Scheffler ausgesprochen worden: Die AEG habe es Behrens ermöglicht, »den leeren Platz Messels einzunehmen«.[29]

Die Industrie – das neue Gesamtkunstwerk – die »Kathedrale der Arbeit«

Es ist ein architekturgeschichtlicher Unglücksfall, daß weder Schinkel die Erfahrungen seiner Englandreise 1826, noch Messel den Riesenschritt seines Kaufhauses Wertheim in einen großen Fabrikbau einbringen konnten. Es war aber ein architekturgeschichtlicher Glücksfall, daß die AEG einen Architekten berufen hatte, der für seine Berufskollegen gar keiner war, der die Lektion von Schinkel und Messel vollkommen lernte und der sich zeitlebens einen »Autodidakten« nannte.

Auf der Exposition Internationale d'Electricité in Paris 1881 hatte der 43jährige, aus einer alten Berliner

acumen and incomparable genius."[30] Rathenau purchased a license, and in the shadow of Siemens, with the aid of circumspect and thrifty banker friends, founded a company in 1883 to produce and distribute Edison's incandescent lamps in Germany. This rapid success led to the establishment of the Allgemeine Elektricitaets-Gesellschaft in 1887. The rise of this firm is one of the success stories of German manufacturing, on a veritably American scale. When Behrens was appointed as artistic adviser to the AEG in 1907, the company was in its twenty-fifth year and, along with General Electric, Westinghouse, and Siemens &

jüdischen Familie stammende Ingenieur Emil Rathenau (1838–1915) »die Erfindung des berühmten Einsiedlers von Menlo Park ... Thomas Alva Edisons Beleuchtungssystem« kennengelernt. Rathenau fand es »bis in die Einzelheiten so genial erdacht und durchgearbeitet als sei es jahrzehntelang erprobt gewesen ... alles war mit staunenswertem Verständnis und unvergleichlichem Genie durchgebildet«. Rathenau kaufte die Lizenz, gründete im Schatten von Siemens, von vorsichtigen und sparsamen Bankiersfreunden unterstützt, 1883 eine Firma zur Einführung der Edisonschen Glühlicht-Beleuchtung in Deutschland. Schnelle Er-

Fig. 119 *Bruno Taut. Row houses: design, before 1933; construction by the Gehag building company, 1933–34. Berlin-Zehlendorf, Hartmannsweiler Weg (1972 photo).*
Subjected to National Socialist pressure, Taut was forced to flee Germany before this project could be built The Gehag building company handled its construction in his absence, but not without drastically altering the design. The introduction of steeply pitched roofs with chimneys, tightly squeezed balconies, and monochromatic plaster contributed to the destruction of Taut's formal language.

Abb. 119 *Bruno Taut. Reihenhäuser; Entwurf vor 1933; Ausführung »Gehag«, 1933–34. Berlin-Zehlendorf, Hartmannsweiler Weg (Zustand 1972). Die Veränderung, ja Zerstörung der Formensprache Bruno Tauts durch steiles Dach mit Schornsteinen, eingeklemmte Balkongruppen, einfarbigen Putz, wird drastisch deutlich.*

Halske AG, was a leader on the international market. In five large manufacturing complexes in and around Berlin it offered a livelihood to "a populace of 150,000 souls," as Le Corbusier put it in 1912.[31]

From the start, AEG set great store by architectural talent, employing Franz Schwechten from 1889, Cremer and Wolffenstein in 1892, Otto Eckmann as advertising artist from 1900, and Alfred Messel in 1905. The next year, Messel received a huge commission for the Pergamon Museum, so a new man had to be found to plan the extensions made necessary by the company's breathtaking expansion.

The choice of Peter Behrens for this job must have rested primarily on his skill in advertising and promotion. In 1906 he had begun doing graphic design for AEG, including the binding and cover for *Mitteilungen der Berliner Elektricitäts-Werke (Newsletter of the Berlin Electric Company)*, an in-house paper for which he brought out a completely new design in January

folge führten zur Gründung der Allgemeinen Elektricitäts-Gesellschaft im Jahre 1887. Der Aufstieg dieser Firma gehört zu den Erfolgsstorys der deutschen Industrie von durchaus amerikanischem Ausmaß.[30] Als Behrens 1907 zum künstlerischen Beirat berufen wurde, bestand die Firma 25 Jahre und gehörte mit der General Electric Company, Westinghouse und Siemens & Halske zu den Großunternehmen der Weltwirtschaft. In fünf großen Fabrikkomplexen in und bei Berlin bot sie einem »Volk von 150.000 Seelen ... Brot und Arbeit«.[31]

Von Anfang an legte die AEG Wert auf den Rang seiner Architekten: Franz Schwechten ab 1889, Cremer und Wolffenstein 1892, Otto Eckmann als Werbegraphiker ab 1900, Alfred Messel 1905. Da Messel 1906 den großen Auftrag für das Pergamon-Museum erhielt, mußte eine neue Kraft für die Planung der Neubauten, die das atemberaubende Wachstum der Firma notwendig machte, gefunden werden. Die

Fig. 120 *Cremer & Wolffenstein. Administration building of the AEG and the Berliner Elektricitäts-Werke, 1892. Berlin-Mitte, Schiffbauerdamm (destroyed).*

Abb. 120 *Cremer & Wolffenstein. Verwaltungsgebäude der AEG und der Berliner Elektricitäts-Werke, 1892. Berlin-Mitte, Schiffbauerdamm (zerstört).*

Fig. 121 *Alfred Messel. AEG Administration Building, 1905. Berlin-Mitte, Friedrich-Karl-Ufer (destroyed).*

Abb. 121 *Alfred Messel. Verwaltungsgebäude der AEG, 1905. Berlin-Mitte, Friedrich-Karl-Ufer (zerstört).*

1907. In June 1908 he erected the octagonal AEG Pavilion at the German Shipbuilding Exhibition in Berlin, for which he also designed an unusually fine little catalogue.

Behrens apparently earned the full confidence of management with these small jobs, because in June 1908 they entrusted him with a commission that was to send reverberations through all modern architecture: the Turbine Factory on Huttenstrasse *(figs. 20–21, 122–125)*. The reassessment of values this building represented can be understood only against the European background of nineteenth-century achievements in engineering, which in many cases limited the architect's role to that of applier of ornament and decorator of facades. The "space-shaper" Behrens, untrained in architecture and with a building experience encompassing only his own house in Darmstadt and a few other relatively small projects, was now

Berufung von Behrens muß vordringlich unter dem Gesichtspunkt der Werbung erfolgt sein. Seit 1906 hat er graphische Arbeiten für die AEG ausgeführt, so Einband und Umschlag der »Mitteilungen der Berliner Elektricitaets-Werke«, von Nr. 1, Januar 1907, an. Im Juni 1908 errichtet er den achteckigen AEG-Pavillon zur Deutschen Schiffbauausstellung in Berlin, für die er auch einen ungemein schönen, kleinen Katalog entwirft.

Diese kleinen Arbeiten dürften zur vollen Zufriedenheit der Firmenleitung verlaufen sein. Denn im Juni 1908 erhält Behrens einen der folgenreichsten Aufträge in der Architekturgeschichte des 20. Jahrhunderts, – die Turbinenhalle an der Huttenstraße *(Abb. 20–21)*. Nur vor dem europäischen Hintergrund der großen Ingenieurleistungen des 19. Jahrhunderts mit ihrer Abwertung der Architektenarbeit als bloßer Fassadenapplikation oder Materialdekoration ist die »Immer

asked to design a colossal structure that could not be built without the skills of an engineer. He first projected a "space-defining configuration," then developed a "structural idea" to suit it. Only at this point did he request a structural engineer, Karl Bernhard, to make the "calculations necessary . . . for actual construction" and bring his "technical inventiveness" into play, thanks to which the final structure had a "beautiful, cathedral-like effect" and a "superb silhouette." And, as most observers have noted only in passing, it was a plant perfectly suited to manufacturing needs, which has served its function to this day.

Space-defining configuration, cathedral-like effect, and superb silhouette – all these were attributes proper to cathedrals, palaces, courtly buildings of the past that Behrens, the self-taught architect, now lent to the architecture of industry. "This modern building with its powerful outward forms is an image of the tremendous labor that goes on within," said Oskar Lasche, production engineer and one of the building's three designers. The effect was achieved not by quotations from past architectural styles but through the new materials of industry itself – glass, steel, and concrete.

Behrens reduced his vocabulary of forms radically, to a small number of structural elements that were easily manufactured and could be combined in endless sequences. These elements, beyond the function they were calculated to fulfill, were formally emphasized in terms of space and plane to the point where their rhythmical sequence and the grouping between projecting concrete base and riveted cornice consciously recalled cathedral or temple *(figs. 122–125)*.

The formalism of the turbine plant has often been criticized, but this cuts both ways. Of course the unnecessary filling of the space between the facade and the steel supports, which carry the roof like the columns of a temple, is an architectural "lie." In "truth," the supports are an integral part of Bernhard's three-joint tie system, whose lateral reinforcement serves primarily to take up the tremendous loads and lateral forces of the wall-mounted and traveling cranes. These interior workloads and the instrumental character of the supports, emphasized by separating them from the inwardly inclined wall, have simply been given visual expression by Behrens, just as earlier architects underscored the load-bearing quality of columns. Goethe once admired in Palladio "the force of a great poet . . . who shaped from truth and falsehood a third quality whose borrowed existence fascinates us."[32]

tung der Werte«, die sich hier ereignet, verständlich. Der »Raumbildner« Behrens, der nie eine Ausbildung als Architekt erfahren, nur sein eigenes Wohnhaus in Darmstadt 1901 und kleinere Bauten errichtet hatte, erhält den Auftrag für einen gewaltigen Ingenieurbau. Er entwirft seine »raumbildnerische Erscheinung« und entwickelt dafür eine »konstruktive Idee«. Erst danach wird der Bauingenieur Karl Bernhard beauftragt, »die konstruktive Durchführung« durch »die nötigen Berechnungen« zu organisieren und dieser »Raumgestaltung« durch »technische Erfindungsgabe« zu ihrer »schönen domartigen Wirkung« und ihrer »ausgezeichneten Silhouette« zu verhelfen. Nur beiläufig nimmt man zur Kenntnis, daß sozusagen trotzdem eine betriebstechnisch vollkommene Werkstatt gelang, die bis heute funktioniert.

Raumbildnerische Erscheinung, domartige Wirkung und ausgezeichnete Silhouette, – das waren Attribute, die für Kathedralen, Paläste und Schloßbauten der Vergangenheit galten und die Behrens, der Autodidakt als Architekt, nun den Bauten der Industrie verleiht.

»Dieser moderne Bau ist in seinen wuchtigen äußeren Formen ein Abbild der gewaltigen Arbeit, die im Inneren des Gebäudes geleistet wird«, so sah es der Betriebsingenieur und einer der drei Erbauer, Oskar Lasche. Dies geschieht nicht durch Zitate aus der Baukunst alter Stile, sondern gelingt mit den neuen Materialien der Industrie selbst, – mit Glas, Stahl und Beton.

Konsequent wird die Formensprache auf wenige Bauelemente reduziert, die technisch leicht zu produzieren und unendlich zu reihen waren. Deren Formen werden über ihren errechneten Funktionsauftrag hinaus plastisch, räumlich und flächig so betont, daß die rhythmische Reihung und Gruppierung solcher Elementarformen zwischen profiliertem Betonsockel und dem genieteten Gesims zur gewollten Erinnerung an Dom und Tempel wird *(Abb. 122–125)*.

Der viel kritisierte Formalismus der Turbinenhalle ist ein doppelter. Natürlich ist die Suggestion der unnötig vollwandigen Stahlstützen, die ein Dach tragen, und damit die Erinnerung an Tempelsäulen, »Lüge«. In »Wahrheit« sind die Stützen konstruktiver Teil des Bernhardschen Dreigelenkbinders, der durch Querversteifungen vor allem die Wand- und Laufkrane und deren gewaltige Lasten und seitliche Schubkräfte zu tragen hat. Diese Arbeitsleistung im Inneren, diesen Instrumentalcharakter der Stützen bringt Behrens aber durch ihre Sichtbarmachung, in der Ablösung von

---

Fig. 122 *Peter Behrens. AEG Turbine Factory, 1909. (now owned by Kraftwerk-Union AG). Berlin-Moabit, base along Berlichingenstrasse (1986 photo).*

Abb. 122 *Peter Behrens. Turbinenfabrik der AEG, 1909, (heute Kraftwerk-Union AG). Berlin-Moabit, Sockelzone entlang der Berlichingenstraße (Zustand 1986).*

Fig. 122 / Abb. 122

This same force brings the turbine plant, with the "eloquent power" of collective labor, into proximity with temple and cathedral. To cite Behrens, who read his Nietzsche, "Architecture is a sort of eloquence of power in form ...."[33]

The rich variety of the more than twenty-six buildings Behrens designed for AEG *(figs. 22, 126–128)* speaks for an imagination capable of inventing ever-new configurations that "embraced" the activities performed in them, "expressed" these activities, and "corresponded" to their function. In other words, Behrens set out to find an adequate architectural expression for the unprecedented building tasks of industry, though he did not go so far as to postulate industrial architecture as the basis for all future architecture. That conclusion was drawn by his gifted students. Their teacher's giant step, to them, meant an opportunity to take the next step. Gropius, in his Fagus Shoe Last Factory of 1911, turned the structure of the turbine plant inside out – the temple supports disappeared behind a glass skin that continues around the entire building, rendering it, not without a bit of forcing, almost facadeless. The "eloquence" of the earlier structure is reduced to weightlessness, transparency, rationality, which from this point on became applicable to any structure. "Now the role of the wall," Gropius said, "is merely to keep out rain, cold, and noise."

Mies expanded the lesson of the turbine plant – with a backward glance at Schinkel – to cover architecture from start to finish. To Mies's way of thinking, Behrens did not realize just what he had achieved in the turbine plant.[34] Le Corbusier, on his journey from there to the Parthenon, declared the latter to be the better machine. And Mendelsohn discovered the route to his own architecture by criticizing Behrens's turbine plant.

The Cult of Shell and Skin

"My activity began with the design of an arc lamp," Behrens recalled in 1929. From the start, he had taken it for granted that "the same factors that determine architecture also hold for the smaller objects manufactured by industry"; this was the simple formula to which, in 1910, he reduced his design work on lamps *(figs. 129)*, kettles *(figs. 133–134)*, fans *(fig. 135)*, and clocks *(figs. 130–132)*. "Following an artistic path," i. e. applying the method of geometric abstraction, Behrens would "arrive at those forms which ... suit the

der einwärts geneigten Wand als ein Tragen, wie früher von Säulen, zur Anschauung. Goethe hat an Palladio »die force des großen Dichters« bewundert, »der aus Wahrheit und Lüge ein Drittes bildet, dessen erborgtes Dasein uns bezaubert«.[32] Diese »force« bringt die Turbinenhalle mit der neuen »Machtberedsamkeit« kollektiver Arbeit in die Nähe von Tempel und Kathedrale. Behrens, der Nietzsche-Leser: »Architektur ist eine Art Machtberedsamkeit in Formen ...«[33]

Der Variantenreichtum der etwa 26 Bauwerke, die Behrens für die AEG entwarf *(Abb. 22, 126–128)*, spricht für seine Phantasie, immer neue Gehäuse zu erfinden, die sich den Tätigkeiten in ihnen »anschmiegten«, sie »zum Ausdruck« brachten, ihrer Funktion »entsprachen«. Behrens wollte also den neuen Bauaufgaben der Industrie einen adäquaten architektonischen Ausdruck verleihen, keineswegs die Erfahrungen der Industriearchitektur zur Grundlage aller künftigen Architektur machen. Das war die Konsequenz seiner begabten Schüler. Ihnen erschien der Riesenschritt des Meisters nur Anlaß, den nächsten zu tun. Gropius drehte im Faguswerk *(Abb. 23)* von 1911 das System der Turbinenhalle von 1909 um: Die Tempelstützen verschwanden hinter der freitragenden Glashaut, die das ganze Gebäude nicht ohne Mühe beinahe fassadenlos umzieht. Die »Beredsamkeit« des Baues reduziert sich auf Schwerelosigkeit, Durchsichtigkeit, auf Rationalität, nunmehr applizierbar auf jedes Bauwerk. Die Rolle der Wand ist jetzt nur noch, »Regen, Kälte und Lärm abzuhalten«. (Gropius)

Mies erweiterte das Lehrstück Turbinenhalle über den Umweg des Schinkelschen Klassizismus in die gesamte Architektur. Dem Sinne nach meinte er, Behrens habe nicht gewußt, was ihm in der Turbinenhalle gelungen war[34]. Le Corbusier erkannte auf der Reise von der Turbinenhalle zum Parthenon letzteren als die bessere Maschine. Und in der Kritik an der Turbinenhalle fand Mendelsohn zu seiner Architektur.

Der Kultus der Hülsen und Hüllen

»Meine Tätigkeit begann mit dem Entwurf einer Bogenlampe«, erinnert sich Behrens 1929. Von Anfang an war ihm dabei selbstverständlich, daß »dieselben Gesichtspunkte, die maßgebend für den Hochbau sind, auch für die kleineren Objekte, die von der Industrie hergestellt werden, gelten«, – auf diese einfache Formel bringt Behrens 1910 das Prinzip seiner Gestal-

Fig. 123   *Peter Behrens. AEG Turbine Factory, 1909. (Now owned by Kraftwerk-Union AG). Berlin-Moabit, detail of the base (1986 photo).*

Abb. 123   *Peter Behrens. Turbinenfabrik der AEG, 1909, (heute Kraftwerk-Union AG). Berlin-Moabit, Detail des Sokkels (Zustand 1986).*

Fig. 123 / Abb. 123

154

machine and mass production."[35] Thanks to the visual language he developed, appliances of the most varied kind became recognizably the products of a *single* company. Yet the aesthetic of their color scheme and forms avoided the mechanical appearance of tools and opened the doors to their users' private realm. Their unornamented, smooth surfaces retained no suggestion of preindustrial commodities, the hand-made look, or merely ornamental decoration. The mechanical parts of these appliances were no longer hidden away in sheet-metal tubes with arbitrarily applied beading and knobs simply grafted onto tradi-tional craft objects, or, as in the case of fan motors, attached to the appliances as a formally unrelated appurtenance. Behrens invented a new relationship between appliance and power source, perceiving the possibility of variation within a series. Their precision of manufacture was reflected in a geometric lucidity of form that was easy to die-cut, pressure-mold, and sol-der. The mechanical compulsion to reduce a formal vocabulary to serial standardization and to employ

tungsarbeit für die Bogenlampen *(Abb. 129)*, Wasser-kessel *(Abb. 133–134)*, die Ventilatoren *(Abb. 135)* und Uhren *(Abb. 130–132)*: »Auf künstlerischem Wege«, d. h. mit der Methode der geometrischen Abstraktion, »zu denjenigen Formen gelangen, die der Maschine und der Massenfabrikation... gleichgeartet sind«.[35] Seine Formensprache verlieh den verschiedensten Geräten den sichtbaren Ausdruck, Produkte *einer* Firma zu sein. Die betonte Ästhetik ihrer Farb- und Formgebung befreite sie aus dem technoiden Werk-zeug- und Maschinencharakter und öffnete den Weg in den privaten Lebensbereich des Käufers. Die schmucklose, glatte Form vermied jeden Bezug auf vorindustrielle Geräte, deren handwerkliche Herstel-lung und ornamentale Verzierung. Die Mechanik der Geräte wurde nicht mehr in rohen Blechröhren mit beliebigen Profilen und Wülsten versteckt oder den traditionellen handwerklichen Gebrauchsgeräten ein-fach einverleibt oder als Motor dem Gerät formal folgenlos angeschlossen (Ventilator). Behrens erfand einen neuen Zusammenhang zwischen Gerät und

Fig. 124   *Peter Behrens. AEG Turbine Factory, 1909. (Now owned by Kraftwerk-Union AG). Berlin-Moabit, elevation of inner court (1986 photo).Designed by Mies van der Rohe in Behrens's office, according to Mies.*

Abb. 124   *Peter Behrens. Turbinenfabrik der AEG, 1909, (heute Kraftwerk-Union AG). Berlin-Moabit, Hofseite (Zu-stand 1986). Die von der Straßenfront stark abweichende Hofseite ist, nach eigener Aussage, von Mies van der Rohe im Atelier von Behrens entworfen worden.*

Fig. 125 *Peter Behrens. AEG Turbine Factory, 1909. (Now owned by the Kraftwerk-Union AG). Berlin-Moabit, detail of the Berlichingenstrasse side (1986 photo).*

Abb. 125 *Peter Behrens. Turbinenfabrik der AEG, 1909, (heute Kraftwerk-Union AG). Berlin-Moabit, Detail der Längsseite an der Berlichingenstraße (Zustand 1986).*

similar parts for a number of different models was raised to an artistic principle, that of the variation of pure forms and types.

This innovative planning of a product line is well illustrated by the electric kettle *(figs. 133–134)* manufactured almost unaltered from 1909 to 1930. Three basic shapes were offered: a flat oval, an octagonal, or a water-drop form, mounted on a profiled base, and ending in a semicircular or rectangular wicker handle inserted in a sleeve that is identical for all versions. The spouts of the oval and drop-shaped kettles are identical down to their sockets, as are their bases and the domed lids of the octagonal and drop-shaped kettles. The three versions were available in three materials (brass, nickel-plated brass, and copper-plated brass), with three surface treatments (smooth, hammered, and striated), in three sizes (0.75, 1.25, and 1.75 liters). From these three designs thirty variations were derived; mathematically, the system would have allowed eighty-one.

Energiequelle, die Möglichkeit einer seriellen Variation desselben Gerätetyps (Wasserkessel, Ventilatoren). Die Exaktheit der technischen Herstellung spiegelt sich in der geometrischen Klarheit der Form, die leicht zu stanzen, zu drücken und zu löten ist. Der technische Zwang zur Reduktion des Formenapparates auf dessen serielle Vereinheitlichung und auf die Verwendbarkeit gleicher Bestandteile in einer Vielzahl von Gerätetypen wird zum künstlerischen Prinzip der Variation reiner Formen und Typen erhoben.

Am Beispiel der elektrischen Wasserkessel *(Abb. 133–134)*, die von 1909 bis um 1930 fast unverändert produziert wurden und die bis heute benutzt werden, läßt sich das neuartige Planungsverfahren einer Produktserie erkennen. Es wurden drei Grundformen geliefert: flaches Oval, Achteck und Tropfenform stehen auf einem profilierten Sockel, enden in halbrunden oder rechteckigen rohrgeflochtenen Henkeln, die in gleichen Hülsen stecken. Die Tüllen des ovalen und des tropfenförmigen Kessels sind bis auf den Ansatz

Fig. 126 *Peter Behrens. AEG Small Motor Factory, 1910–13. Berlin-Wedding, AEG complex at Humboldthain, detail of Voltastrasse facade (1984 photo).*

Abb. 126 *Peter Behrens. AEG Fabrik für Kleinmotoren, 1910–13. Berlin-Wedding, AEG-Anlage am Humboldthain, Detail der Fassade Voltastraße (Zustand 1984).*

Fig. 127 *Peter Behrens. AEG Small Motor Factory, 1910–13, with Gerhard Schmieder's AEG Heavy Machinery Factory, 1965–66. Berlin-Wedding, AEG complex, Humboldthain, Voltastrasse (1984 photo).*

Abb. 127 *Peter Behrens. AEG Fabrik für Kleinmotoren, 1910–13, und Gerhard Schmieder, Fabrik für Schwermaschinen der AEG, 1965–66. Berlin-Wedding, AEG-Anlage am Humboldthain, Voltastraße (Zustand 1984).*

In addition AEG produced a multiplicity of kettles in traditional designs and preciously "artistic" shapes, which, taken together, offered an incomparable seventy-five models for every taste – but not for every pocketbook, for initially these appliances were expensive. While the Behrens kettles cost between 18 and 25 Reichsmarks in 1912 (equivalent, approximately, to 4 to 6 dollars), simple ones cost 13 and silver-plated deluxe versions up to 128 Reichsmarks.

All kettles were equipped with the same easily replaceable hidden heating element. Here, Behrens found a design solution that met mass production's need for "standardization" of products; that is, their division into separate replaceable components, easily machine-produced, installed, and assembled. The modern appliance had two basic aspects: its invisible

gleich, ebenso deren Sockel und die gewölbten Deckel des Achteck- und Tropfenformkessels. Die drei Formen wurden in drei Materialien geliefert: Messing, Messing vernickelt, Messing verkupfert; in drei Oberflächenstrukturen: glatt, gehämmert und geflammt; in drei Größen: 0,75, 1,25 und 1,75 Liter. Nicht mehr als drei Entwürfe von Behrens wurden in dreißig Variationen angeboten, das System hätte genau 81 zugelassen.

Daneben produzierte die AEG eine Vielzahl traditioneller Kesselformen und preziöser »künstlerischer« Kessel, die zusammen eine unvergleichliche Auswahl von etwa 75 Variationen für jeden Geschmack anboten – jedoch nicht für jeden Geldbeutel, denn die Geräte waren am Anfang teuer: die von Behrens kosteten 1912 zwischen 18 und 25 Reichsmark, einfache

mechanical innards, which Behrens considered "ugly"; and its "elegant" shell, which protected both the mechanical parts and the user. The artist became a designer because, unlike Cellini, he could no longer shape a saltcellar as a whole but only the shell and skin of a machine-made product.

The porcelain by Marguerite Friedlaender-Wildenhain *(figs. 75–77)* and Trude Petri, the tubular-steel furniture by Mies *(fig. 1)* and Breuer *(figs. 96–97)*, the glassware of Wilhelm Wagenfeld *(figs. 78–80)*, all followed similar principles of serial coherence with forms based on exhaustive study of highly developed materials and sophisticated manufacturing procedures. Wagenfeld's extensive collaboration from 1934 to

Kessel 13, versilberte Luxuskannen bis zu 128 Reichsmark. Alle Wasserkessel waren mit der gleichen leicht austauschbaren, unsichtbaren Heizpatrone ausgestattet. Behrens erfüllt damit im Formausdruck die Bedingungen der modernen Massenfabrikation, die Bestandteile eines Produktes zu »normalisieren«, d. h. in austauschbare, leicht und fehlerfrei montierbare, maschinell herstellbare Einzelteile zu zerlegen. Das moderne Gerät zerfällt damit in seine immer unsichtbare, von Behrens als »häßlich« bezeichnete Mechanik und eine »anmutige« Hülle, die jene Mechanik und den Benutzer schützt. Der Künstler wird zum Designer, weil er nicht mehr wie Cellini das Salzfaß als Ganzes, sondern nur noch die Hüllen und Hülsen gestaltet.

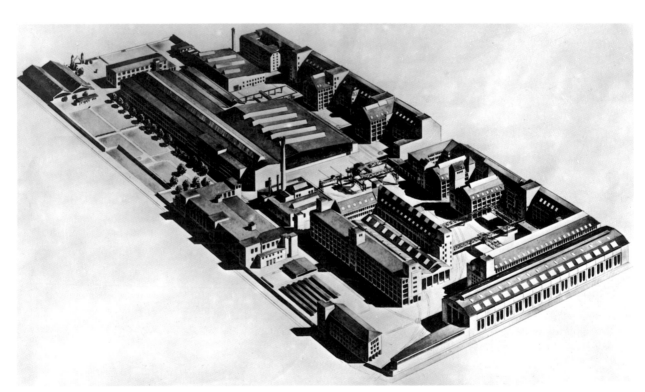

Fig. 128 *AEG factories at Humboldthain. Berlin-Wedding (photo before 1930). This bird's eye rendering of the AEG complex indicates the location of Behrens's projects in relation to the overall plan. The complex itself was bordered on the left by the Humboldthain public park, and, moving clockwise, by Brunnenstrasse, Voltastrasse, and Hussitenstrasse. Behrens's Large Motor Factory is located at the lower right corner of the drawing, at the corner of Hussitenstrasse and Voltastrasse. His Railway Equipment Factory is nestled along its side, above. Around the corner along the Voltastrasse corridor stands the Small Motor Factory. Inside the complex, Behrens's High Voltage Factory from 1909 can be located parallel to the Small Motor Factory. Its structure, a massive, open-ended rectangle, dominates the lower half of the AEG grounds.*

Abb. 128 *AEG Fabriken am Humboldthain. Berlin-Wedding (Zustand vor 1930). Links wird der Komplex vom Humboldthain begrenzt, rechts unten liegt die Fabrik für Großmaschinen entlang der Hussitenstraße. Parallel ist die Fabrik für Bahnmaterial zunächst im Hofinnern, dann im rechten Winkel entlang der Voltastraße angeordnet. Es folgt die Kleinmotorenfabrik. Das rechte Hofinnere beherrscht das offene Rechteck der Hochspannungsfabrik von Behrens, 1909.*

AEG-FLAMMENBOGENLAMPE

Fig. 129   *Peter Behrens. Publicity leaflet for AEG Flammen-bogenlampe, 1908. AEG-Archiv, Frankfurt.*

Abb. 129   *Peter Behrens. Werbeprospekt für AEG Flam-menbogenlampe, 1908. AEG-Archiv, Frankfurt.*

Fig. 130   *Peter Behrens. AEG two-sided electric clock, before 1914. Private collection.*
Abb. 130   *Peter Behrens. Elektrische AEG-Doppeluhr, vor 1914. Privatbesitz.*

1947 with the Vereinigte Lausitzer Glaswerke AG (VLG) in Weisswasser, at the time Europe's leading manufacturer of blown and pressed glass, has to be viewed in relation to the AEG model. Wagenfeld's appointment took place immediately after Karl Mey (b. 1879) was nominated as director of the board. Mey had been assistant to Emil Rathenau, then director of the AEG lightbulb factory, from 1911 to 1920, and was thus familiar with Behrens's work. According to a recent remark of Wagenfeld, Mey wanted to duplicate the Behrens-AEG collaboration at Weisswasser.[36] This means that the two twentieth-century examples of large factories whose mass production was organized almost totally by artists – the AEG and the VLG – are directly related. But in no company did the design of advertising and products expand even close to the dimensions of the social utopia envisioned by Emil Rathenau and his son Walther for AEG. Their well-designed appliances and factory facilities were meant not only to please the buyer, but to release the factory worker from dingy tenements to company housing, from dark, noisy

Die Porzellangeschirre von Marguerite Friedlaender-Wildenhain *(Abb. 75–77)* und Trude Petri, die Stahlrohrmöbel von Mies *(Abb. 1)* und Breuer *(Abb. 96–97)*, die Glasgefäße von Wagenfeld *(Abb. 78–80)* verfolgten ganz ähnliche Prinzipien einer seriellen Kohärenz von Geräten. Sie entwarfen die Formen nach genauestem Studium der technisch weit entwickelten Materialien und der industriellen Produktionsbedingungen. Die umfassende Mitarbeit von Wagenfeld an den Vereinigten Lausitzer Glaswerken, Weisswasser, dem größten europäischen Hohlglashersteller der damaligen Zeit, im Jahre 1934 ist in der direkten Nachfolge des AEG-Modelles zu sehen: Die Berufung erfolgte durch den neuen Vorstandsvorsitzenden Karl Mey (geb. 1879), der die Arbeit von Behrens als Assistent von Emil Rathenau und als Direktor der AEG-Glühlampenfabrik in Berlin von 1911–1920 aus eigener Anschauung kannte. Nach der Aussage von Wagenfeld strebte Mey mit ihm die gleiche gestalterische Arbeit an, die Behrens für die AEG leistete.[36] Damit sind die beiden umfassendsten Produktionsplanungen nach künstlerischen Gesichtspunkten im 20. Jahrhundert, der AEG und der VLG, direkt miteinander verbunden.

Bei keiner anderen Firma weitet sich aber eine solche Designtätigkeit in die von Emil und Walther Rathenau gewollten Dimensionen einer Sozialutopie aus. Bei den wohlgestalteten Geräten und Fabriken dachte man nicht nur an den Käufer, sondern auch an die Erlösung des Industriearbeiters aus den Mietskasernen in werkseigene Siedlungen und aus schmutzigen und dunklen Fabriken in lichtdurchflutete Hallen. Die Arbeiter sollten nicht mehr durch billigen »Massenkram« ermüdet, sondern mit Qualitätsprodukten ihrer Arbeit »Sinn« und Erfüllung verleihen. Das war Werkbundideologie, die uns heute furchtbar veraltet erscheint.

Die AEG-Idee der Ganzheit des neuen »Sozialgebildes« der Großindustrie hat Walther Rathenau intensiv beschäftigt. Er glaubt an diese neue Führungsrolle der Industrie; denn die alte Elite, der Adel, hatte keine »Stütze in der mechanistischen Gesellschaft«. Er dachte an die buchstäbliche Besitznahme der alten Lebensformen des preußischen Adels und ihrer klassizistisch-spartanischen Kultur durch die neuen Machthaber der Industrie. Es ist das dauernde Verdienst Emil und Walther Rathenaus, durch Behrens, dem »Hofkünstler« dieser »Großunternehmung«, dieser Utopie einer Führungsrolle der Industrie in der modernen Gesellschaft zu einer kulturellen Rechtfertigung verholfen zu haben – ein deutsches Gesamtkunstwerk einer Berliner Industriekultur.

Es ist nun sehr bezeichnend, daß Walther Rathenau die Bemühungen von Muthesius, Behrens, Naumann,

factories to light-flooded halls. The end result of the worker's toil was no longer to be cheap, "mass-produced junk"; his labor was to be given meaning by quality products. That was Werkbund ideology, which may appear terribly outmoded to most of us today.

The AEG idea of the wholeness of a new "social configuration," with large industry at the helm, concerned Walter Rathenau especially. He believed industry had a leading role to play simply because the old elite, the aristocracy, had no "support in a mechanized society." He envisioned a literal takeover by the new captains of industry of the lifestyle of the Prussian nobility and their classically Spartan culture. It is to Emil and Walther Rathenau's lasting credit that through Behrens, the "court artist" of their corporate empire, they lent cultural justification to this distant utopia of industry's guiding role in modern society.

Nevertheless, Walther Rathenau was skeptical of the efforts of Muthesius, Behrens, Naumann, Osthaus, and the Werkbund to find new forms appropriate for the products of the Industrial Age. He never tired of defending the complete autonomy of art. To him, art

Fig. 132 *"Synchron" electric clock, 1931. AEG-Berlin. Private collection.*
Abb. 132 *»Synchron« elektrische Uhr, 1931. AEG-Berlin. Privatbesitz.*

Osthaus und dem Werkbund, den Gehäusen und Produkten des Industriezeitalters einen angemessenen, neuen Formenausdruck zu verleihen, mit Mißtrauen verfolgte. Nimmermüde verteidigte er die vollkommene Zweckfreiheit der Kunst, die er nur als »hohe Kunst«, verkörpert in der Musik, gelten lassen wollte. Alle Versuche, den »Massenkram der Zweckgewerbe« künstlerischen Gestaltungsprinzipien zu unterwerfen, betrachtete er als »unerhörten Mißbrauch«. Jede rationale Planung, jedes »Zweckdenken« ziehe die Kunst »in Staub und Lärm der Alltäglichkeit«. Die Architektur wie die gewerblichen Künste waren ihm »unrettbar vernichtet durch die Mechanisierung der Produktion«.[37]

So finden wir unter dem gleichen Dache der AEG eine bewegte Diskussion über Wesen, Grenzen und Dimensionen der Gestaltungsmöglichkeiten des Menschen: hier die extremste Subjektivität eines abgehobenen Begriffs der Kunst, die es vor der modernen Welt der Mechanisierung zu schützen gilt, dort der kolossale Versuch, diese materielle Welt der Mechanisierung als eine künstlerisch geformte, ästhetisch

Fig. 131 *Peter Behrens. AEG "Elektrochronos," c. 1930. Private collection.*
Abb. 131 *Peter Behrens. Elektrische AEG-Uhr »Elektrochronos«, um 1930. Privatbesitz.*

162

Fig. 133   *Peter Behrens. AEG electric tea- and water-kettle after 1909. Private collection.*
Abb. 133   *Peter Behrens. Elektrischer AEG- Tee- und Wasserkessel, seit 1909. Privatbesitz.*

meant fine art, particularly as embodied in music. Every attempt to subject the "mass-produced junk of applied commerce" to artistic principles, he declared an "incredible abuse." All rational planning, all "utilitarian thinking" pulled art through "the dust and noise of banality." Both architecture and the applied arts, said Rathenau, would be "irrevocably destroyed by the mechanization of production."[37]

Thus under the roof of the AEG we find a heated debate on the nature, limitations, and potentialities of human creativity, a debate whose implications have lost none of their force: on the one hand, the extreme subjectivity of a transcendent concept of art, which had to be protected from modern mechanization; on the other, a colossal attempt to gain control of this materialistic, mechanized world by shaping it artistically, organizing it rationally, ordering it aesthetically. To quote Nietzsche, the issue was no less than "reshaping the world in order to be able to stand living in it."

gestaltete und rational geordnete zu bewältigen. Es ging, um Nietzsche zu zitieren, um eine »Umformung der Welt, um es in ihr auszuhalten«.

Anmerkungen

1 Zu Ludwig Hoffmann siehe seine: Neubauten der Stadt Berlin, 12 Bde. (Berlin 1902 ff.); Fritz Stahl, Ludwig Hoffmann (Berlin 1914); Paul Westheim, Helden und Abenteurer (Berlin 1931), S. 172 ff.; Eine Neubewertung versucht Julius Posener, Berlin auf dem Wege zu einer neuen Architektur (München 1979), S. 107 ff.; Ludwig Hoffmann, Lebenserinnerungen eines Architekten, hrsg. von Wolfgang Schäche (Berlin 1983); Ludwig Hoffmann in Berlin, Die Wiederentdeckung eines Architekten, hrsg. von Hans J. Reichhardt und Wolfgang Schäche (Berlin 1986).
2 Paul Westheim, Helden und Abenteurer (Berlin 1931), S. 173.
3 Walter Curt Behrendt, Alfred Messel (Berlin 1911); M. Rapsilber, Alfred Messel (Berlin 1912); Adolf Behne, »Die Museumsinsel – eine Tragödie Berliner Städtebaus«, in: Das Neue Frankfurt 9, (1930, Nachdruck Dresden 1984, S. 366 ff.).
4 Zur Villa Oppenheim, mit knapper Not dem Abriß entgangen und von der »Neuen Heimat« umzingelt, siehe: Behrendt, op. cit., S. 115, 117, 123. Der verschwundene berühmte Garten war von Messel entworfen und mit Ratschlägen von Lichtwark ausgeführt, siehe Alfred Lichtwark, Briefe an Max Liebermann, hrsg. von Carl Schellenberg (Hamburg, 1947), S. 335 f., ferner Lichtwarks Briefe an die Kommission für die Verwaltung der Hamburger Kunsthalle, Bd. XIX, 1911 (Hamburg 1919), S. 85, 124 f.
5 Siehe J. Posener, S. 375, 479.
6 Adolf Behne, Der moderne Zweckbau (Berlin 1926), S. 20.
7 Otto Wagner, Baukunst unserer Zeit (Wien 1895).
8 Hermann Muthesius, Stilarchitektur und Baukunst (Mülheim 1901), S. 43.
9 Zum Reichstag siehe Michael S. Cullen, Der Reichstag, Die Geschichte eines Monumentes (Berlin 1983); ders. und Wolfgang Volz, Christo, Der Reichstag, Suhrkamp Taschenbuch 960 (Frankfurt 1984), S. 146–156, darin: Tilmann Buddensieg, »Der Reichstag und die Künstler«, geschrieben 1977 zur Unterstützung der Verhüllung des Baues durch Christo, die für 1988 endlich zu erwarten ist.
10 H. Albrecht, »Wohnungsfürsorge«, in: Soziale Kultur und Volkswohlfahrt während der ersten 25 Regierungsjahre Kaiser Wilhelm II., ein Gedenkwerk (Berlin 1913), S. 793. Früher aber: H. Albrecht, Das Arbeiterwohnhaus mit Entwürfen von A. Messel (Berlin 1896).
11 R. Eberstadt, Handbuch des Wohnungswesens und der Wohnungsfrage (Jena 1917³), S. 296.

Fig. 134   *Peter Behrens. AEG electric tea- and water-kettle, after 1909. Private collection.*

Abb. 134   *Peter Behrens. Elektrischer AEG- Tee- und Wasserkessel, seit 1909. Privatbesitz.*

Fig. 135   *Peter Behrens. AEG table fan, c. 1908. Private col-lection.*

Abb. 135   *Peter Behrens. AEG-Tischventilator, um 1908. Pri-vatbesitz.*

Footnotes

1 On Ludwig Hoffmann, see his own *Neubauten der Stadt Berlin,* 12 vols. (Berlin, 1902); Fritz Stahl, *Ludwig Hoffmann* (Berlin, 1914); Paul Westheim, *Helden und Abenteurer* (Berlin, 1931), pp. 172 ff.; the reassessment by Julius Posener, *Berlin auf dem Wege zu einer neuen Architektur* (Munich, 1979), pp. 107 ff.; Ludwig Hoffmann, *Lebenserinnerungen eines Architekten,* ed. by Wolfgang Schäche (Berlin, 1983); and *Ludwig Hoffmann in Berlin, Die Wiederentdeckung eines Architekten,* ed. by Hans J. Reichhardt and Wolfgang Schäche (Berlin, 1986).

2 Westheim, *op. cit.,* p. 173.

3 Walter Curt Behrendt, *Alfred Messel* (Berlin, 1911); M. Rapsilber, *Alfred Messel* (Berlin, 1912); Adolf Behne, "Die Museumsinsel – eine Tragödie Berliner Städtebaus," *Das Neue Frankfurt,* 9 (1930, reprinted, Dresden, 1984), pp. 366 ff.

4 For the Oppenheim Residence, which escaped destruction at the last minute and is closely surrounded by new structures, see Behrendt, *op. cit.,* pp. 115, 117, 123. The garden, designed by Messel with suggestions by Alfred Lichtwark, has disappeared; see Alfred Lichtwark, *Briefe an Max Liebermann,* ed. by Carl Schellenberg (Hamburg, 1947), pp. 335–336. See also Lichtwark's *Briefe an die Kommission für die Verwaltung der Hamburger Kunsthalle,* vol. 19, 1911 (Hamburg, 1919), pp. 85, 124 f.

5 See Posener, *op. cit.,* pp. 375, 479.

6 Adolf Behne, *Der moderne Zweckbau* (Berlin, 1926), p. 20.

7 Otto Wagner, *Baukunst unserer Zeit* (Vienna, 1895).

8 Hermann Muthesius, *Stilarchitektur und Baukunst* (Mülheim, 1901), p. 43.

9 On the Reichstag Building, see Michael S. Cullen, *Der Reichstag, Die Geschichte eines Monumentes* (Berlin, 1983); Michael S. Cullen and Wolfgang Volz, *Christo: Der Reichstag,* Suhrkamp Taschenbuch 960 (Frankfurt, 1984), pp. 146-156, including Tilmann Buddensieg, "Der Reichstag und die Künstler," written in 1977 in support of Christo's project for the wrapping of the Reichstag, which seems finally to be scheduled for 1988.

10 H. Albrecht, "Wohnungsfürsorge," in *Soziale Kultur und Volkswohlfahrt während der ersten 25 Regierungsjahre Kaiser Wilhelm II, ein Gedenkwerk* (Berlin, 1913), p. 793. Also Albrecht's earlier discussion, *Das Arbeiterwohnhaus mit Entwürfen von A. Messel* (Berlin, 1896).

11 R. Eberstadt, *Handbuch des Wohnungswesens und der Wohnungsfrage,* 3rd edition (Jena, 1917), p. 296.

12 On this, see Tilmann Buddensieg, "Messel und Taut," *Archithese,* 12 (1974), pp. 23 ff.; reprinted in the Bruno Taut issue of *Neue Heimat, Monatshefte für neuzeitlichen Wohnungs- und Städtebau,* 5 (1980). And, in the same issue, Rolf Bothe, "Die Siedlung Schillerpark in Berlin Wedding von Bruno Taut," pp. 38 ff.; also Posener, *op. cit.,* pp. 343 ff. See also the fundamental study by Nicholas Bullock and James Read, *The Movement for Housing Reform in Germany and France 1840–1914* (Cambridge 1985), pp. 131 ff.

12 Zu diesem Aspekt siehe T. Buddensieg, »Messel und Taut«, in: Archithese 12, (1974), S. 23 ff., abgedruckt im Bruno Taut-Heft der Neue Heimat, Monatshefte für neuzeitlichen Wohnungs- und Städtebau 5, (1980), darin auch: Rolf Bothe, »Die Siedlung Schillerpark in Berlin Wedding von Bruno Taut«, S. 38 ff.; J. Posener, op cit., S. 343 ff. Ferner grundlegend: Nicholas Bullock und James Read, *The Movement for Housing Reform in Germany and France 1840–1914* (Cambridge 1985), S. 131 ff.

13 Siehe Berlin und seine Bauten, Teil IV, Band B (Berlin 1974), Nr. 603, S. 119 ff. Hier auch Ernst Heinrichs grundlegende Einleitung, S. 39 ff.

14 Friedrich Nietzsche, »Über Wahrheit und Lüge im außermoralischen Sinn« (1873), in: Gesammelte Werke, (München 1922), Bd. 6, S. 88, 90.

15 Tilmann Buddensieg, »To build as one will... Schinkel's Notions on the Freedom of Building«, in: Daidalos 7 (1983), S. 93 ff.

16 Siehe jetzt Gottfried Riemann, Karl Friedrich Schinkel, Reise nach England, Schottland und Paris im Jahre 1826 (München 1986), S. 168.

17 Friedrich Nietzsche, Unzeitgemäße Betrachtungen, Erstes Stück, 1.

18 Zu den Vergleichsbeispielen siehe: Eva Börsch-Supan, Berliner Baukunst nach Schinkel, 1840–1870 (Berlin 1977), Abb. 53, 209, 210. Das Vorbild ist offenbar ein Mietshaus von M. Gropius und Schmieden um 1875 am Lützowplatz 11, siehe Janos Frecot u. a., Berlin im Abriß, (Berlinische Galerie 1981), Abb. S. 238.

19 Bruno Taut, »Genossenschaftsarchitektur«, in: Wohnungswirtschaft (1926), S. 13; ders., »Von der architektonischen Schönheit des Serienbaues«, in: Der Aufbau 1 (1926), S. 106.

20 Tilmann Buddensieg, in: Frankfurter Allgemeine Zeitung (30. 4. 1977) und: Neue Heimat, Monatshefte für neuzeitlichen Wohnungs- und Städtebau 5 (1980), S. 20 ff.

21 Zitat in: T. Buddensieg, Loc. cit., (Anm. 12), aus: Die Neue Stadt (Frankfurt 1933), S. 270 f.; El Lissitzky 1929, Bauwelt Fundamente 14 (1965), S. 203 f.

22 Siehe A. Sigrist, Das Buch vom Bauen (Berlin 1930), S. 63 ff.

23 Siehe Anm. 20 und 21. Zu Britz und den anderen Berliner Siedlungen der Weimarer Zeit siehe Kurt Junghanns, Bruno Taut 1880–1938 (Berlin 1983[2]); Lieselotte Ungers, Die Suche nach einer neuen Wohnform. Siedlungen der zwanziger Jahre damals und heute (Stuttgart 1983); Norbert Huse, Hrsg., *Siedlungen der zwanziger Jahre heute* (Ausstellung Bauhaus-Archiv, Berlin 1984).

24 Zitate aus: Ernst Bloch, Geist der Utopie (zweite Fassung 1923), Werkausgabe Suhrkamp, Bd. 3 (Frankfurt 1977), S. 294 ff.

25 Siehe Anna Teut, Architektur im 3. Reich (Berlin 1967), S. 126.

26 Brief Messels an Herwarth Walden vom 12. 10. 1908, »Sturm« – Archiv, im Schiller-Archiv Marbach.

27 Siehe Buddensieg, Industriekultur, S. 22 ff.

28 Peter Behrens, Nachruf auf Messel, in: Frankfurter Zeitung (6. 4. 1909).

166

13 See *Berlin und seine Bauten,* part 4, vol. B (Berlin, 1974), no. 603, pp. 119 ff. Also the illuminating preface to the same volume by Ernst Heinrich, pp. 39 ff.

14 Friedrich Nietzsche, "Über Wahrheit und Lüge im aussermoralischen Sinn" (1873), in *Gesammelte Werke* (Munich, 1922), vol. 6, pp. 88, 90.

15 Tilmann Buddensieg, "To build as one will . . . Schinkel's Notions on the Freedom of Building," *Daidalos,* 7 (1983), pp. 93 ff.

16 See now Gottfried Riemann, *Karl Friedrich Schinkel, Reise nach England, Schottland und Paris im Jahre 1826* (Munich 1986), p. 168.

17 Friedrich Nietzsche, *Unzeitgemässe Betrachtungen,* Part One, 1.

18 For the examples given in comparison, see Eva Börsch-Supan, *Berliner Baukunst nach Schinkel, 1840–1870* (Berlin, 1977), figs. 53, 209, 210. The model was apparently an apartment house by Martin Gropius and Schmieden, c. 1875, at Lützowplatz 11. See Janos Frecot, et al., *Berlin im Abriss* (Berlinische Galerie, 1981), fig. p. 238.

19 Bruno Taut, "Genossenschaftsarchitektur," *Wohnungswirtschaft* (1926), p. 33; Bruno Taut, "Von der architektonischen Schönheit des Serienbaues," *Der Aufbau,* 1 (1926), p. 106.

20 Tilmann Buddensieg, in *Frankfurter Allgemeine Zeitung,* April 30, 1977, and *Neue Heimat, Monatshefte für neuzeitlichen Wohnungs- und Städtebau,* 5 (1980), pp. 20 ff.

21 Quotation in: Buddensieg, *op. cit.* (note 12), from *Die Neue Stadt* (Frankfurt, 1933), pp. 270 f.; El Lissitzky 1929, *Bauwelt Fundamente,* 14 (1965), pp. 203 f.

22 See A. Sigrist, *Das Buch vom Bauen* (Berlin, 1930), pp. 63 ff.

23 See notes 20 and 21. On Britz and the other Berlin complexes of the Weimar period, see Kurt Junghanns, *Bruno Taut, 1880–1938* (Berlin, 2nd edn., 1983); Lieselotte Ungers, *Die Suche nach einer neuen Wohnform. Siedlungen der zwanziger Jahre damals und heute* (Stuttgart, 1983); and Norbert Huse, ed., *Siedlungen der zwanziger Jahre heute* (Ausstellung Bauhaus Archiv, Berlin, 1984).

24 Quotation from Ernst Bloch, *Geist der Utopie,* 2nd edn., 1923, *Werkausgabe Suhrkamp,* vol. 3 (Frankfurt, 1977), pp. 294 ff.

25 See Anna Teut, *Architektur im 3. Reich* (Berlin, 1967), p. 126.

26 Letter from Messel to Herwarth Walden dated October 12, 1908, "Sturm"-Archiv, in Schiller-Archiv, Marbach.

27 See Tilmann Buddensieg in collaboration with Henning Rogge, *Industriekultur: Peter Behrens und die AEG, 1907–14* (Berlin, 1979), pp. 27 ff; translated by Iain Boyd Whyte, *Industriekultur: Peter Behrens and the AEG, 1907–1914* (Cambridge, Mass., 1984, cited hereafter as *Industriekultur.*

28 Peter Behrens, Obituary for Messel in the *Frankfurter Zeitung* April 6, 1909.

29 Karl Scheffler, in *Kunst und Künstler,* 8 (1910), p. 419.

30 On these aspects, see the detailed discussion in Buddensieg, *Industriekultur.*

29 Karl Scheffler, in: Kunst und Künstler 8 (1910), S. 419.

30 Zu diesen Aspekten siehe umfassend Buddensieg, Industriekultur.

31 Ch.-E. Jeanneret, Étude sur le mouvement d'Art Décoratif en Allemagne (La Chaux-de Fonds 1912).

32 J.W. v. Goethe, Italienische Reise, ed. Herbert von Einem (München 1978[9]), S. 53.

33 Friedrich Nietzsche, Götzendämmerung, Streifzüge eines Unzeitgemässen, 11.

34 "Behrens did not seriously apply the method to other buildings. Funny. It takes quite a while before people realise what they are doing," (1968), zit. in: Fritz Neumeyer, Mies van der Rohe (Berlin 1986), S. 104. Hier auch der wichtige Hinweis, daß Mies sich als Entwerfer der kaum beachteten Hofwand der Turbinenhalle bezeichnete.

35 Buddensieg, Industriekultur, S. 32.

36 Diese Mitteilung verdanke ich meiner Doktorandin Dagmar Altgeld. Zu Karl Mey siehe Georg Wenzel, Deutsche Wirtschaftsführer (Hamburg, Berlin, Leipzig 1929), Sp. 1484 f. Zu Wagenfelds Arbeit für die Lausitzer Glaswerke siehe: Wilhelm Wagenfeld, 50 Jahre Mitarbeit in Fabriken (Ausstellung Kunstgewerbemuseum Köln, bearb. von Carl Wolfgang Schümann 1973), Nr. 81–295.

37 Buddensieg, Industriekultur, S. 63 ff.

31 Ch.-E. Jeanneret, *Étude sur le mouvement d'Art Décoratif en Allemagne* (La Chaux-de Fonds, 1912).

32 J. W. v. Goethe, *Italienische Reise,* ed. Herbert von Einem, 9th edn., Munich, 1978, p. 53.

33 Friedrich Nietzsche, *Götzendämmerung, Streifzüge eines Unzeitgemässen,* 11.

34 "Behrens did not seriously apply the method to other buildings. Funny. It takes quite a while before people realize what they are doing" (1968), quoted in Fritz Neumeyer, *Mies van der Rohe* (Berlin, 1986), p. 104. This book also contains an important reference to Mies's statement that he designed the back (courtyard) wall of the turbine factory, which has attracted little notice.

35 Buddensieg, *Industriekultur,* p. 34.

36 This information I owe to a student of mine, Dagmar Altgeld. For Karl Mey, see Georg Wenzel, *Deutsche Wirtschaftsführer* (Hamburg, Berlin, and Leipzig, 1929), col. 1484 f. On Wagenfeld's work for the Lausitzer Glaswerke, see Carl Wolfgang Schümann, *Wilhelm Wagenfeld, 50 Jahre Mitarbeit in Fabriken* (Ausstellung Kunstgewerbemuseum, Cologne, 1973), nos. 81–295.

37 Buddensieg, *Industriekultur,* pp. 69 ff.

Fig. 136   *Jan Tschichold. Poster for "Laster der Menschheit,"*
1927. SMPK Kunstbibliothek, Berlin.

Abb. 136   *Jan Tschichold. Plakat für »Laster der*
Menschheit«, 1927. SMPK Kunstbibliothek, Berlin.

Michael Esser

Spaces in Motion: Remarks on Set Design in the German Silent Film

German film architecture of the 1920s was a product of the inflation that followed the First World War. Nothing could have corresponded more perfectly to banknotes successively overprinted with ever more vertiginous sums than locomotives made of plywood or sunsets in plaster of Paris and tinfoil; behind studio doors, everyday experiences found expression in a world of shams, mock-ups, and crazily out-of-kilter facades. Quite naturally, the production of moving pictures was concentrated in and around Berlin – where the most beautiful illusions shone behind plate-glass windows, where boulevards whispered of the pleasures of the night, where manufacturing and commerce determined the hectic pace of life.[1]

Being inseparably connected with modern technology as well as with the national economy, cinema was a new art form with no need to search for the zeitgeist of the era; it was its expression. Cinema had an existence that was independent of the traditional arts, and it was eagerly taken up by the artistic avant-garde. "A new rhythm, a new motion seized the world," Erich Mendelsohn wrote in his manifesto, *Dynamik und Funktion*. "Mold art out of the actual assumption, mass and light out of the inconceivable space." Mendelsohn's programmatic statements were undoubtedly influenced by the spirit of cinema and by the ideas of such early set designers as Hermann Warm, Erich Kettelhut, Robert Herlth, Franz Schroedter, and the well-known Hans Poelzig, designer of the sets for Paul Wegener's *Golem*.

Das Cabinet des Dr. Caligari

Germany, 1919–20
Directed by Robert Wiene
Script by Carl Mayer and Hans Janowitz
Photography by Willy Hameister
Sets by Walter Röhrig, Walter Reimann and Hermann Warm
With Werner Krauss, Conrad Veidt, Lil Dagover, et al.

Michael Esser

Räume in Bewegung: Einige Hinweise zur Architektur des deutschen Stummfilms

Die deutsche Filmarchitektur ist eine Blüte der Inflationszeit. Nichts hätte den mit immer schwindelerregenderen Beträgen überstempelten Geldscheinen genauer entsprechen können als Eisenbahnlokomotiven aus Sperrholz oder Sonnenuntergänge aus Gips und Stanniol; hinter den Toren der Ateliers fanden die alltäglichen Eindrücke ihren Ausdruck in einer Welt der Vorspiegelungen, Fälschungen und schiefen Ebenen. Selbstverständlich konzentrierten sich die Produktionsstätten der bewegten Bilder dort, wo illuminierte Schaufenster den schönen Schein propagierten, wo nächtliche Boulevards von halbseidenen Attraktionen flüsterten, wo die Warenzirkulation das hektische Tempo bestimmte: in und um Berlin.[1]

Das Kino hatte es nicht nötig, nach dem Ausdruck der neuen Zeit zu suchen: es war Ausdruck der neuen Zeit. Entstanden an der Schwelle zum 20. Jahrhundert, war es untrennbar verbunden mit der modernen Technologie und Ökonomie. Gerade weil es in seinen ersten Jahren die traditionellen Künste ignorierte und die Tradition der Künste, konnte es zum Maßstab werden für die künstlerische Avantgarde. »Ein neuer Rhythmus erfaßt die Welt, eine neue Bewegung«, schrieb Erich Mendelsohn in seinem Manifest »Dynamik und Funktion«.

»Formt aus den realen Voraussetzungen die Kunst, aus Masse und Licht den unfaßbaren Raum...« Die programmatischen Erklärungen der zeitgenössischen Moderne sind unbestreitbar beeinflußt vom Geist des Kinos und den Ideen der Bühnenbildner Hermann Warm, Erich Kettelhut, Robert Herlth, Franz Schroedter und des bekannten Hans Poelzig, der die Kulissen für Paul Wegeners *Golem* entwarf.

Das Cabinet des Dr. Caligari

Deutschland 1919/1920
Regie: Robert Wiene
Buch: Carl Mayer, Hans Janowitz
Kamera: Willy Hameister
Bauten: Walter Röhrig, Walter Reimann, Hermann Warm
Mit Werner Krauß, Conrad Veidt, Lil Dagover u. a.

Fig. 137   *Hermann Warm. Design for Alan's bedroom "Das Cabinet des Dr. Caligari," 1920. Colored pencil. Stiftung Deutsche Kinemathek, Berlin.*

Abb. 137   *Hermann Warm. Entwurf für Alans Zimmer »Das Cabinet des Dr. Caligari«, 1920. Farbstift. Stiftung Deutsche Kinemathek, Berlin.*

The Expressionist axioms compress reality to essentials, concentrated appearances. Expressionism as a style is perfectly suited to the film world and its figures, its hallucinations and weird happenings. It lends everything a ghostly, nightmarish effect.[2]   *Hermann Warm*

With *Das Cabinet des Dr. Caligari*, a morality play about a demonic psychiatrist who makes use of a somnambulist to commit grisly murders, German filmmaking demonstrated what it had learned from the French director Méliès and his fantastic journeys to the moon: how to evoke the reality of dreams cinematically *(figs. 137–138)*. With shadowy images painted on the sets, the interiors in *Caligari* are infused with dream-fears

»Die expressionistischen Axiome komprimieren die Wirklichkeit, die Realistik, so daß nur das Wesentliche konzentriert zur Erscheinung kommt. Der Expressionismus als Stil dient am besten der Welt und den Figuren des Filmes, ihren Halluzinationen, sowie den absonderlichen Geschehnissen. So erhält alles eine gespenstisch-alptraumhafte Wirkung.« (Hermann Warm)[2]

Mit der Moritatengeschichte vom dämonischen Irrenarzt, der eines Somnambulen zur Ausführung schrecklicher Mordtaten sich bedient, mit dem *Cabinet des Dr. Caligari* demonstriert 1919/1920 das deutsche Kino, was es vom Franzosen Méliès und seinen phantastischen Mondreisen gelernt hat: Die Wirklichkeit des Traumes ist sein Vorbild *(Abb. 137–138)*. Die

Fig. 138   *Hermann Warm. Design for roof tops, "Das Cabinet des Dr. Caligari," 1920. Colored pencil. Stiftung Deutsche Kinemathek, Berlin.*

Abb. 138   *Hermann Warm. Entwurf für die Dächer »Das Cabinet des Dr. Caligari«, 1920. Farbstift. Stiftung Deutsche Kinemathck, Berlin.*

that floodlights are no longer capable of banning from the bedroom.

> The room in threatening obscurity – nightmarish, the shadows like bats' wings, deep blacks in the corners. With wedge-shaped windows thrown wide open, behind them moonlight, whose rays, almost dagger-sharp themselves, point to the bed. And cast an accent of garish light on the wall.[3]

With *Caligari*, a film architect liberated architecture from its static function and a film designer liberated the sets from their decorative function. All that counted now was cinematic effect; only within the cinematic discourse does film architecture have its function.

Ängste erhalten ihre Bilder, und kein Scheinwerferlicht kann mehr die Schrecken aus dem Wohnzimmer bannen; denn die Schatten sind den Kulissen aufgemalt.

»Der Raum im drohenden Dunkel – alptraumhaft, die Schatten wie von Fledermausflügeln, tiefe Schwärze in den Winkeln. Mit aufgerissenen keiligen Fenstern, dahinter Mondschein, dessen Strahlen beinahe selbststechend wie Messer, hinweisend auf das Bett. An die Wand einen grellen Lichtakzent werfend.« (Hermann Warm)[3]

Mit dem *Cabinet des Dr. Caligari* befreit der Filmarchitekt die Architektur von ihrer statischen Funktion, befreit der Filmbildner das Bühnenbild von seiner dekorativen Funktion. Entscheidend ist einzig und allein der Effekt im Kino, nur im filmischen Diskurs hat Filmarchitektur ihre Funktion.

Der Golem, wie er in die Welt kam

Germany, 1920
Directed by Paul Wegener
Script by Paul Wegener and Henrik Galeen
Photography by Karl Freund
Sets by Hans Poelzig
With Paul Wegener, Albert Steinrück, Lyda Salmo-nova, et al.

Hans Poelzig's Gothic-style ghetto for *Der Golem*, with its tortuously twisting lanes, its black gaping portals, narrow stairwells, and mysteriously shadowed bays, exudes that occult and mystical mood without which the clay colossus brought to life would not convince when he comes on the scene *(fig. 139)*. Poelzig's Jewish quarter encompassed an entire world, a hermetic world, which, according to the story, the Golem is meant to protect, but which he instead wants to destroy. The film itself, however, reveals something else: that the streets are too steep for the actor Paul Wegener's clumsy clay feet, the ornament too delicate and intricate for his harsh gesticulations. The decor clashes with the acting, and for split seconds, cinematic reality is suspended. Wegener's cinematic renditions of architecture and his settings for the action on occasion can dominate the actors' interpretations. Out of this, Wegener develops the actors' conflicts.

Die Nibelungen

Part One: *Siegfried*
Part Two: *Kriemhilds Rache*
Germany, 1923–24
Directed by Fritz Lang
Script by Thea von Harbou
Photography by Carl Hoffmann and Günther Rittau
Sets by Otto Hunte, Erich Kettelhut, and Karl Vollbrecht
With Margarethe Schön, Paul Richter, Rudolf Klein-Rogge, et al.

What can emerge from mathematics, technology and imagination will become evident in the Nibelung film, in its northern lights and in its petrified dwarves, whose mouths are still alive and open in a scream, while their bodies have already turned to stone.[4]   *Fritz Lang*

Lang treated *Das Lied der Nibelungen* as an epic poem; instead of shooting the story, he invented images that presupposed a knowledge of the saga. Every trace of immediacy was eliminated; stationary camera, ornamented rooms, stylized costumes, the

Der Golem, wie er in die Welt kam

Deutschland 1920
Regie: Paul Wegener
Buch: Paul Wegener, Henrik Galeen
Kamera: Karl Freund
Bauten: Hans Poelzig
Mit Paul Wegener, Albert Steinrück, Lyda Salmonova u. a.

Hans Poelzigs gotisch-spitzgieblige Ghettostadt für *Der Golem, wie er in die Welt kam* verbreitet mit ihren winkligen Gassen, dunklen Torbögen, schmalen Treppen und geheimnisvollen Erkern jene mystisch-düstere Stimmung, die das Erscheinen eines zum Leben erweckten Tonkolosses erst glaubhaft macht *(Abb. 139)*. Dies jüdische Städele umfaßt eine ganze Welt, in sich geschlossen; und diese Welt, davon handelt die Geschichte, soll der Golem schützen, diese Welt will der Golem zerstören. Was aber in dem Film auch zu sehen ist: Die Straßen sind zu steil für die dicken Klotzsohlen des Schauspielers Paul Wegener, die Verzierungen eines Brunnen zu filigran für seine derben Gesten. Der Dekor widersteht der Darstellung; so klafft für Momente ein Riß in der filmischen Realität. Die Bauten als filmische Darstellung von Architektur und Schauplatz können die dargestellten Figuren beherrschen: Auch daraus entwickeln Paul Wegeners Filme ihre Konflikte.

Die Nibelungen

Teil 1: Siegfried
Teil 2: Kriemhilds Rache
Deutschland 1923/1924
Regie: Fritz Lang
Buch: Thea von Harbou
Kamera: Carl Hoffmann, Günther Rittau
Bauten: Otto Hunte, Erich Kettelhut, Karl Vollbrecht
Mit Margarethe Schön, Paul Richter, Rudolf Klein-Rogge u. a.

»Was aus Mathematik, Technik und Phantasie entstehen kann, das wird im Nibelungenfilm das Nordlicht zeigen und die versteinerten Zwerge, deren lebendiger Mund noch zum Schrei geöffnet ist, während der Körper schon zu Stein erstarrt.« (Fritz Lang)[4]

Lang behandelt das Nibelungenlied als Epos; statt es zu verfilmen erfindet er Bilder, die das Überlieferte voraussetzen. Jeder Anschein von Gegenwärtigkeit wird entfernt, der feste Kamerastandort, die ornamentalisierten Räume, die stilisierten Kostüme, die rhythmisierten Bewegungen der Schauspieler weisen auf

Fig. 139   *Hans Poelzig. Scene from "Der Golem, wie er in die Welt kam," 1920. Street in the Golem's village. SMPK Kunstbibliothek, Berlin.*

Abb. 139   *Hans Poelzig. Szene aus »Der Golem, wie er in die Welt kam«, 1920. Gasse in der Golemstadt. SMPK Kunstbibliothek, Berlin.*

Fig. 140   *Erich Kettelhut. Design for scene of Hagen and Volker keeping night watch, "Die Nibelungen", 1924. Pencil and pastel. Stiftung Deutsche Kinemathek, Berlin.*

Abb. 140   *Erich Kettelhut. Entwurf für die Szene: Hagen und Volker halten Nachtwache, »Die Nibelungen«, 1924. Bleistift und Pastell. Stiftung Deutsche Kinemathek, Berlin.*

actors' exaggeratedly rhythmic movements, all emphasize the fictional nature of the tale and point out that this is a narration in the historic past tense.

On the lots, we began building the forest. I say "building" advisedly, because this was no naturally grown forest but a cathedral, created by enigmatic powers, whose tree-trunk columns, over two meters in diameter, extended limbless into obscurity above. The roof of foliage, never visible, let an occasional swath of sunlight through into the shadows. We had long discussions about this forest during meetings with the director. It was clear from the start that it had to be a stylized forest, so as not to destroy the visual unity of the sequences. I consider this one of the first rules that every designer of film sets should take to heart – never agree to a stylistic inconsistency.[5]   *Erich Kettelhut*

das Ausgedachte, auf das Erzählen in der Vergangenheitsform.

»Auf dem Gelände wurde mit dem Bau des Waldes begonnen. Ich sage bewußt Bau, denn dieser Wald war nicht gewachsene Natur, sondern ein von geheimnisvollen Kräften erschaffener Dom, dessen über zwei Meter im Durchmesser betragende Raumpfeiler sich astlos in ein dämmriges Dunkel reckten. Einzelnen breiten Sonnenbahnen gestattete das nie sichtbare Laubdach, das Dunkel zu erhellen. Über diesen Wald ist bei Regiesitzungen lange diskutiert worden. Von vornherein war klar, daß es sich nur um einen stilisierten Wald handeln könne, um die Einheit der Bildfolge nicht zu zerstören. Ich halte das für eine der obersten Regeln, von denen sich jeder Gestalter einer Filmausstattung leiten lassen sollte, nie einem Stilbruch zuzustimmen.« (Erich Kettelhut)[5]

Fig. 141 *Otto Hunte, Erich Kettelhut, Karl Vollbrecht. Scene from "Die Nibelungen," 1924. Kriemhild with the dead Siegfried. Stiftung Deutsche Kinemathek, Berlin.*

Abb. 141 *Otto Hunte, Erich Kettelhut, Karl Vollbrecht. Szene aus »Die Nibelungen«, 1924. Kriemhild mit dem toten Siegfried. Stiftung Deutsche Kinemathek, Berlin.*

Kettelhut's designs for *Die Nibelungen* were eclectic. The characters Volker and Hagen hold their nightwatch before a circular structure that recalls Poelzig's or Rudolf Steiner's cavernous earth-architecture *(fig. 140)*; the interior spaces might have been borrowed from Bernhard Hoetger's pseudo-prehistoric mead halls; Brunhild's castle is a reference to the crystal domes that Bruno Taut envisioned in the Alps. These diverse components merge only in the film medium itself, where Fritz Lang's "architectural" narrative style[6] combines them with other elements – screenplay, acting, lighting, composition, and framing – into the structure of a plot. The decor in Lang's films writes the laws to which the characters are subject, laws they are unable to decipher and which thus seem to be emanations of fate – to the characters, if not to the viewers, who can match the wild, chaotic actions of the Huns

Kettelhuts Entwürfe für *Die Nibelungen* sind eklektizistisch. Volker und Hagen halten Nachtwache vor einem an Poelzigs oder Steiners erdentwachsenen Höhlen erinnernden Rundbau *(Abb. 139)*, die Innenräume könnten Bernhard Hoetgers prähistorisierenden Wohnhallen entlehnt sein, Brunhildens Burg zitiert Bruno Tauts alpine Kristalldome. Erst der Film schließt die Einzelteile zusammen, Fritz Langs ›architektonische‹ Erzählweise [6] fügt sie mit den anderen Elementen (Drehbuch, Darsteller, Beleuchtung, Bildausschnitt) zur Konstruktion einer Geschichte. Der Dekor in den Fritz Lang-Filmen gestaltet die Gesetze, denen die Figuren unterworfen sind; Gesetze, die sie nicht erkennen können und die ihnen daher schicksalhaft erscheinen; Gesetze, die sich vom Zuschauer jedoch entziffern lassen: Dem wilden, chaotischen Treiben der Hunnen entsprechen die gedrungenen, primitiven Erdhöhlen;

with their primitive underground hovels, or see that the courtly manners of the Nibelungs' castle are governed by austere arches and columns, spacious halls, and the geometric patterns on the roof-beams *(fig. 141)*. Every detail of Lang's sets has its visual function.

During the early years of moving-pictures, scenery had to be painted in tones of gray. By 1920, however, it was already possible for cameramen like Carl Hoffmann, Fritz Arno Wagner, or Karl Freund to capture subtle nuances with black-and-white photography, and color sets such as those by Erich Kettelhut became commonplace. These color sets not only animated actors and directors; they made use of film's capabilities and provided a much broader range of contrasts.

Faust

Eine Deutsche Volkssage
Germany, 1925–26
Directed by Friedrich Wilhelm Murnau
Script by Hans Kyser
Photography by Carl Hoffmann
Sets by Robert Herlth and Walter Röhrig
With Gösta Ekman, Emil Jannings, Camilla Horn, et al.

> I go on the premise that the concept of the film image is not so much controversial as simply unknown; after all, this image is what we have in mind when we talk about film architecture. The architecture itself is nonexistent as such, just as everything that happens in front of the camera during shooting is in a strict sense nonexistent, since it merely serves as a medium for the projected image. This holds just as much for the space as for the action, and even for the actors themselves. That is the reason why film sets, as technically real and logical as they may look in the studio, can be convincing and meaningful only if the filmmaker's planning eye designs and employs them as they must appear during the actual projection, on the screen. So there can be no sets as such, but only sets imagined for planning purposes, whether this plan be realistic, romantic, or surreal in character.[7]
>
> *Robert Herlth*

In their sketches for Murnau's *Faust,* Robert Herlth and Walter Röhrig conceived not so much architectural as pictorial spaces *(figs. 142–144)*. There is no trace in their drawings of the solidity of the studio sets that were constructed from them. Their effect derives from great smudged swaths of graphite blacks and a dissolution of definite contour lines in favor of subtle chiaroscuro gradations. Everything in them aims at creating a mood

die höfischen Beziehungen in der Nibelungenburg dagegen werden von strengen Bögen und Pfeilern, von weiten Hallen und den geometrischen Mustern der Deckenbalken reguliert *(Abb. 141)*. Jedes Ausstattungsteil bei Fritz Lang hat seine visuelle Funktion.

Um 1920 bereits bedeutete es für Kameramänner wie Carl Hoffmann, Fritz Arno Wagner oder Karl Freund kein Problem, zarteste Nuancierungen mit Hilfe der Schwarzweiß-Photographie abzubilden. In den allerersten Jahren des Films mußten die Kulissen in Grautönen angestrichen werden, um böse Überraschungen bei der Umsetzung von Farbwerten in die Schwarzweiß-Skala zu vermeiden; für den avancierten Stummfilm dagegen waren die farbig ausgeführten Dekors eines Erich Kettelhut keine Besonderheit. Farbige sets belebten die Imaginationskraft der Darsteller und Regisseure; vor allem jedoch boten sie die Möglichkeit, den Kontrastumfang des materiellen Filmträgers in seiner ganzen Breite auszunutzen.

Faust

Eine deutsche Volkssage
Deutschland 1925/1926
Regie: Friedrich Wilhelm Murnau
Buch: Hans Kyser
Kamera: Carl Hoffmann
Bauten: Robert Herlth, Walter Röhrig
Mit Gösta Ekman, Emil Jannings, Camilla Horn u. a.

> »Ich gehe von der Voraussetzung aus, daß der Begriff des Filmbildes nicht so sehr umstritten als unbekannt ist; denn nur um dieses kann es sich ja handeln, wenn von einer Architektur die Rede ist. Sie ist als solche gar nicht existent, wie ja alles, was vor der Kamera im Prozeß der Arbeit geschieht, nicht existent im eigentlichen Sinne ist, sondern lediglich als Medium für die Projektion dient. Das gilt für den Raum sowohl als für das Spiel, ja für die Darsteller selber. Filmbauten sind daher, wie sehr sie sich technisch real und deutlich im Studio präsentieren mögen, nur dann möglich oder sinnvoll, wenn sie vom planenden Auge des Filmschaffenden so gestaltet und verwendet werden, wie sie im Ablauf der Projektion erscheinen müssen. Es kann also keine Kulisse als solche, sondern nur eine für die Planung gedichtete geben, ob sie nun realistisch, romantisch oder surreal ist.« (Robert Herlth)[7]

Robert Herlth und Walter Röhrig entwerfen in ihren Skizzen für Murnaus *Faust* weniger einen Architektur- als einen Bildraum *(Abb. 142–144)*. Nichts ist in ihren Zeichnungen zu spüren von der Materialität der Atelierbauten, denen sie doch als Vorlage dienen sollen. Ihre Wirkung beziehen sie aus den breit hingewischten

– a mood that is characteristic of F. W. Murnau's films.[8] No viewer who is familiar with Murnau's style will have difficulty in detecting in these drawings the compositional elements of diagonal and circle, which dominated the visual thinking of a director indebted to Renaissance and Romantic art.[9] Street and town wall block the view of the two figures in the Easter procession who were barred from church; the perspective lines in the night scene on the heath converge on Mephisto's round and gnomelike face; the oval mouth of a volcano illuminates a meditative Faust.

The designs of Herlth and Röhrig are suffused with cinematic vision. By eschewing detail, they gain an evocation of motion – the motion of Faust airborne on Mephisto's cloak, in a flight over the town and mountains, past waterfalls and storm clouds, but above all, the motion of glances and gestures, creating the emotion that itself seems to call the space around the figures into being.

Graphitschwärzen und der Auflösung fester Umriß-linien zugunsten abgestufter Helldunkel-Valeurs. Alles zielt hier auf Stimmung, – auf eben jene Stimmung, die so charakteristisch ist für die Filme F. W. Murnaus.[8]

Der mit Murnaus Filmen vertraute Betrachter findet in den Blättern bereits die Kompositionselemente Diagonale und Kreis; sie prägen die bildnerische Gestaltung dieses den Werken der Renaissance und der Romantik verpflichteten Künstlers.[9] Straße und Stadtmauer durchschneiden den Blick der beiden vom Kirchenbesuch ausgeschlossenen Figuren auf die Osterprozession, die perspektivischen Fluchtlinien im nächtlichen Heidemoor weisen auf Mephistos rundliches Gnomengesicht, die ovale Vulkanöffnung beleuchtet den sinnierenden Faust.

Robert Herlths und Walter Röhrigs Arbeiten sind zutiefst von einer filmischen Sichtweise durchdrungen. Aus dem Verzicht auf das Detail gewinnen sie die Vorstellung von Bewegung: der Bewegung des flie-

Fig. 142 *Robert Herlth. Design for stairway, "Faust," 1925. Graphite. Stiftung Deutsche Kinemathek, Berlin.*

Abb. 142 *Robert Herlth. Entwürfe für eine Treppe »Faust«, 1925. Graphit. Stiftung Deutsche Kinemathek, Berlin.*

Fig. 143 *Robert Herlth and Walter Röhrig. Scene from "Faust," 1925. Mephisto in front of Gretchen's house. Stiftung Deutsche Kinemathek, Berlin.*

Fig. 143 *Robert Herlth und Walter Röhrig. Szene aus »Faust«, 1925. Mephisto vor dem Haus Gretchens. Stiftung Deutsche Kinemathek, Berlin.*

These sketches invoke a utopia, for the space they project can be fully expressed only in an entirely different medium. Only in the film, in a cinematic space defined by the director in terms of staging and montage, are movement, glance, and gesture fully realized.

Zuflucht

Germany, 1928
Directed by Carl Froelich
Script by Friedrich Raff
Photography by Gustave Preiss
Sets by Franz Schroedter
With Henny Porten, Franz Lederer, Margarete Kupfer

It goes without saying that interiors, particularly in historical films, should conform to the conditions of their period in every detail. Even more important, however, is that the character of a film's story be expressed in the sets themselves. The motifs of the

genden Faust auf Mephistos Mantel, des von der Kamerafahrt suggerierten Fluges über Stadt und Berge, vorbei an Wasserfällen und Wetterwolken; vor allem jedoch der Bewegung des Blickes und der Geste, der Emotion, die den Raum um die Figuren erst hervorzurufen scheint.

Diese Skizzen beschwören eine Utopie, denn sie entwerfen einen Raum, dem nur ein anderes künstlerisches Verfahren Ausdruck geben kann. Erst im Film, in dem vom Regisseur mittels der Inszenierung und der Montage beschriebenen Filmraum, werden Bewegung, Blick und Geste realisiert.

Zuflucht

Deutschland 1928
Regie: Carl Froelich
Buch: Friedrich Raff
Kamera: Gustave Preiss
Bauten: Franz Schroedter
Mit Henny Porten, Franz Lederer, Margarete Kupfer

rooms should definitely serve to characterize, and what a person is like should become immediately and clearly evident from his surroundings. Then there is the necessity of combining the natural with the practical, to make the cameraman's work on the scene easier, especially in the case of long passages, which are generally handled by using dolly shots. This almost always involves reaching a compromise between creative ideals and construction ideas, two things that are all too often at loggerheads.[10]   *Franz Schroedter*

In *Zuflucht*, Martin, a disappointed revolutionary from the November 1919 uprising in Berlin and son of a well-to-do family, returns to his hometown after trying years in socialist Russia to find refuge with Hanne, a girl who works in a market vendor's booth.

»Selbstverständlich sollen die Räume bis in die kleinsten Einzelheiten, namentlich bei historischen Filmen, den Verhältnissen ihrer Zeit entsprechen. Vor allem aber ist es notwendig, schon in den Bauten zu einem Film den Charakter seiner Handlung zum Ausdruck zu bringen. Die Raummotive sollen unbedingt charakterisierend und die Art eines Menschen muß schon in seiner Umgebung deutlich und schnell faßbar sein. Dazu kommt die Forderung, das Natürliche mit dem Praktischen zu vereinen, um innerhalb der Bauten die Arbeit des Kameramannes – besonders im Hinblick auf lange Passagen, die in der Regel durch Fahraufnahmen bewältigt werden – zu erleichtern. Es gilt darum fast immer, einen Kompromiß zu schließen zwischen den ideell-schöpferischen und den konstruktiven Ideen, die gar zu leicht hart aufeinanderprallen.« (Franz Schroedter)[10]

Fig. 144   *Walter Röhrig. Design for a cathedral, "Faust", 1926. Pencil. Stiftung Deutsche Kinemathek, Berlin.*

Abb. 144   *Walter Röhrig. Entwurf für einen Dom »Faust«, 1926. Bleistift. Stiftung Deutsche Kinemathek, Berlin.*

Fig. 145 *Franz Schroedter. Design for waiting room, "Zuflucht," 1928. Chalk. Stiftung Deutsche Kinemathek, Berlin.*

Abb. 145 *Franz Schroedter. Entwurf für einen Warteraum »Zuflucht«, 1928. Kreide. Stiftung Deutsche Kinemathek, Berlin.*

After taking in the low doorways in the wings of a Berlin apartment building and the gray, flaking walls of its airshaft, the camera moves behind the facade to reveal a single, small room, partitioned into cubicles. A night-lodger sleeps on a shelf under the ceiling, a rabbit-hutch has been installed beside the door; there is a litter of crates, baskets, a shabby sofa, plain chairs, three beds shared by five, sometimes six, people who live, eat, wash, sleep, make love, and, of course, fight here.

The rear courtyard facade is existing Berlin reality; the apartment is invented Berlin reality, built in the studio. The two have been synthesized into the cinematic reality of a Berlin slum tenement by means of montage.

Hanne and Martin, the story goes on to relate, are fed up with the constricting circumstances and their fellow lodgers' snide remarks. They run away and spend the night in the waiting room of a train station. With its standard-time clock, diagonal iron beams, and the oppressive inertia of locomotives waiting to depart, the film's production designer, Franz Schroedter, not only created an ambience for the pair's loneliness and homelessness but found a formal correspondence for

Zuflucht, ein Film von 1928. Martin, enttäuschter Revolutionär der Berliner Novembertage und Sohn wohlhabender Eltern, kehrt nach Jahren der Strapazen aus dem sozialistischen Rußland in seine Heimatstadt zurück; bei der jungen Marktverkäuferin Hanne findet er Unterschlupf.

Niedrige Eingangstüren zu den Seitenflügeln und grau-fleckige Wände: der enge Schacht des Hinterhofes; hinter der Fassade die Wohnküche, ein Raum aufgeteilt in Verschläge, auf dem Hängeboden nächtigt der Schlafbursche; neben der Wohnungstür ein Kaninchenstall, Kisten, Körbe, ein abgewetztes Sofa, rohe Holzstühle; auf drei Betten verteilen sich fünf, sechs Menschen, hier wird zugleich gegessen, geschlafen, gewaschen, geliebt und natürlich gestritten.

Die Hinterhoffassade ist vorgefundene Berliner Realität, die Hinterhofwohnung ist erfundene, im Atelier gebaute Berliner Realität. Die Montage, an das Bild ›Hinterhof‹ das Bild ›Wohnung‹ koppelnd, synthetisiert beides zur filmischen Realität eines Berliner Elendsquartiers.

Hanne und Martin, so geht die Geschichte weiter, ertragen nicht die Enge der Kammer und die anzüg-

them *(fig. 145)*. Perhaps even more than through the actors' gestures, the drama here, as in other films of the period, is stated through spatial settings with which the viewer tends to identify even more directly than with the faces and expressions of the actors.

Eventually Martin finds work on a subway construction project at Tempelhof Field, but, being too weak to perform heavy labor, he dies exhausted in the arms of his mother. That *Zuflucht* is a melodrama comes as no surprise once we have seen Schroedter's eloquent waiting room.

F. P. 1 antwortet nicht

Germany, 1932
Directed by Karl Hartl
Script by Walter Reisch, based on the novel by Kurt Siodmak
Photography by Günther Rittau, Konstantin Irmen-Tschet, and Otto Baecker
Sound effects by Fritz Thiery
Sets by Erich Kettelhut
With Hans Albers, Sybille Schmitz, and Peter Lorre

With the addition of sound, filmmaking obviously entered new territory. Suddenly, in a pinch, a director could bridge great distances in space by introducing a few bars from a hit tune, a few allusive words from a

lichen Bemerkungen ihrer Mitbewohner. Sie laufen davon und verbringen eine Nacht in einem Bahnhofswartesaal.

Der Architekt Franz Schroedter hat mit Normaluhr, schrägen Eisenträgern, mit der lastenden Ruhe abfahrbereiter Lokomotiven der Einsamkeit und Unbehaustheit des Paares nicht nur ein Ambiente, sondern Ausdruck verschafft *(Abb. 145)*. Vielleicht mehr noch als durch Gesten werden im Kino Figuren durch räumliche Situationen charakterisiert, mit den räumlichen Situationen der Figuren identifiziert sich der Zuschauer vielleicht mehr noch als mit ihren Physiognomien.

Martin findet Arbeit beim U-Bahn-Bau am Tempelhofer Feld, doch entkräftet stirbt er in den Armen seiner – wenn auch begüterten, so doch gütigen – Mutter: Daß *Zuflucht* ein Melodrama ist, das wissen wir spätestens beim Anblick des beredten Wartesaals.

F. P. 1 antwortet nicht

Deutschland 1932
Regie: Karl Hartl
Buch:
Walter Reisch, nach dem Roman von Kurt Siodmak
Kamera: Günther Rittau, Konstantin Irmen-Tschet, Otto Baecker
Ton: Fritz Thiery
Bauten: Erich Kettelhut
Mit Hans Albers, Sybille Schmitz, Peter Lorre

Fig. 146 *Erich Kettelhut. Design for gangway below deck, "F.P.1 antwortet nicht," 1932. Hand-colored photos of drawings. Stiftung Deutsche Kinemathek, Berlin.*

Abb. 146 *Erich Kettelhut. Entwurf für einen Gang unter Deck der F. P. 1 »F. P. 1 antwortet nicht«, 1932. Handkolorierte Photos von Zeichnungen. Stiftung Deutsche Kinemathek, Berlin.*

narrator could transform the UFA lot at Neubabelsberg, shots of a Baltic Sea island called Oie, and a tiny model into the floating airfield F. P. 1, a relay station for transatlantic flights by airlines accommodating three hundred passengers in opulent staterooms. In some ways, F. P. 1 can be likened to Germany in 1932: a mammoth technological project *(figs. 146–147)*, the utopian character of which becomes obvious through the interior decorations, which are straight out of the Bauhaus catalogue.

Sadly, film sets are more transient than anything else in the world. For the space of a few scenes, all interest focuses on them, and we lavish more loving care on them than on flesh-and-blood human beings. But after that, they are expendable and can crash and burn, and what remains of uncountable days of nerve-racking work, done to entertain an audience for two hours, is nothing but an unsightly pile of junk that gets carted to the next best trash dump.[11]   *Franz Schroedter*

Ein anderes Kapitel ist der Tonfilm. Ihm hilft notfalls ein flotter Schlager über räumliche Grenzen hinweg, ihm genügen einige verbindende Worte, um aus dem Ufa-Gelände in Neubabelsberg, der Ostseeinsel Oie und einem Modell die schwimmende Flugplattform F. P. 1 zu konstruieren, Zwischenstation für Transatlantikflüge mit dreihundert Hotelkabinen. Deutschland 1932: den utopischen Charakter dieses technischen Großprojekts illustriert die Innenarchitektur aus dem Bauhaus-Katalog *(Abb. 146–147)*.

»Leider sind Filmbauten kurzlebiger als alles andere auf dieser Erde. Wenige Szenen lang sind sie Mittelpunkt jedes Interesses; man behandelt sie sorgfältiger als Menschen von Fleisch und Blut. Doch dann sind sie überflüssig, in Schutt und Asche werden sie gelegt, und von der nervenaufreibenden Arbeit unzähliger Tage, die geleistet wurde, um das Publikum zwei Stunden lang zu unterhalten, bleibt nichts übrig als ein armseliger Haufen Gerümpel, der auf den ersten besten Schuttplatz gebracht wird.« (Franz Schroedter)[11]

Footnotes

1 *Das Cabinet des Dr. Caligari* was shot in the Lixie Studio, Berlin-Weissensee. Marlene Dietrich played her first leading role *(Die Frau, nach der man sich sehnt)* in the Terra-Glashaus Studio at Berlin-Marienfelde, and other UFA studios were located in Berlin-Tempelhof and the suburb of Neubabelsberg. In addition to further studios and lots in Wedding, Grunewald, Woltersdorf, and other parts of Berlin, locations throughout the metropolitan area were used to shoot countless films.

2 Hermann Warm, *Dekorationen für den Film "Das Kabinett [sic] des Dr. Caligari"* (unpublished typescript, in the collection of Stiftung Deutsche Kinemathek, Berlin).

3 Warm, "Das Wohnzimmer Alan," in *ibid.*

4 Fritz Lang, "Arbeitsgemeinschaft im Film," *Der Kinematograph*, February 17, 1924.

5 Erich Kettelhut, *Erinnerungen.*

6 Cf. Stephen Jenkins, ed., *Fritz Lang: The Image and the Look* (London, 1981), and Frieda Grafe, "Für Fritz Lang. Einen Platz, kein Denkmal," in Peter W. Jansen, Wolfram Schütte, and Stiftung Deutsche Kinemathek, eds., *Fritz Lang* (Munich and Vienna, 1976), Reihe Film 7.

7 Robert Herlth, "Vortrag vor dem Club deutscher Filmjournalisten am 22. Februar 1951," in Wolfgang Längsfeld, ed., *Filmarchitektur Robert Herlth* (Munich, 1965).

8 Cf. Lotte H. Eisner, *F. W. Murnau* (Paris, 1964).

9 Cf. Eric Rohmer, *L'Organisation de l'espace dans le "Faust" de Murnau* (Paris, 1977).

10 Franz Schroedter, in Hans-Joachim Hahn, *Die Arbeit des Architekten* (typescript of a conversation published in 1935 in an as yet unidentified Berlin newspaper; in the collection of Stiftung Deutsche Kinemathek, Berlin).

11 *Ibid.*

Anmerkungen

1 *Das Cabinet des Dr. Caligari* wurde im Lixie-Atelier, Berlin-Weißensee gedreht, Marlene Dietrich interpretierte ihre erste Hauptrolle *(Die Frau, nach der man sich sehnt)* im Terra-Glashaus-Atelier in Berlin-Tempelhof und dem Vorort Neubabelsberg; neben weiteren Ateliers und Freigeländen, unter anderem in Berlin-Wedding, Berlin-Grunewald oder Woltersdorf, diente das ganze Stadtgebiet als Drehort zahlloser Filme.

2 Hermann Warm: Dekorationen für den Film »Das Kabinett des Dr. Caligari« (sic!). (Unveröffentlichtes Typoscript, im Besitz der Stiftung Deutsche Kinemathek, Berlin)

3 Hermann Warm: Das Wohnzimmer Alan. In: Dekorationen für den Film »Das Kabinett des Dr. Caligari«; a. a. O.

4 Fritz Lang: Arbeitsgemeinschaft im Film. In: Der Kinematograph vom 17. 2. 1924

5 Erich Kettelhut: Erinnerungen. A. a. O.

6 Vgl. Stephen Jenkins (Ed.): Fritz Lang. The Image And the Look. London 1981; und Frieda Grafe: Für Fritz Lang. Einen Platz, kein Denkmal. In: Peter W. Jansen, Wolfram Schütte, Stiftung Deutsche Kinemathek (Hrsg.): Fritz Lang. München, Wien 1976 (Reihe Film 7)

7 Robert Herlth: Vortrag vor dem Club deutscher Filmjournalisten am 22. Februar 1951. In: Wolfgang Längsfeld (Red.): Filmarchitektur Robert Herlth. München 1965

8 Vgl. Lotte H. Eisner: F. W. Murnau. Paris 1964

9 Vgl. Eric Rohmer: L'Organisation de l'espace dans le »Faust« de Murnau. Paris 1977

10 Franz Schroedter in Hans-Joachim Hahn: Die Arbeit des Architekten. (Typoscript eines 1935 in einer bisher noch nicht identifizierten Berliner Tageszeitung erschienenen Gesprächs; im Besitz der Stiftung Deutsche Kinemathek, Berlin)

11 ebd.

Fig. 147   *Erich Kettelhut. Design for flotation tanks under F.P.1, "F.P.1 antwortet nicht," 1932. Hand-colored photo of drawing. Stiftung Deutsche Kinemathek, Berlin.*

Abb. 147   *Erich Kettelhut. Entwurf für Schwimmtanks unter F.P.1 »F.P.1 antwortet nicht«, 1932. Handkoloriertes Photo einer Zeichnung. Stiftung Deutsche Kinemathek, Berlin.*

Further Reading –   Weiterführende Literatur

Argan, Giulio. *Gropius und das Bauhaus.* Hamburg: Rowohlt, 1962; Braunschweig: Vieweg, 1983.

Banham, Reyner. *Die Revolution der Architektur.* Hamburg: Rowohlt, 1964; *Theory and Design in the First Machine Age.* London: Architectural Press, 1969.

Behne, Adolf. *Der moderne Zweckbau.* Munich: 1926; reprint, Berlin: Ullstein, 1964.

Benevolo, Leonardo. *Geschichte der Architektur des 19. und 20. Jahrhunderts.* Munich: Callwey, 1964; *History of Modern Architecture.* London: Routledge, 1971.

Buddensieg, Tilmann, in collaboration with Henning Rogge. *Industriekultur. Peter Behrens und die AEG 1907–1914.* Berlin: Gebr. Mann, 2d ed. 1981; *Industriekultur: Peter Behrens and the AEG 1907–1914.* Cambridge: MIT Press, 1984.

Burckhardt, Lucius, ed. *The Werkbund: History and Ideology, 1907–1933.* New York: Barrons, 1980; *Der Werkbund in Deutschland, Österreich und der Schweiz. Form ohne Ornament.* Stuttgart: Deutsche Verlags-Anstalt, 1978.

Campbell, Joan. *The German Werkbund.* Princeton, N.J.: Princeton University Press, 1978.

Conrads, Ulrich, and Hans G. Sperlich. *Fantastische Architektur.* Stuttgart: Hatje, 1960.

Curtis, William J.R. *Modern Architecture Since 1900.* Oxford: Phaidon, 1982.

Drexler, Arthur. *Mies van der Rohe.* New York: Braziller, 1960.

Frampton, Kenneth. *Modern Architeture. A Critical History.* London: Thames & Hudson, 1980; *Die Architektur der Moderne. Eine kritische Baugeschichte.* Stuttgart: Deutsche Verlags-Anstalt, 1983.

Franciscono, Marcel. *Walter Gropius and the Creation of the Bauhaus in Weimar: The Ideals and Artistic Theories of Its Founding Years.* Urbana, Ill.: University of Illinois Press, 1971.

Geest, Jan van and Otokar Máčel. *Stühle aus Stahl. Metallmöbel 1925–1940.* Cologne: Walter König, 1980.

Giedion, Siegfried. *Befreites Wohnen.* Zurich: Orell Füssli, 1929; reprint, Frankfurt: Syndicat, 1985.

– *Mechanization Takes Command.* Cambridge: Harvard University Press, 1947; *Die Herrschaft der Mechanisierung.* Frankfurt: Europäische Verlags-Anstalt, 1982.

– *Space, Time and Architecture.* Cambridge: Harvard University Press, 1941; *Raum, Zeit, Architektur.* Munich: Artemis, 1965, 3d ed. 1984.

Heuss, Theodor. *Hans Poelzig. Lebensbild.* Tübingen: Wasmuth, 1939.

Hilberseimer, Ludwig. *Berliner Architektur der 20er Jahre.* Neue Bauhausbücher, no. 7. Mainz and Berlin: Florian Kupferberg (Berlin: Gebr. Mann), 1967.

– *Großstadt-Architektur.* Stuttgart: Julius Hoffmann, 1927; 2d ed., 1979.

Hitchcock, Henry-Russell. *Architecture: Nineteenth and Twentieth Centuries.* Baltimore: Penguin Books, 1958.

– and Philip Johnson. *The International Style: Architecture Since 1922.* New York: W.W. Norton, 1932; *Der Internationale Stil 1932.* Braunschweig: Vieweg, 1985.

Huse, Norbert. *Neues Bauen 1818–1933.* Rev. ed. Munich: Heinz Moos, 1985.

Johnson, Philip C. *Mies van der Rohe.* New York: Museum of Modern Art, 1947; 3d ed., 1978.

Junghanns, Kurt. *Bruno Taut 1880–1938.* Berlin: Henschel, 1970.

Lampugnani, Vittorio Magnago, ed. *Encyclopaedia of Twentieth-Century Architecture.* London: Thames & Hudson, 1986; *Lexikon der Architektur des 20. Jahrhunderts.* Stuttgart: Hatje, 1983.

Lane, Barbara M. *Architektur und Politik in Deutschland 1918–1945.* Braunschweig: Vieweg, 1965; *Architecture and Politics in Germany, 1918–1945.* Cambridge: MIT Press, 1968.

Müller-Wulckow, Walter. *Architektur der zwanziger Jahre in Deutschland.* Königstein, Taunus: Langewiesche, 1929; 3d ed. 1979.

Nerdinger, Winfried. *Der Architekt Walter Gropius. Zeichnungen, Pläne und Fotos ... Werkverzeichnis.* Berlin: Gebr. Mann, 1985.

Neumeyer, Fritz. *Mies van der Rohe. Das kunstlose Wort. Gedanken zur Baukunst.* Berlin: Siedler, 1986.

Pehnt, Wolfgang. *Expressionist Architecture.* New York: Praeger, 1973; *Die Architektur des Expressionismus.* Stuttgart: Hatje, 1973.

Pevsner, Nikolaus. *Der Beginn der modernen Architektur und des Designs.* Cologne: DuMont, 1968.

Posener, Julius. *Berlin auf dem Wege zu einer neuen Architektur: Das Zeitalter Wilhelms II.* Munich: Prestel, 1979.

– *From Schinkel to the Bauhaus.* London: Lund Humphries, 1972.

Roters, Eberhard, et al. *Berlin 1910–1933.* New York: Rizzoli, 1982.

Scarpa, Ludovica. *Martin Wagner e Berlino.* Rome: Officina Edizioni, 1983.

Scheerbart, Paul, and Bruno Taut. *Glass Architecture and Alpine Architecture*. New York: Praeger, 1972; *Glasarchitektur*. Munich 1971.

Schlösser, Manfred. *Arbeitsrat für Kunst, 1918–1921* (exhibition catalogue, Akademie der Künste, 1980). Berlin: Akademie der Künste, 1980.

Schulze, Franz. *Mies van der Rohe. A Critical Biography*. Chicago: University of Chicago Press, 1985; *Mies van der Rohe. Leben und Werk*. Berlin: Ernst & Sohn, 1986.

Tafuri, Manfredo, and Francesco Dal Co. *Architettura Contemporanea*. Milan: 1976; *Modern Architecture*. London: Abrams, 1980.

Taut, Bruno. *Die neue Baukunst in Europa und Amerika*. Stuttgart: Julius Hoffmann, 1927; 2d ed. 1978.

– *Bruno Taut* (exhibition catalogue, Akademie der Künste). Berlin: Akademie der Künste, 1984.

Tegethoff, Wolf. *Die Villen und Landhausprojekte von Mies van der Rohe*. Essen: Richard Bacht, 1981.

Waetzoldt, Stephan, ed. *Tendenzen der Zwanziger Jahre* (catalogue of the 15th European art exhibition). Berlin: Dietrich Reimer, 1977.

Whitford, Frank. *Bauhaus*. London: Thames & Hudson, 1984.

Whyte, Iain Boyd. *Bruno Taut. Baumeister einer neuen Welt. Architektur und Aktivismus. 1914–1920*. Stuttgart: Hatje, 1981; *Bruno Taut and the Architecture of Activism*. Cambridge: Cambridge University Press, 1982.

Willet, John. *The Weimar Years*. New York: Abbeville Press, 1984.

Wingler, Hans M. *The Bauhaus*. Cambridge: MIT Press, 1969; *Das Bauhaus*. Bramsche/Cologne: Rasch/DuMont, 3d ed. 1975.

Zevi, Bruno. *Erich Mendelsohn. Opera Completa*. Milan: Etas Kompass, 1970.

Photo credits

Photonachweis

Hans Joachim Bartsch, Berlin   81
Bauhaus-Archiv, Berlin   25, 45, 56, 57, 58, 94
Berlinische Galerie, Berlin   16
Bildarchiv Preußischer Kulturbesitz, Berlin   104
Busch-Reisinger-Museum, Harvard   47
Axel Feuß, Hamburg   34
Hans Finsler   75
Vera Frowein-Ziroff   119
Peter Grunwald, Berlin   8
Gruppe Nord, Berlin   46
Otto Hagemann, Bauhaus-Archiv, Berlin,   10, 108, and Cover
Scott Hyde, New York   17, 39, 66, 68, 69, 73, 82, 93, 95, 96, 97a
Arthur Köster, Akademie der Künste, Berlin   109
Kranich-Photo, Berlin   137, 138
Kunsthistorisches Institut der Freien Universität Berlin   128
Landesbildstelle Berlin   99
Museum of Modern Art, Mies van der Rohe Archive, New York   24, 41, 42, 50
Niggemeyer, Berlin   38
Knud Peter Petersen, Berlin   4, 5, 11, 19, 20, 21, 22, 30, 44, 61, 70, 72, 76, 78, 79, 80, 84, 85, 88, 105, 106, 107, 110, 112, 113, 114, 118, 122, 123, 124, 125, 126, 127, 130, 131, 133, 134, 136
Arne Psille, Berlin   83
Henning Rogge, Berlin   101
Lothar Schnepf, Köln   35, 36
Siemens-Museum, München   87, 89
Staatliche Museen Preußischer Kulturbesitz SMPK, Kunstbibliothek, Berlin   31, 32, 40, 48, 49, 51, 52, 60, 100, 139
Stiftung Deutsche Kinemathek, Berlin   140, 141, 142, 143, 144, 145, 146, 147,
Dr. Franz Stoedtner, Photo Marburg   2, 3, 6, 9, 18, 59, 102, 115, 116, 117
Wolfgang Volz, Düsseldorf   1, 12, 13, 14, 15, 77, 97, 135
Wenzel-Hablik-Stiftung, Itzehoe   33

From/Aus:

Berlin und seine Bauten, 1896   120
Blätter für Architektur und Kunsthandwerk, 1915   26
Deutsche Kunst und Dekoration   1902/02: 63, 64, 65; 1904/1905: 62; 1905: 71
Die Form   1930: 74; 1931: 91, 92, 98
Werner Graeff, *Jetzt wird Ihre Wohnung eingerichtet,* 1933   90
Jahrbuch des Deutschen Werkbundes, 1915   27, 28, 29
Udo Kultermann, *Wassili und Hans Luckhardt,* 1958   53, 54, 55
Erich Mendelsohn, *Das Gesamtschaffen des Architekten,* 1930   43

Berlin 1900–1933: Architecture and Design has been made possible by generous grants from the Auswärtiges Amt, Bonn; the Senator für Kulturelle Angelegenheiten, Berlin; and the Smithsonian Institution Regents Special Exhibition Fund. It has also been supported by Lufthansa German Airlines.